FISHERIES AND AQUACULTURE

FISHERIES AND AQUACULTURE

Edited by

Prof. Neelima Gupta
Ph.D., D.Sc.
Department of Animal Science
M.J.P. Rohilkhand University
Bareilly - 243 006
(INDIA)

Dr. D.K. Gupta
Head, Department of Zoology &
Head, Department of Biotechnology
Bareilly College
Bareilly - 243 005. U.P.
(INDIA)

DPH

DISCOVERY PUBLISHING HOUSE PVT. LTD.
NEW DELHI-110 002

Published by:
Tilak Wasan
DISCOVERY PUBLISHING HOUSE PVT. LTD.
4383/4B, Ansari Road, Darya Ganj
New Delhi - 110 002 (India)
Phone : +91-11-23279245, 43596064-65
Fax : +91-11-23253475
E-mail : discoverypublishinghouse@gmail.com
sales@discoverypublishinggroup.com

website : www.discoverypublishinggroup.com

***First Edition:* 2015**

ISBN: 978-93-5056-736-4

Fisheries and Aquaculture

Printed at:
Infinity Imaging Systems
Delhi

Preface

Human population growth has placed a significant demand on fish as a food source placing it as a significant source of protein for millions of people in the world. It is estimated that approximately 25 per cent of all protein consumed by people comes from fish. For some developing nations fish provides a large percentage of protein for its own people as well as a source of income as an export product.

Fish research has become an increasingly important study as fish populations decline throughout the world. The decline of fish has an immense impact on ocean eco-systems as well as a significant impact on one of the primary food sources for people around the world. Overfishing in the past 50 years has significantly reduced fish populations across a large number of species. Research in ichthyology helps policy-makers determine what course of action to take in order to maintain fish populations throughout the world. National and international policies are determined based on the data provided by fish research.

India is known for fishing and has seen rapid advances in this sector. Indian central government initiated a dedicated organization focussed on fisheries, under its Ministry of Agriculture. Fish production rose from 800,000 tons in 1950 to 4.1 million tons in the early 1990s and through 2010, Indian fish industry growth has accelerated, reaching a total marine and freshwater fish production to about 8 million metric tonns.

An International Conference on Recent Trends in Climate Change Researches vis-a-vis Biodiversity was organized at MJP Rohilkhand University, Bareilly during 3rd to 4th December, 2012 under the auspices of 'Centre of Excellence', Government of Uttar Pradesh and the Indian Academy of Environmental Sciences, Hardwar. This is the third volume of the publication of the Proceedings, the first (Modern Parasitology) and second (Environment and Biodiversity) volumes have already been published.

We place on record our appreciation to all the contributors of this volume for their unabated co-operation extended at every step which has made it possible to publish this piece of work.

We dedicate this volume to meet the objectives of 'Blue Revolution'.

Neelima Gupta
D.K. Gupta

Contents

[I] Prospects, Management and Diversity in Fishes

Fisheries and Aquaculture
Edited by: **Prof. (Mrs.) Neelima Gupta** and **Dr. D.K. Gupta**
Edition: **2015**
ISBN: 978-93-5056-736-4
Published by: **Discovery Publishing House Pvt. Ltd., New Delhi (India)**

1

Prospects of Fisheries in India

Dileep K. Gupta

Department of Zoology, Bareilly College, Bareilly 243 005. U.P. India.
Email: guptaby@gmail.com

INTRODUCTION

India has a vast coastline and fishing has emerged as a major industry in coastal India, employing over 14 million people. Fish production in India has multiplied more than tenfold since independence. According to the Food and Agriculture Organization (FAO) of the United Nations, fish production has doubled between 1990 and 2010 in India (FAO, 2011). India has rich fishery resources including 8,118 km. of marine coastline, 3,827 fishing villages, and 1,914 traditional fish landing centres. India's fresh water resources consist of 1,95,210 km. of rivers and canals, 2.9 million hectares of minor and major reservoirs, 2.4 million hectares of ponds and lakes, and about 0.8 million hectares of flood plain wetlands and water bodies (FAO, 2006). Due to these rich resources, the marine and freshwaters offered a combined sustainable catch fishing potential of over 4 million metric tonnes of fish according to 2010 data. In addition, India's water and natural resources offer a tenfold growth potential in farm fishing from 2010 harvest levels of 3.9 million metric tonnes of fish. The marine fish harvested in India include about 65 commercially important species. Marine and freshwater catch fishing combined with aquaculture fish farming is a rapidly growing industry in India. India is the second largest producer of fish in the world contributing to about 5-43 per cent of global fish production. India is also a major producer of fish through aqua culture and ranks second in the world after China. In 2006, India exported over 600,000 metric tonnes of fish to 90 countries, earning a revenue over $1.8 billion (CIFT, 2008). Exported species include shrimps, the giant tiger prawn (*Penaeus monodon*) and the Indian white prawn (*Fenneropenaeus indicus*). Farmed shrimp accounts for about 60 per cent of shrimp exported from the country. In 2008, India was the sixth largest producer of marine and freshwater capture fisheries, and the second largest aquaculture farmed fish producer in the world (FAO, 2010). The total production during 2011-12 is at 8.67 million tonnes with a contribution as 5.3 million tonnes from inland sector and 3.37 million tonnes from the marine sector. During 2010-11, the volume of fish and fishery products exported from India was 8,13091 tonnes worth Rs. 12901.47 crore and during 2011-12, the export earnings have crossed 3.5 billion USD and it is expected to reach USD 4.7 billion by 2014. Indian fishers quickly overfished their own waters and production plummeted in 2013 as the access to Sri Lankan waters closed after the defeat of the Liberation Tigers of Tamil Eelam.

Fisheries is a state subject and as such the primary responsibility for its development rests with the state Government. The major thrust is to generate employment and improve welfare of fisherman and their socio-economic state. Fish production in India is set to cross 13 million tonnes (MT) mark by 2016 from the current level of over 9 million tonnes according to a study of Associate Chamber of Commerce and Industries of India. Indian marine waters are home of over 1,700 fish species including 200 commercially significant species while the sector employs over 15 million people. Fish eaters account for over half of India's total population. Therefore, the prospects of utilizing fish as food offers India one of the easiest and fastest way to address acute problems of malnutrition and food security. However, the situation of fish economy in India is not so pleasant: a fish farmers' average annual production in India is only 2 metric tonnes per person, compared to 172 tonnes in Norway, 72 tonnes in Chile, and 6 tonnes per fisherman in China (FAO, 2010). The living standards of Indian fishermen are rather poor and can be appreciably enhanced by achieving higher productivity, knowledge transfer for sustainable fishing, continued growth in fish production with a corresponding increase in fish exports. Fish harvest distribution is difficult in India because of poor rural road infrastructure, lack of cold storage facilities and absence of organized retail.

Fishing in India: Historical Perspective

The history of fishing and aquaculture in India is rich and long. Kautilya's Arthashastra (321-300 B.C.) and King Someswara's Manasottara (1127 A.D.) each refer to fish culture (FAO, 2009). India is known for its traditional practice of fish culture in small ponds in Eastern India. There was a significant increase in fish productivity in West Bengal in the early nineteenth century with the controlled breeding of carp in *Bundhs* (tanks or impoundments where river conditions are simulated). Tamil Nadu is a state where as early as 1911, fish culture started receiving notable attention, subsequently, other states followed such as: West Bengal, Punjab, Uttar Pradesh, Gujarat, Karnataka and Andhra Pradesh which initiated fish culture by establishing Fisheries Departments in the respective states. In 2006, under the Ministry of Agriculture, Indian Central Government initiated a dedicated organization focussed on fisheries development in the country.

Brackish water farming in India also has an ancient history confined mainly to the *Bheries* (manmade impoundments in coastal wetlands) of West Bengal and *pokkali* (salt resistant deepwater paddy) fields along the Kerala coast. With no additional knowledge and technology input, except that of trapping the naturally bred juvenile fish and shrimp seed, these systems have been sustaining production levels between 500 and 750 kg/ha/year with shrimp contributing 20 to 25 per cent of the total Indian production (FAO, 2009).

Fish Production

Awareness on fish production was generated in 1950 with a meagre 800,000 tonnes which bloomed to 4.1 million tonnes in the early 1990's. Indian fish industry growth accelerated, from 1990 to 2010, reaching a total marine and freshwater fish production to about 8 million metric tonnes. During these years, special efforts have been made to promote extensive and intensive inland fish farming, modernize coastal fisheries, and encourage deep-sea fishing through joint efforts. These led to a more than fourfold increase in coastal fish production from 520,000 tonnes in 1950 to 2.4 million tonnes in 1990. The situation of inland fish production was even better, increasing almost eightfold from 218,000 tonns in 1950 to 1.7 million tonnes in 1990. The value of fish and processed fish exports increased from less than 1 per cent of the total value of exports in 1960 to 3.6 per cent in 1993.

Between 1990 to 2007, fish production in India has grown at a higher rate as compared to eggs, food grains, milk, and other food items (TNAU, 2007) which clearly indicates increased interest in the fisheries sector.

The Economic Perspective of Fishing Industry

There has been a steady rise in the productivity of fish products in India. Fishing in India contributed over 1 per cent of India's annual gross domestic product in 2008. About 14.5 million people are employed in this sector. The country's rich marine and inland water resources, fisheries and aquaculture offer an attractive and promising sector for employment, livelihood, and food security. Fish products from India are exported to almost half of world's countries, creating export-driven employment opportunities in India and greater food security all over the world. There have been improvements in craft, tackle and farming methods during the recent decades. Creation of required harvest and post-harvest infrastructure has been receiving due attention of the central and state governments inducing a steady growth (FAO, 2006). India is adopting exclusive economic zone, stretching 370 km into the Indian ocean, thereby harvesting economic benefits from fishing. In the mid-1980's, only about 33 per cent of that area was being exploited. The potential annual catch from the area has been estimated at 4.5 million tonnes. In addition to this marine zone, India has about 14,000 km^2., of brackish water available for aquaculture, of which only 600 km^2., were being farmed in the early 1990's; about 16,000 km^2., of freshwater lakes, ponds, and swamps; and nearly 64,000 kms., of rivers and streams.

Statistical picture indicates that in 1990, there were 1.7 million full-time, 1.3 million part-time, and 2.3 million occasional fishermen, many of whom worked as salt-makers, ferrymen, or seamen, or operated hired boats. In the early 1990's, the fishing fleet consisted of 180,000 traditional craft powered by sails or oars, 26,000 motorized traditional craft, and 34,000 mechanized boats.

Aquaculture

India is rich in carp production. Between 1970 and 1980, India initiated scientific carp farming in the country by demonstrating high production levels of 8 to 10 tonnes/ hectare/year. Aquaculture dawned in India in late 1980's and transformed fish culture into a modern enterprise and during economic liberalization of early 1990's, fishing industry got a major investment boost and started growing at a rapid pace.

Breeding and culture technologies of different species of carp became popular in India; later on, catfishes, murrels and prawns also picked up.

Fish Culture Systems in India

Different culture systems have been adopted in India depending on the regional inputs and investment capabilities of farmers. The following culture systems are adopted in the country (FAO, 2009):

1. Intensive pond culture with supplementary feeding and aeration (10-15 tonnes/ha/yr).
2. Composite carp culture (4-6 tonnes/ha/yr).
3. Weed-based carp polyculture (3-4 tonnes/ha/yr).
4. Integrated fish farming with poultry, pigs, ducks, horticulture, etc., (3-5 tonnes/ha/yr).
5. Pen culture (3-5 tonnes/ha/yr).
6. Cage culture (10-15 $kg/m^2/yr$).
7. Running-water fish culture (20-50 $kg/m^2/yr$).

The aquaculture resources in India are rich including 2.36 million hectares of ponds and tanks, 1.07 million hectares of *'beels'*, *'jheels'* and derelict waters in addition to 0.12 million kms., of canals, 3.15 million hectares of reservoirs and 0.72 million hectares of upland lakes that have a potential for aquaculture. Although the prime resources for freshwater aquaculture in India are ponds and tanks but only less than 10 per cent of India's natural potential is at present used for aquaculture purposes. Therefore, the prospects for freshwater aquaculture are high.

About 1.2 million hectares of potential brackish water area available in India are estimated to be suitable for farming according to FAO . In addition, around 8.5 million hectares of salt affected areas are also available, of which about 2.6 million hectares could be exclusively utilised for aquaculture due to the unsuitability of these resources for other agriculture based activities. However, just like India's fresh water resources, the total brackish water area under cultivation is only just over 13 per cent of the potential water area available. The prospects for shrimp farming in its brackish waters in India are high.

In order to improve fish production, attention has been focussed on enhancing seed output. There has been an increase in seed production from 6321 million fry in 1985-86 to over 18500 million fry in 2007 in carp hatcheries in both, the public and private sectors. There are 35 freshwater prawn hatcheries in the coastal states producing over 200 million seed per annum. The 237 shrimp hatcheries with a production capacity of approximately 11.425 billion post larvae per year meet the seed requirement of the brackish water shrimp farming sector (FAO, 2009).

Freshwater aquaculture activities are prominent in the eastern states, West Bengal, Orissa and Andhra Pradesh and new areas are coming up in the states of Punjab, Haryana, Assam and Tripura. Brackish water aquaculture is mainly concentrated on the coasts of Andhra Pradesh, Tamil Nadu, Orissa and West Bengal. Fish are mainly consumed in Bihar, Orissa, West Bengal and northeast India.

State-wise Distribution of Fish Industry

Freshwater prawn farming in India has grown rapidly between 2000 and 2010. Andhra Pradesh dominates the sector with more than 86 per cent of the total production in India with approximately 60 per cent of the total water area dedicated to prawn farming, followed by West Bengal. A viable option for enhancing farm income is composite farming of freshwater prawn along with carp, a technologically sound culture practice. Thirty five freshwater prawn hatcheries, at present producing about 200 million seed per annum, cater for the requirements of the country (FAO, 2009).

Legal Perspectives

Indian government has a federal structure, the power of enacting laws is split between India's central government and the Indian states. The state legislatures of India have the power to make laws and regulations with respect to a number of subject-matters, including water (*i.e.*, water supplies, irrigation and canals, drainage and embankments, water storage and water power), land (*i.e.*, rights in or over land, land tenure, transfer, and alienation of agricultural land), fisheries, as well as the preservation, protection and improvement of stock and the prevention of animal disease. There are many laws and regulations that may be relevant to fisheries and aquaculture adopted at the state level.

At the central level, several key laws and regulations are relevant to fisheries and aquaculture. The important ones include the British-era Indian Fisheries Act (1897), which penalizes the killing of fish by poisoning water and by using explosives; the Environment (Protection) Act (1986), containing provisions for all environment related issues affecting fisheries and aquaculture industry in India. India also has enacted the Water (Prevention and Control of Pollution) Act (1974) and the Wild Life Protection Act (1972). A full picture of the law and regulations that are applicable to fisheries and aquaculture in India can be gained by not only reading all these legislations in conjunction with one another but also with the local laws of the specific state in question.

Fish Research

The scenario of fish and aquaculture research in India indicates that about 460 papers, roughly 5.5 per cent of the world output, are published from India every year, of which 82 per cent are journal articles. Nearly 70 per cent of journal articles have appeared in 113 Indian journals. Less than a third of the journal articles are published in journals indexed in SCI, about 61 per cent of publications are contributed by government laboratories and over 25 per cent by academic institutions. Government laboratories publish most of their work in low impact and low visibility journals and academic institutions in journals of medium impact. However, even those papers appearing in better-rated journals are not cited well. Kochi, Chennai, Mumbai and Mangalore are the cities and Tamil Nadu and Kerala are the states contributing the maximum research papers states contributing large number of papers (Table 1.1, Jayashree and Arunachalam, 2000).

Fisheries research and training institutions are supported by central and state governments that owe credit for the improvements in the Indian fishing industry.

Table 1.1: Indian cities and states contributing to the world literature of fisheries (arranged by number of papers) (According to Jayashree and Arunachalam, 2000)

City/Town	No. of Papers	State	No. of Papers
Kochi	242	Tamil Nadu	390
Chennai	185	Kerala	370
Mumbai	128	Uttar Pradesh	281
Mangalore	117	West Bengal	244
Hyderabad	83	Karnataka	204
Calcutta	81	Andhra Pradesh	200
Thiruvanthapurum	73	Maharashtra	166
New Delhi	69	Bihar	99
Bhubaneshwar	65	Madhya Pradesh	81
Visakhapatnam	61	Orissa	79
Bangalore	60	New Delhi	70
Kalyani	58	Punjab	41
188 other cities	1232	10 other states and 2 union territories	229

Principal Fisheries Research Institutions

The principal fisheries research institutions, operating under the Indian Council of Agricultural Research are:

1. Central Marine Fisheries Research Institute at Kochi (formerly Cochin), Kerala.
2. Central Inland Fisheries Institute at Barrackpore, West Bengal.
3. Central Institute of Fisheries Technology at Willingdon Island near Kochi.
4. Central Institute for Fishery Education in Mumbai, which has ancillary institutions in Barrackpore (Bengal), Agra (Uttar Pradesh), and Hyderabad (Andhra Pradesh).
5. Central Fisheries Corporation in Kolkata is instrumental in bringing about improvements in fishing methods, ice production, processing, storing, marketing, and constructing and repairing fishing vessels.

6. Marine Products Export Development Authority (MPEDA), operating under a 1972 law, headquartered in Kochi, has made several market surveys abroad and has been instrumental in introducing and enforcing hygiene standards that have gained for Indian fishery export products a reputation for cleanliness and quality.

National Fisheries Development Board

The Government of India launched National Fisheries Development Board in 2006 having its headquarters in Hyderabad, located in a fish shaped building. Its activity focus areas are (NFDB, 2008).

- Intensive Aquaculture in Ponds and Tanks.
- Fisheries Development in Reservoirs.
- Coastal Aquaculture.
- Mariculture.
- Seaweed Cultivation.
- Infrastructure: Fishing Harbours and Landing Centres.
- Fish Dressing Centres and Solar Drying of Fish.
- Domestic Marketing.
- Technology Up-gradation.
- Deep Sea Fishing and Tuna Processing.

Inland Fisheries Programmes

Two programmes have been launched for inland fisheries:

(i) Fish farmers' development agencies.

(ii) National Programmes of Fish Seed Development.

These programmes have facilitated increased production, which reached 1.5 million tonnes during financial year FY 1990, up from 0.9 million tonnes in FY 1984. A network of 313 fish farmers' development agencies was functioning in 1992. Under the National Programme of Fish Seed Development, forty fish-seed hatcheries were commissioned. Fish-seed production doubled from 5 billion fry in FY 1983 to 10 billion fry in FY 1989. A new programme using organic waste for aquaculture was started in FY 1986. Inland fish production as a per cent of total fish production increased from 36 per cent in FY 1980 to 40 per cent by FY 1990.

Harbours

There are five main fishing harbours:

1. Mangalore (Karnataka).
2. Kochi (Kerala).
3. Chennai (Tamil Nadu).
4. Vishakhapatnam (Andhra Pradesh).
5. Roychowkin Kolkata (West Bengal).

In addition, twenty-three minor fishing harbors and ninety-five fish-landing centres are designated to provide landing and berthing facilities to fishing craft. The harbors at Vishakhapatnam, Kochi, and Roychowk were completed by 1980; the one at Madras was completed in the 1980s. A major fishing harbor was under construction at Sassoon Dock in Mumbai in the early 1990s, as were thirteen additional minor fishing harbors and eighteen small landing centres. By early 1990, there were 225 deep-sea fishing vessels operating in India's exclusive economic zone. Of these, 165 were owned by Indian shipping companies, and the rest were chartered foreign fishing vessels.

Restrictions

The banning of trawling by chartered foreign vessels and the speedy motorization of traditional fishing craft in the 1980s led to a quantum jump in marine fish production in the late 1980s. The export of marine products rose from 97,179 tonnes (Rs. 531 billion) in FY 1987 to 210,800 tonnes (Rs. 17.4 trillion) in FY 1992, making India one of the world's leading seafood exporting nations. This achievement was largely a result of significant advancements in India's freezing facilities since the 1960's, advancements that enabled India's seafood products to meet international standards. Frozen shrimp, a high-value item, has become the dominant seafood export. Other significant export items are frozen frog legs, frozen lobster tails, dried fish, and shark fins, much of which is exported to seafood-loving Japan. During the eighth plan, marine products were identified as having major export potential.

Training Institutes

Several specialized institutes have been established to train fishermen.

1. The Central Institute of Fisheries Nautical and Engineering Training (CIFNET) was established in 1963 at Kochi, Kerala, India and produces trained manpower for manning the fishing vessels. It has two Units in Chennai (1968), Tamil Nadu and Vishakhapatnam (1981). Andhra Pradesh.
2. An Institute named: 'Fisheries Institute of Technology and Training' (FITT) was established with the participation of TATAs in Tamil Nadu, to improve the socio-economic condition of fishers.
3. The Integrated Fisheries Project, also headquartered in Kochi, was established for the processing, popularizing, and marketing of unusual fish.
4. Another training organization, the Central Institute of Coastal Engineering for Fisheries in Bangalore, has done techno-economic feasibility studies on locations of fishing harbor sites and brackish-water fish farms.

Presently, there are 19 Fisheries colleges and one fisheries university (CIFE: Central Institute of Fisheries Education, Mumbai) functioning in various states of the country, providing Professional Fisheries education for developing Professionalism in Fisheries. Among the fisheries colleges, Fisheries College and Research Institute located in Tuticorin, Tamil Nadu is more popular due to the maximum number of intake of MFSc and PhD., candidates every year. Other colleges such as the College of Fisheries, Panangad, College of Fisheries, and Mangalore are also playing a significant role.

Several states have organized marketing cooperatives for fishermen in order to improve returns to fishermen and provide better products for consumers. Nevertheless, most traditional fishermen rely on household members or local fish merchants for the disposal of their catches. In some places, marketing is carried on entirely by fisherwomen who carry small quantities at a time to nearby places.

Thus the prospects of utilizing fish as a food item, for generating employment and for utilizing it as research tool are high in India. This sector demands great attention and careful planning by the farmers, researchers and administrators will contribute in achieving the goals set forth for the 'Blue Revolution'.

REFERENCES

CIFT (2008). "Export of Marine Products from India". Central Institute of Fisheries Technology, India. 2008.

FAO (2006). Food and Agriculture Organization of the United Nations. 2006.

FAO (2009). "National Aquaculture Sector Overview: India". Food and Agriculture Organization of the United Nations. 2009.

FAO (2010). "The State of World Fisheries and Acquaculture, 2010". FAO of the United Nations. 2010.

FAO (2011). "Fishery and Aquaculture Country Profiles: India". Food and Agriculture Organization of the United Nations. 2011.

Jayashree B and Arunachalam S. (2000). Mapping Fish Research in India. Curr. Sci., 79,(5): 613-619.

NFDB (2008). About Indian Fisheries". National Fisheries Development Board – A Government of India Sponsored Autonomous Organization. 2008.

TNAU (2007). Fisheries". Tamil Nadu Agricultural University, Coimbatore. 2007.

Page 16-46

Fisheries and Aquaculture
Edited by: **Prof. (Mrs.) Neelima Gupta** and **Dr. D.K. Gupta**
Edition: **2015**
ISBN: 978-93-5056-736-4
Published by: **Discovery Publishing House Pvt. Ltd., New Delhi (India)**

2

Fish Bio-diversity Status and Eco-Characteristics of Aquatic Resources of Western Himalayan Region
A Review

B.D. Joshi

Department of Zoology and Environmental Sciences, Gurukula Kangri Vishwavidyalaya, Hardwar, 249 404, India. Email: joshi_bd@rediffmail.com

ABSTRACT

This review describes the salient features of the aquatic resources and fish fauna, spread through the Western Himalayan mountain region of Indian side, which include about 12 major rivers, 22 lakes and 03 man made reservoirs. Eco-biological characteristics and classification of these aquatic bodies, present status and impact of anthropogenic activities have been included. The paper describes fish fauna as reported in the hitherto available literature, besides partly worked out by the author. Accordingly, there are as many as about 256 species of fresh water teleosts distributed among the water bodies of the Himalayan region. Out of these, around 60 species are endemic, 7-8 species are transplanted ones and about 35 species are regarded as threatened or endangered. Most of other fish species have gradually moved up to these Himalayan hill streams, or rivers under natural course of local and seasonal or courtship migration.

INTRODUCTION

Mother nature has been quite benevolent to our Indian sub-continent in equipping it with most varied geo-geographical and climatological zones, spread through the length and breadth of this country. This has consequently resulted in equally most varied biospheric regions, harbouring myriad types of terrestrial and aquatic habitats, further sub-divided in innumerable micro-habitats and highly specific ecological niches. Such abiotic diversity is further manifested by mother nature in equally one of the richest bio-diversity within the geo-political boundaries of India, falling under the Oriental zoo-geographical region.

Himalayas form the northern boundaries of this country, partly also maneuvering over the western and the eastern boundaries, too. The Himalayas offer a wide area of a unique mega-bio-sphere region with very dynamic and diverse eco-climatological sub-regions spread through 2500 km. long and about 135-450 km wide belt built of almost a parallel row of mountains full of usual troughs, peaks and valleys.

The whole of the Himalayan region has been vertically divided into three major zones *viz;*

1. The greater Himalaya.
2. Lesser Himalaya.
3. The Shiwaliks.

The Greater Himalaya by and large serve as the source of almost all the major rivers and lakes for the northern part of India. This region is relatively eco-climatologically quite hostile, being predominantly an alpine region.

The lesser Himalayan zone is full of diverse forests, throughout. This region is also full of a variety of aquatic resources, making a vast net of catchment areas for all the rivers originating in deeper mountain zones. There are also a number of small to large lakes spread in the whole area. The whole of the aquatic realms, despite many basic similarities offer wide variations in their individual topographical and ambient ecological conditions. This has given birth to equally diverse evolution of their faunistic components and a very characteristic endemism. The Himalayan region of Indian sub-continent is well known for three groups of vertebrates *viz;* *(i)* Mammals, *(ii)* Birds and *(iii)* Fishes.

The endemic fish fauna of Himalayan region finds its record from our most ancient Vedic era. The most famous Mahseer fish species of *Tor putitora* finds its mention under the name of Mahasalka, most probably on account its large sized body scales. However, as for the recent historical past, it was most probably Hamilton (1822), who for the first time documented a number of hill stream fishes from the sub Himalayan region. During the same period, Haeckel (1838) documented the presence of about 16 species of fresh water fishes from the Jhelum valley of Kashmir, based on the field collection of Kari Alexander Anslem Von Hugel, during his surveys (1831-36). Hugel is reported to have deposited his collection samples in the Museum of Natural History in Vienna, Austria Where Jacob Heckel was working as an Ichthyologist. These authors are followed by Gunther (1861) and Day (1878-79), who described a record number of fishes from the Himalayan mountain region. During the 20th century work on various aspects of Himalayan mountain fish fauna were carried out by a number of authors (Hora 1922 a, b; Hutchinson 1939; Menon 1949, 1954, 1962, 1992; Misra 1962; Das 1965; Pant 1970; Badola and Pant 1973, Badola and Singh 1977a, b, Jhingran and Sehgal 1978; Joshi *et al.* 1978; Sehgal *et al.* 1988; Sehgal, 1990, 1992). Most of these authors have described fish fauna of western and north central Himalayan states.

In fact, the Himalayan fish fauna includes even those fishes too, which are found in the Nepal part of the Himalayas. Similarly, the north eastern states of India *viz;* Assam, Manipur, Sikkim, Arunanchal etc., are also part of the Himalayan aquatic system. However, its published literature is not available to the author of this paper, till now. Hence, this paper primarily enlists the distribution of fishes from the states of Jammu and Kashmir, Himachal Pradesh and Uttar Pradesh. It is mainly on account of the fact that these three states harbor relatively, commercially more important fishes than rest of the Himalayan region. Further, the fish fauna of the whole Himalayan belt is by and large almost common, but for specific endemic diversity.

General Ecological Conditions of the Himalayan Region

The Himalayan region is usually regarded as a cold water regime, though this is not fully so. But still as compared to the Indo Gangetic plains and rest of the Indian peninsular region, the Himalayan waters are relatively colder. Apart from the thermal factor, the geo-topography of whole of the mountain region is highly varied and hostile, with very fast turbulence to very narrow deep encaved gorges on one hand to highly bouldered rocky substratum to soft sandy bottom. On the basis of elevation and temperature regime the Himalayan streams are classified in three principal types, by Jhingran and Sehgal, (1978) and Sehgal (1983 - Table 2.1). These water bodies usually have higher dissolved oxygen contents, high transparency, very low bio-chemical and chemical oxygen demands and relatively a low productivity.

A high velocity of water current is a major constraint in the lower primary productivity of the aquatic bodies of this region. In the recent years interest to know the general eco-biological characteristics of the Himalayan streams has increased and adequate information is available about a number of water bodies from this region (Sunder *et al.* 1978, Joshi, Seghal and Sunder 1978; Joshi 1988, a, b; Joshi *et al.* 1992 a, b; Joshi and Singh 1998; Joshi and Kathait 1998; Kishore *et al.* 1998; Joshi and Singh 1999 and Bhatt *et al.* 2000). However, the major aquatic net work of the Himalayan belt is still virgin and offers a wide scope, to explore the hydro-biological characteristics of various water bodies.

The Aquatic Resources of the Himalayan Region

The whole of the Himalayan belt towards Indian side, that is south of the Himalayas is well endowed with a number of major rivers (Table 2.1) having wide spread catchment areas. Sehgal (1992) has enlisted 15 major rivers, 12 high altitude lakes, 10 low altitude lakes and 03 reservoirs (Table 2.2), spread between greater Himalayas and lesser Himalayas and its foot hills. The hydrobiological characteristics of many of these water bodies have been partially worked out, as briefly included in the foregoing description. But most of the eco-biological reports on these aquatic resources are repeatedly site/location/region specific and hardly one or two are holistic in their approach. Apart from being micro-regional, the ambient environmental conditions are far from routinely seasonal, on account of number of anthropogenic activities, which have reached to the root of these various Himalayan rivers or up to the peak of the Himalayan mountains. As a result, there are wide fluctuations and abnormal variations in all sorts of ecosystems around us; the Himalayan aquatic eco-system is no exception. For example there is still no agreement among few of the Indian limnologists that what criterion should be applied in describing the various types of water bodies spread in this region. This is mainly due to two main reasons:

Table 2.1: Major Himalayan rivers holding cold water fisheries (Sehgal, 1992)

Sl. No.	Name	Origin	Length (km)	Area (km^2) Drained	App. Fishery Area (km)
1.	Indus	Trans Himalaya	709	117,844	600
2.	Jhelum	North Pirpanjal	400	28,490	400
3.	Chenab	Lahaul Himalayas	1180	26,755	1000
4.	Ravi	Barabanghal Himalayas	725	5,957	494
5.	Beas	South of Rohtang	470	25,900	470
6.	Sutlej	Trans Himalaya	1050	24,087	963
7.	Yamuna	Banderpunch peak	1300	359,700	1050
8.	Ganga	Gangotri Himalaya	2071	951,600	1010
9.	Ramganga	Kumaon Himalaya	609	32,800	609
10.	Ghagra	Lesser Himalaya	1080	127,500	1080
11.	Gandak	Central Himalaya	425	9540	425
12.	Kosi	Trans Himalaya	730	21,500	Not estimated
13.	Manas	Bhutan	–	34,480	Not estimated
14.	Teesta	Darjeeling	–	–	-do-
15.	Brahmaputra	Trans Himalaya	855	240,000	-do-

Table 2.2: The important Himalayan lakes and reservoirs: (Modified vide Sehgal, 1992)

Sl. No.	Name	Location	Total Area (ha) for Fishery	Remark
1.	Nilnag	Himalaya	6	Remain frozen for>6months
2.	Kishensar	Kashmir Himalaya	40	
3.	Vishensar	-do-	10	
4.	Gangabal	Kashmir Himalaya	157	
5.	Nundhkol	-do-	10	
6.	Tarsar/Marsar	Kashmir Himalaya	7	
7.	Sheshnag	-do-	51	
8.	Kounsernag	Kashmir Himalaya	40	
9.	Pangar Tso	Ladakh	290	Brackish water lake
10.	Tso Moriri	-do-	2100	-do-
11.	Khajjear	Chamba (H.P.)	2	
12.	Devariatal	Garhwal Himalaya	12	Remain frozen for<5 months
Low Altitude Lakes				
13.	Surnsar	Jammu	29	
14.	Mansar	-do-	45	
15.	Dal	Kashmir	1170	
16.	Manasbal	-do-	280	
17.	Wular	-do-	1600	
18.	Renuka	Himachal Pardesh	23	
19.	Bhimtal	Kumaun Himalaya	86	
20.	Nainital	-do-	74	
21.	Sattal	-do-	93	
22.	Naukuchital	-do-	65	
Himalayan Reservoir				
23.	Gobindsagar	Simla hills	16,870	
24.	Pong	Kangra Valley	2,900	
25.	Pandoh	Kulu Valley	2,000	

Firstly there are highly discernible conspicuous differences in the geographical placement of these water bodies. These differences are related mainly to altitude, topography of the region, river beds, gradients, types of the mountain on one hand and *secondly* the related physico-chemical characteristics like temperature, transparency, turbidity, pH, depth, river span and water velocity on the other make each system, different from the other (Table 2.3: Joshi, 1993). All these parameters cumulatively exert a very unique influence on the primary productivity of a given system, which ultimately become a deterministic characteristic on its total biotic community (Joshi and Singh 1998).

Despite a variable dynamism, each system tries to attain sort of a stable predictable behavioural pattern. And this tendency of an eco-system creates various types of adaptive divergences, leading to species diversity. Now all these abiotic and the biotic components make a system quite specific. This specificity is not an entire one, but is segmented in various regions of the same water body (Table 2.4: Sehgal, 1992; Joshi and Singh 1998, Kishore *et al.* 1998; Nautiyal 1995 and Singh and Kumar, 2000). These characteristics have been used by few authors in suggesting classifications of Himalayan rivers (Table 2.5: Sehgal *et al.* 1988; Nautiyal 1995 and Joshi *et al.* 1978) and Kashmir valley lakes (Zutshi and Khan, 1978: Table 2.5, 2.6).

Even the same river can be classified in to several altitudinal zones on the basis of just three parameters *viz;* altitude, temperature and dissolved oxygen contents in the water (Nautiyal, 1995). And this does not include the short term ambient influences of minor tributaries, besides the pollutional impacts of myriad types, which are soon mitigated on account of self-rejuvenating characteristics of these aquatic ecosystems, unless there is no recurrence of an hostile feeder stream. The whole of the Bhagirathi – Ganga system is a very good example, reflecting a high rejuvenating capacity in the uplands, which gets diluted once it enters the indo-ganetic plains and is almost totally lost by the time Ganga crosses the Kanpur zone. Similarly most of the lacusterine systems of up land valleys have lost their originality, productivity and are fast getting eutrophicated on account of various types of effluents being discharged in to them. As a result most of these lotic as well as lentic water bodies of the Himalayan

Table 2.3: Pooled mean values of some important physico-chemical parameters of glacier fed river (GFR) and spring fed rivers/rivulets (SFR) Garhwal Himalayas (vide Joshi, 1993 and Singh and Kumar, 2000)

S. No.	Parameter	Mandakini (GFR)	Khanda (SFR)	Nayar (SFR)	Bhagirathi (GFR)			Dwari Gad (SFR)	Ganga (GFR)	
	Station->	-1-	-2-	-3-	-4-	-5- U.Kashi	-6- Tehri	-7- U.Kashi	-8- D. Prayag	-9- R.Kesh
1.	Altitude(msl)	4000	–	3000	3812	2350	1750	2400	1600	290
2.	Velocity(M/S)	1.56	0.58	0.46	1.82	1.27	1.06	0.62	1.70	1.06
3.	Temperature(°C)	14.0	18.0	17.0	16.0	12.5	15.1	19.8	16.0	16.8
4.	DO(mg/l)	10.1	9.8	9.6	9.4	11.38	10.4	10.8	10.9	10.3
5.	BOD(mg/l)	1.34	1.26	1.71	2.16	2.90	3.55	3.87	2.85	4.17
6.	pH	7.2	7.4	7.6	7.3	7.5	7.6	7.7	7.6	7.7
7.	Tot. Alkal.(mg/l)	31.0	53.0	49.0	42.0	48.7	50.2	–	–	–
8.	Hardness(mg/l)	51.0	59.0	61.0	55.0	–	–	–	–	–
9.	Transparency(Cm)	–	–	–	–	54.7	62.9	80.0	52.0	50.8
10.	Turbidity	56 (NTU)	37 (NTU)	43 (NTU)	152 (NTU)	201.6 (JTU)	246.6 (JTU)	65.0 (JTU)	209.0 (JTU)	305.0 (JTU)
11.	Primary. Product. ($mg/c/m^3/h$)	–	–	–	–	62.3	102.7	181.4	93.7	98.7

Note: *Value given for parameter at column/station 1,2,3,4, are vide Singh and Kumar (2000). The name of station for their rivers and station has not been given by authors. *Values given for station column 5,6,7,8 are from authors project work (Joshi, 1993).

region are fast loosing their primary productivity (Joshi and Singh 1998) on one hand and there are observable break downs in the complicated food chains/webs with in each system, independent of each other, for similar systems, with in the same geographical habitat or else where.

Table 2.4: Comparison of major hydrobiological parameters of R. Beas in Himachal Pradesh up-stream (Between Manali and Bhakhili) and down stream (Below Pandoh Dam) during 1985-87 (Vide Seghal, 1992)

S. No.	Parameters	Up Streem	Down Stream
1.	Flow rate (cm s^{-1})	103.5	64.2
2.	Water temperature (°C)	12.0	16.2
3.	pH	7.6	7.6
4.	Dissolve Oxygen (ppm)	10.0	9.5
5.	Total alkalinity (ppm)	40.2	43.3
6.	Specific conductivity (mho s^{-1})	118.3	123.1
7.	Hardness (Ca+Mg) (ppm)	33.2	35.2
8.	Chlorides (ppm)	4.5	16.0
9.	Silicates (ppm)	2.0	3.5
10.	Calcium (ppm)	10.2	11.8
11.	Phosphates (ppm)	Traces	Traces
12.	Density of plankton (unit 1^{-1})	2220	2458
13.	Density of benthic microbiota (unit per cm^{-2} in lakhs)	2.30	5.84
14.	Bacillariophyceae (%)	90.2	63.1
15.	Chlorophyceae (%)	1.0	0.6
16.	Cyanophyceae (%)	8.3	2.9
17.	Density of benthic invertebrates (unit/m^{-2})	97	80
18.	Major constituents of benthic invertebrates (%)		
	18.1. Nymphs of Ephemeroptera	40.2	44.2
	18.2. Nymphs of Plecoptera	3.0	0.2
	18.3. Larvae of Caddis flies	14.3	22.2
	18.4. Larvae and adults of Coleoptra	2.7	2.2
	18.5. Larvae of Diptera	19.2	21.4

Table 2.5: Classification of Himalayan streams-based on water quality parameters, altitude, average percentage of major benthic invertebrates per square meter area and predominant fish species (Modified from Sehgal *et al.* 1988)

S. No.	Particulars	Streams of		
		Greater Himalaya	Lesser Himalaya	Siwalik
1.	Water temperature °C	13.4	18.7	22.9
2.	pH	7.4	7.9	8.0
3.	Dissolve oxegen (ppm)	9.3	8.7	7.9
4.	Elevation above (msl)	4000-2000	2000-1000	Below 1000
5.	Substratum	Rocks and boulders	Stones with sandy patches	Pebbles and muddy
6.	Benthic invertebrates (%): Out of total observed:			
(i)	Naids of Odonata	...	3.2	16.0
(ii)	Nymphs of Ephemeroptera	59.7	46.8	20.7
(iii)	Nymphs of Plecoptera	12.9	7.1	2.2
(iv)	Larvae of Trichoptera	23.6	21.8	26.8
(v)	Adults and larvae of Coleoptera	2.9	9.0	12.2
(vi)	Larvae of Diptera	22.5	10.7	7.4
7.	Predominant fish species			
(i)	*S. esocinus*	+	–	+
(ii)	*S. richardsonii*	+	+	(winter)
(iii)	*D. maculates*	+	+	–
(iv)	*G. reticulatum*	+	+	–
(v)	*T. putitora*	–	+(monsoon)	+
(vi)	*L. dero*	–	–	+
(vii)	*L. dyocheilus*	–	–	+
(viii)	*G. stoliczkae*	–	–	+
(ix)	*G. pectinopterus*	–	–	+

All these minor casual faults or variations ultimately, cumulatively blow up in to definite patterns, changing the nich dynamics and there by niche occupancy of the biota, in

Table 2.6: Limnological features of Kashmir vally lake types: (Vide Zutshi and Khan, 1978)

Sl. No.	Parameter	Valley Lake (*e.g.* Dal, Wular, Manasbal)	Forest Lake (*e.g.* Nilnag)	Mountain Lake (*e.g.* Alipathar)
1.	Altitude (m asl)	1580-1600	2000-2200	3000-4000
2.	Origin	River Valley Oxbow	Earth Movement	Glacial Damming
3.	Topography	Flat land	Foothills	High Mountains
4.	Drainage	Through Human Habitations	Partly through Arable Land	Glacial Morains Periphyti and Filamentous Algae
5.	Maximum water depth (m)	12	6	15
6.	Period of ice cover (months)	Absent or Very Short	3-4	7-8
7.	Secchi Disc Transparency	5.5	2-3	1-1.5
8.	Thermal Stratification	Warm monomictic polymictic abnormal	Dimictic	Cold monomictic Dimictic
9.	Summer Water Temp. (°C)	27-30	23-26	8-13 (Low)
10.	Specific Conductivity (uS/25°C), (max)	1000 (High)	370 (Moderate)	75 (Low)
11.	Macrophytes Quantitative Qualitative	Moderate-high All life forms	Moderate Floating types	Absent Absent Low
12.	Phytoplankton	Moderate-high	Moderate	Low
13.	Zooplankton	Moderate-high	Moderate	Low/Absent
14.	Fish population	High	Moderate	

the long food chain affecting the bio-diversity of micro or macro-community component/participant. This is actually happening in many mountain pockets. This is amply reflected in the species dynamics or the biodiversity parameters of these mountain aquatic bodies.

The Status of Fish Fauna of the Himalayan Region

The enlistment (-as described under – The Systematic List of Fishes -) of fish species included here is based on the earlier work of the author and a number of previous researchers. But it must be made clear that this paper, by and large is a brief review on the subject. Till now presence of 256 species of fresh water teleosts, belonging to 62 genera, 11 sub families, 12 families and 05 orders have been reported from various aquatic resources of this western to north-central Himalayan region, during almost last two centuries of fish diversity and taxonomic surveys – till date, by the various authors and groups. It will be interesting to evaluate that what is the real present day status of Fish Diversity in the Himalayan mountain region. From the existing literature three points emerge to my mind:

First still many remote areas are to be explored to find out the species diversity, second in view of reported divergence in speciation for certain species like: *Schizothorax, Puntius, Garra, Glyptosternum, and Noemachilus* there are chances that correct taxonomic identification may show synonimity, and third many species are already on the verge of extinction from this region.

A critical analysis points out that out of 256 species enlisted here as Himalayan Fish Fauna (for the prescribed region) about 93 species fall under Threatened group. This threatened status includes 22 vulnerable species, 16 intermediate species, 48 rare species and 07 endangered species (for the Himalayan region, perhaps?) as described by a few earlier workers of the subject (Menon 1974, Tilak and Sinha 1975; Sehgal 1992). It is quite obvious that many species are highly niche specific and endemic. The typical endemism simply means the organism of the given habitat or area would be critically highly vulnerable to slightest unfavourable variations in its ambient environment.

And as we all know that under the present global scenario and an attitude of – who cares for the environment – (despite a great hullabo about environmental awareness, around), we have severely exposed our aquatic environment to several types of anthropogenic alterations. These alteration pose myriad types of physical (*viz;* mid stream constructions activities, embankment erosions), chemical (use of detergent, chemical fertilizers, pesticides) and biological (introduction of new species exotic or extra territorial ones, introduction or removal or extinction of other community components) challenges to some very micro-habitat oriented and adapted endemic organisms. Absence of even one or two organisms in the long inter-connected food web in any given system would snow ball to grave biological threats at one or other level. And Himalayan ecology, as it stands today is most vulnerable to such conditions, right from the top of say Everest to the base line spots like Hardwar, Haldwani and Jammu to Meghalaya.

Fishery Scenario in Himalayan Region

The present day fishery scenario in Himalayan region can be said almost red (alert) to blackish black (bleak, too) rather being rosy pink. Nearly similar observations have been made by Joshi *et al.* (1978), for western to north central Himalayan fishery, while describing fishery resources of the Jammu region. These authors have mentioned that *Oreinus plagiostomus* constitutes about 29 per cent, and *Barrilius bendelisis* about 28 per cent (in trout streams), while *Tor putitora* constitutes about 30 per cent (in the maser streams) highest for the region. Six common species which contribute to the real fishery to the Uttarakhand (U.P.) Himalayan part are – *Oreinus richardsonii, Tor putitora, Labeo dero, Barilius bendelisis, Garra gotyla gotyla* and *Crossocheilus latius latius*. Our own field surveys show that in the Garhwal Himalayan region it is *Schizothorax sps.*, and *Tor sps.*, which contribute more than 60-70 per cent of the total fish haul (Table 2.7), followed by *Barilius* sps., and *Glptothorax* sps. Joshi (1993) have reported about 47 per cent, 18 per cent and 16 per cent of *Schizothorax, Tor* and *Glyptothorax* species in the random surveys around Tehri.

Table. 2.7: Annual fish haul composition (%) from selected station areas with Garhwal Himalaya, for Bhagirathi, Alaknanada, Ganga and their tributaries (vide Joshi, 1993 and 1998)

S. No.	Station	Year	*Tor* sps.	*Schizothorax* sps.	*Barilius* sps.	*Glyptothorax* sps.	*Pseudecheneis* sps.	*Labeo* sps.	Others
1.	Tehri	19851995	21.417.9	48.343.1	9.28.8	11.714.5	1.82.0	0.92.2	6.711.5
2.	Uttarkashi	19851995	4.13.2	60.052.7	11.410.4	9.614.0	3.42.0	1.60.9	9.916.3
3.	Karan Prayag	19851995	4.06 .8	77.068.4	2.58.4	2.52.4	3.53.0	4.51.2	6.09.8
4.	Rudra Prayag	19851995	8.08.6	72.072.0	4.36.5	3.21.8	4.00.9	3.02.2	5.58.0
5.	Srinagar	19851995	6.24.7	68.056.8	6.89.4	5.34.1	5.04.3	5.34.2	3.416.4
6.	Dev Prayag	19851995	30.232.4	26.028.7	8.26.4	6.34.9	1.11.7	5.75.8	22.520.1
7.	Rishikesh	19851995	49.840.2	2.03.5	6.812.6	0.40.1	0.10.1	19.922.4	21.021.1

Table 2.8: Length-frequency composition of total fish haul at Tehri (Based on Three Random Surveys: Joshi, 1993)

Length Range(CM)	Frequency (%)1985	Frequency (%)1995
05-10	3.8	5.1
11-20	26.8	28.4
21-50	40.7	41.7
51-75	18.0	16.8
76-100	10.7	8.0

Table 2.9: Maximum weight of fish observed during the surveys for (Mean Weight in gm) based for five specimens in each year near, Srinagar

S.No.	Species	Mean Wt. 1985	Mean Wt. 1995
1.	*Barilius barna*	135	205
2.	*Botia dero*	98	67
3.	*Schizothorax* sps.	4570	3895
4.	*Tor* sps.	6390	4720
5.	*Glyptothorax* sps.	354	244
6.	*Pseudechenis* sps.	735	530

A gradual decline (Joshi, 1993) in the length weight frequency of the fish catch/haul for the Garhwal region is also apparent (Tables 2.8, 2.9). There is increasingly greater exploitation of smaller sized fishes at all levels. In the colder mountain regime it is basically *Schizothorax* sps., which predominates others, while at lower mountain altitude or among the spring fed rivers and streams it is *Tor* sps which contributes maximum, at single species consideration. However, increasingly over the years it is almost the juvenile to quite immature age group of these species which are exploited (Nautiyal *et al.* 1988) Joshi, 1993 and Joshi and Singh 1998. In our own observations we found fish weighing about 6-7 kg only, a round Srinagar (Joshi, 1993) and that a general trend in fall of length and weight range of fish hauled between Tehri-Uttarkashi and Srinagar – Rishikesh is quite conspicuous (Tables

2.8, 2.9). Nautiyal *et al* (1988), also found that it is 19-55 cm size range for *Tor putitora,* which is exploited maximum; though these authors have quoted fishermen capturing fishes weighing 20-25 kg in the Ajeetpur section of river Ganga, in the foot hills at down stream, but that should be taken up as rare instances, under the present scenario, rather than normal catch.

As far as mahseer (*Tor* sps.), the fish of the middle to lower Himalayan region is concerned, there is a general decline through the belt, ranging a fall between 15 to as high as 63 per cent for the Kumaun lakes and the Gobindsagar reservoir (vide Sehgal 1971; Joshi *et al.* 1978; Pathani, 1994). This trend only shows that increasingly more and more amount of immature fishes are being hauled. Certainly this would lead to further decline in fish productivity of the region, for want of appropriate number of new recruiting to spawners in these streams, in near future.

Causes of Fish Decline in Himalayan Region

This part does not require any special elaboration on the question of causes of decline. If a single word can be selected to reply it absolutely then the answer is obviously – Man, himself, is the only and sole reason of such a rapid decline of quality fish fauna and in quantum, besides, in their diversity. However, after spoiling and reaching to the threatened level of over exploitation, we try to act as saviours. In view of our role following major reasons are attributed to the general decline:

(*i*) An over all degradation of ambient micro habitat of fishes at all stages of their life cycle.

(*ii*) Over exploitation of our resources at all levels, irrespective of catch age group, reproductive period and season.

(*iii*) Increasing human activities of human being with the aquatic environment on the name of recreation, tourism, adventurism.

(*iv*) Increasing anthropogenic encroachment of aquatic areas for various developmental and agricultural activities.

(*v*) Increase in deforestation, thereby fall in forest area, leading to enhanced soil erosion and siltation at various levels.

(vi) Break down of aquatic food chains at various levels, on account of loss of one or other types of biotic components.

(vii) Gradual decline of water level in smaller streams, on account of fast deforestation in the catchment areas of the uplands.

(viii) Use of traditional lethal to unnatural clandestine methods of poaching and fishing.

(ix) An apathetic, neutral to careless attitude and role of responsible Government bodies towards conservation, protection and maintenance of fish health and their environment.

(x) Rapid fall in the brooder population of fishes.

(xi) Snow balling impacts of various sorts of pollutional causes and pollutants.

(xii) Erratic and unpredictable changes in the climatilogical trends/patterns at global levels.

(xiii) Appearance of fish epidemics at various levels.

(xiv) Introduction of certain exotic varieties to the Himalayan streams or else where.

(xv) Increasing eutrophication at certain levels, mainly on account of domestic effluents.

(xvi) Developments of minor to major hydro-electric and irrigation projects, without appropriate measures towards fish movements, migration, feeding, spawning and nursery grounds (In Uttarakhand alone about 20 minor to major such projects are under way, at various stages of development).

(xvii) Fall in the biotic components at primary producer level in the aquatic ecosystems, due to various reasons.

(xviii) Fall in carrying capacity of various water bodies due to several anthropogenic and natural reasons.

(xix) Lack of complete knowledge about various aspects of fish eco-biology and their environment.

(xx) Lack of appropriate routine or advanced technology to mitigate various injurious impacts, due to financial or decision-making constraints.

(xxi) Lack of public awareness towards importance of maintenance of proper aquatic environment and fisheries potential in terms of nutritional and economic viability.

(xxii) Lack of manangement expertise with regard to routine fishery management, at various levels.

Systematic List of Fishes

Phylum	Vertebrata
Sub Phylum	Craniata
Super Class	Ganthostomata
Series	Pisces
Class	Teleostomi
Sub Class	Actinopterygii
Order. I:	Cypriniformes
Fam. 1:	Cyprinidae.
Sub Fam. 1:	Cyprininae.

Genus. *Tor*

Species

1.	*T. putitora*	(Ham.)	(V)
2.	*T. tor*	(Ham.)	(V and I)
3.	*T. mosa*	(Ham.)	(V)
4.	*T. mosal mahnadicus*	(Divid)	
5.	*T. khudree*	(Sykes)	(R)
6.	*T. progeneius*	(McCl)	
7.	*T. cheilynoides*	(McCl.)	(R)

Genus. Neolisochilus

8.	*N. hexagonolepis*	(McCl.)	(R)
9.	*N. wynaadensis*	(Day)	(R)

Genus. Oreinus

10.	*O. richardsoni*	(Gray)	(R)
11.	*O. kumaonensis*	(Menon)	

Genus. Chagunius

12.	*C. chagunio*	(Ham.)	

Genus. *Cirrhinus*

13.	*C. fulungee*	(Sykes)	
14.	*C. reba*	(Ham.)	

Genus. *Cirrhinu Schizothorax*

15.	*S. curvifrons*	(Heckel)	
16.	*S. esocinus*	(Heckel)	(R)
17.	*S. hugelii*	(Heckel)	(V)
18.	*S. longipinnis*	(Heckel)	
19.	*S. micropogon*	(Heckel)	
20.	*S. nasus*	(Heckel)	(R)
21.	*S. niger*	(Heckel)	(I)
22.	*S. macrophthalmus*	(Tarashima)	(R)
23.	*S. planifrons*	(Heckel)	(I)
24.	*S. raraensis*	(Tarashima)	
25.	*S. kumaonensis*	(Menon)	(I)
26.	*S. sinuatus*	(Heckel)	
27.	*S. plagiostomus*	(Heckel)	
28.	*S. progastus*	(McCl.)	(V)
29.	*S. labiatus*	(McCl.)	(V)

Genus. *Diptychus*

30.	*D.maccelatus*	(Steindachner)	(R)

Genus. *Lepidopygopsis*

31.	*L. typus*	(Raj)	

Genus. *IX: Schizopygopsis*

32.	*S. stoliczkae*	(Steindachner)	(R)

Genus. *Garra*

33.	*G. gotyla gotyla*	(Gray)	
34.	*G. annandalei*	(Hora)	
35.	*G. bicornuta*	(Rao)	
36.	*G. gravely*	(Annandale)	
37.	*G. hughi*	(Silas)	(I)
38.	*G. kempi*	(Hora)	(I)
39.	*G. lamta*	(Ham.)	

40.	*G. mcclellandi*	(Jerdon)	(R)
41.	*G. lissorhynchus*	(McCl.)	
42.	*G. mullya*	(Sykes)	
43.	*G. naganensis*	(Hora)	(R)
Genus. Crossocheilus			
44.	*C. latius latius*	(Heckel)	(I)
45.	*C. latius deplocheilus*	(Heckel)	(I)
46.	*C. dilocheilus*	(Heckel)	(V)
Genus. Labeo			
47.	*L. dero*	(Ham.)	
48.	*L. bata*	(Ham.)	
49.	*L. calbasu*	(Ham.)	
50.	*L. pangusia*	(Ham.)	(V)
51.	*L. dyocheilus*	(McCl.)	(V)
52.	*L. boga*	(Ham.)	
53.	*L. gonius*	(Ham.)	
Genus. Punhius			
54.	*P. conchonius*	(Ham.)	
55.	*P. ticto*	(Ham.)	
56.	*P arulius*	(Jerdon)	
57.	*P. chola*	(Ham.)	
58.	*P. dorsalis*	(Jerdon)	
59.	*P. filamentosus*	(Vale.)	
60.	*P. maheoda*	(Vale.)	
61.	*P. sophore*	(Vale.)	
62.	*P. waageni*	(Day)	
63.	*P. bovanicus*	(Day)	
64.	*P. jerdoni*	(Day)	(V)
65.	*P. carnaticus*	(Jardon)	
66.	*P. cauveriensis*	(Hora)	
Genus. Bangana			
67.	*B. diplostoma*	(Heckel)	(V)

Genus. *Hypophthalmichthys*

68.	*H. molitrix*	(Vale.)	(V)

Genus. *Ctenopharyngodon*

69.	*C. idella*	(Vale.)	(R)

Genus. *Osteobrama*

70.	*O. cotio cunma*	(Day)	(R)
71.	*O. neilli*	(Day)	
72.	*O. vigorsii*	(Sykes)	

Genus. *Osteochilus*

73.	*O. brevidorsalis*	(Day)	(R)
74.	*O. nashii*	(Day)	(R)

Genus. *Tinca*

75.	*T. tinca*	(Linn.)	(R)

Sub Fam. 2: Cultrinae. Genus. *Chela*

76.	*C. cashius*	(Ham.)	(I)
77.	*C. laubuca*	(Ham.)	
78.	*C. bupis*	(Day)	

Genus. *Salmostoma*

79.	*S. phulo*	(Ham.)	(V)
80.	*S. untrachi*	(Ham.)	(V)
81.	*S. clupeoides*	(Bloch)	(V)

Sub Fam. 3: Danioninae

Genus. *Barilius*

82.	*B. bendelisis*	(Ham.)	
83.	*B. barna*	(Ham.)	
84.	*B. canarensis*	(Jerdon)	
85.	*B. shacra*	(Ham.)	
86.	*B. tileo*	(Ham.)	
87.	*B. vagra*	(Ham.)	
88.	*B. barila*	(Ham.)	(V)
89.	*B. bota*	(Ham.)	(V)

Genus. *Brachydanio*

90.	*B. rerio*	(Ham.)	(R)
91.	*A. meletteies*	(Vale.)	

Sub Fam. 4: Rasborinae

Genus. Danio

92.	*D. rerio*	(Ham.)	(R)
93.	*D. dario*	(McCl.)	
94.	*D. devario*	(Ham.)	
95.	*D. naganensis*	(Chaudhuri)	(R)
96.	*D. neilgherriensis*	(Day)	(R)
97.	*D. aequipinnatus*	(McCl.)	(R)
98.	*D. dangila*	(Ham.)	(R)

Genus. Esomus

99.	*E. barbatus*	(Jerdon)	(R)
100.	*E. danricus*	(Ham.)	

Genus. Rasbora

101.	*R. bola*	(Ham.)	(E)
102.	*R. guttatus*	(Day)	
103.	*R. rasbora*	(Ham.)	
104.	*R. daniconius*	(Ham.)	(E)

Sub Family. 5: Shizothoracinae

Genus. Ptychobarbus

105.	*P. conirostris*	(Steindachner)	(E)
106.	*G. biswasi*	(Talwar)	(R)
107.	*S. curvifrons*	(Heckel)	(V)

Order. II: Siluriformes Family. 2: Sisoridae

Genus. Glyptosternum

108.	*G. pectinopterus*	(McCl.)	
109.	*G. conirostre conirostre*	(Steindachner)	
110.	*G. trilineata*	(Blyth)	(I)
111.	*G. cavia*	(Ham.)	(I)
112.	*G. madraspatanum*	(Day)	(R)
113.	*G. telchitta*	(Ham.)	
114.	*G. annandalei*	(Hora)	
115.	*G. ananmalaiensis*	(Silas)	(R)
116.	*G. gracile*	(Gunther)	

117. *G. indicus*	(Talwar)	
118. *G. kashmirensis*	(Hora)	
119. *G. platypogonoides*	(Bleeker)	(R)
120. *G. prashadi*	(Mukharji)	(R)
121. *G. lonah*	(Sykes)	
122. *G. stoliczkae*	(Steindachner)	
123. *G. striatus*	(McCl.)	
124. *G. dakpathari*	(Tilak and Hussain)	(R)
125. *G. garhwali*	(Tilak)	(R)
126. *G. alaknandi*	(Tilak)	
127. *G. brevipinnis*	(Hora)	
128. *G. trilineadus*	(Hora)	
Genus. *Conta*		
129. *C. conta*	(Ham.)	(R)
Genus. *Erethistes*		
130. *E. pussilus*	(Muler and Trochel)	
131. *E. montana montana*	(Hora)	
132. *E. montana pipri*	(Hora)	(R)
Genus. *Gagata*		
133. *G. cenia*	(Ham.)	(V)
134. *G. gagata*	(Ham.)	
135. *G. sexualis*	(Tilak)	(R)
Genus. *Laguvia* *(R)*		
136. *L. ribeirot*	(Hora)	
137. *L. shawi*	(Hora)	
138. *L. Kapuri*	(Tilak and Hussain)	
139. *L. asperus*	(McCl.)	
Genus. *Sisor*		
140. *S. rhabdophorus*	(Ham.)	(R)
Genus. *Pseudecheneis*		
141. *P. sulcatus*	(McCl.)	
Genus. *Bagarius*		
142. *B. bagarius*	(Ham.)	

Family. 3: Schilbeidae

Genus. Clupesoma

143. *C. garua* (Ham.)
144. *C. Montana* (Ham.)

Sub Fam. 6: Nemacheilinae

Genus. Nemacheilus

145. *N. acuticephalus* (Hora) (I)
146. *N. anguilla* (Annandale) (I)
147. *N. arafi* (Mirza and Banarescu)(I)
148. *N. arunachalensis* (Menon)
149. *N. baluchiorum* (Zugmayer)
150. *N. beavani* (Gunther)
151. *N. botia* (Ham.)
152. *N. brevis* (Boulenger)
153. *N. brunneanus* (Ammandale)
154. *N. carletoni* (Fowler)
155. *N. cincticauda* (Blyth) (I)
156. *N. corica* (Ham.)
157. *N. denisoni denisoni* (Day) (I)
158. *N. densoni dayi* (Hora)
159. *N. devdevi* (Hora)
160. *N. doonensis* (Tilak and Hussian) (R)
161. *N. elongates* (Sen and Nalbant)
162. *N. evezard* (Day)
163. *N. gangeticus* (Mirza and Nalbant)
164. *N. gangeticus* (Menon)
165. *N. guentheri* (Day)
166. *N. himachalensis* (Menon)
167. *N. horai* (Menon) (R)
168. *N. kangjupkhulensis* (Hora) (R)
169. *N. keralensis* (Rita and Nalbant)
170. *N. kessleri* (Gunther)
171. *N. kodaguensis* (Menon) (R)

172. *N. kohatensis* (Mirza and Banarescu)
173. *N. labeosus* (Kottelat)
174. *N. lindbergi* (Banarescu and Mirza)
175. *N. monilis* (Hora)
176. *N. montanus* (McCL)
177. *N. moreh* (Sykes)
178. *N. multifasciatus* (Day)
179. *N. manipurensis* (Chaudhuri) (R)
180. *N. nagaensis* (Menon)
181. *N. nilgiriensis* (Menon)
182. *N. notostigma* (Bleeker)
183. *N. pakistanicus* (Mirza and Banarescu)(R)
184. *N. pavonaceus* (McCl.)
185. *N. peguensis* (Hora)
186. *N. petrubanarescui* (Menon)
187. *N. parshadi* (Hora)
188. *N. reticulofasciatus* (Singh, Sen and Banar.)
189. *N. rivulicola* (Hora)
190. *N. rubidipinnis* (Blyth)
191. *N. rueppelli* (Sykes)
192. *N. rupicola* (McCl.)
193. *N. savona* (Ham.)
194. *N. scaturigina* (McCl.)
195. *N. semiarmatus* (Day)
196. *N. sijuensis* (Menon)
197. *N. sikmaiensis* (Hora)
198. *N. shanensis* (Hora)
199. *N. singhi* (Menon)
200. *N. striatus* (Day)
201. *N. triangularis* (Day)
202. *N. urophthalmus* (Gunther)
203. *N. vinciguerrae* (Hora)
204. *N. zonalternans* (Blyth)

Genus. *Aborichthys*

205. *A. elongatus*	(Hora)	
206. *A. garoensis*	Hora)	
207. *A. kempi*	(Chaudhuri)	
208. *A. tikaderi*	(Barman)	

Genus. *Schistura*

209. *S. punjabensis*	(Hora)	(R)
210. *T. marmorata*	(Heckel)	(R)
211. *T. kashmirensis*	(Hora)	

Sub Family. 7: Balitorinae

Genus. *Balitora*

212. *B. brucei*	(Gray)	
213. *B. mysorensis*	(Hora)	
214. *B. australis*	(Jerdon)	

Genus.*Homaloptera*

215. *H. bilineata*	(Blyth)	
216. *H. montana*	(Herre)	
217. *H. rupicola*	(Prashad and Mukeriji)	

Genus. XLVII: *Travancoria*

218. *T. jonesi*	(Hora)	(R)

Sub Fam. 8: Botiinae Family. 5: Cobitidae.

Genus. *Botia*

219. *B.almorhae*	(Gray)	
220. *B. berdmorei*	(Blyth)	
221. *B. birdi*	(Chaudhuri)	
222. *B. Dario*	(Ham.)	
223. *B. striata*	(Rao)	
224. *B. histrionic*	(Blyth)	
225. *B. lohachata*	(Chaudhuri)	
226. *B. rostrata*	(Gunther)	

Sub Fam. 9: Cobitinae

Genus. *Lepidocephalus*

227. *L. guntea*	(Ham.)	

228. *L. annanbalei* (Chaudhuri)
229. *L. berdmorei* (Blyth)
230. *L. irrorata* (Hora) (E)
231. *L. menoni* (Piuai and Yazdani)
232. *L. thermalis* (Vale.)
233. *L. caudofurcatus* (Tilak and Hussain)

Genus. Somileptes

234. *S. gongota* (Ham.) (R)

Genus. Pangio

235. *P. pangio* (Ham.)
236. *P. longipinnis* (Menon)

Genus. Neoencirrhichthys

237. *N. maydelli* (Bana and Nal.) (E)

Family. 6: Amblyceitidae

Genus. Amblyceps

238. *A. mangosis* (Ham.)
239. *A. laticees* (McCl.)

Family. 7: Bagridae

Genus. Mystus

240. *M. cavasius* (Ham.)
241. *M. bleekeri* (Day)
242. *M. aor* (Ham.)
243. *M. seenghala* (Sykes)

Genus. Batasio

244. *B. batasio* (Ham.)
245. *B. travancoria* (Hora and Law)

Family. 8: Channidae

Genus. Channa

246. *C. gachua* (Ham.)
247. *C. orientalis* (Bloch and Schneider)
248. *C. punctatus* (Bloch)

Family. 9: Adlocheilidae

Genus. Aplocheilus

249. *A. panchax* (Ham.) (E)'

Order. III: Mastacembeliformes

Family. 9: Mastacembelidae

Genus. Mastacembelus

250. *M. armatus* (Lacepede)

251. *M. pancalus* (Ham.)

Family. 10: Belonidae

Genus. Xenthodon

252. *X. cancila* (Ham.)

Order. IV: Salmoniformes

Family. 11: Salmonidae

Sub Fam. 10: Salmoninae Genus. LX: Salmo

Genu. Salmo

253. *S. trutta fario* (Linnaeus) (V)

254. *S. gairdenerii* (Richardson) (V)

Genus. Onchorhynchus

255. *O. mykiss* (Woldaum) (V)

Family. 12: Poeciliidae Order. V: Cyprinodontiformes

Sub Fam. 11 : Poeciliilae.

Genus. Gambusia

256. *G. holborooki* (Girard)

Note: E=Endangered I=Intermediate
R=Rare V=Vulnerable

Recommendation

In general we have the required basic knowledge of our infrastructural and natural resources of all kinds *viz;* abiotic and the biotic as well. We have more than often discussed these and many such related problems and prospects with suggestive remedial measures. Therefore I very strongly believe that the only recommendation I can make is that we require just one thing, and that is a very honest and strong objective oriented work culture and ethics – that's all. Once we all collectively as well as individually vow for it, sooner than later we shall have worlds best of our ecological and environmental status best maintained and ultimately one of the world's strongest and richest bio-diversity at all levels, terrestrial and the aquatic one.

REFERENCES

Badola SP and Pant MC (1973). Fish Fauna of the Garhwal Hills. Part I. *Indian J.Zoot.* 14:37-44.

Badola SP and Singh HR (1977a). Fish Fauna of Garhwal Hills. Pt. III. Chamoli District. *Ibid.* 18:119-122.

Badola S.P., and Singh HR (1977b). Fish Fauna of Garhwal Hills. Pt. IV. Tehri District. *Ibid.* 18:115-118.

Bhatt JP, Nautiyal P and Singh HR (2000). Population Structure of Himalayan Masher a Large Cyprinid Fish in the Regulated Foothill Section of the River Ganga. *Fish. Res.* 44:267-271.

Day F (1978). In: The Fishes of India: Being A Natural History of Fishes Known to Inhabit the Seas and Freshwaters of India Burma and Ceylon. Reproduced in 1958. William Dawson and Sons Ltd. London.

Day F (1889). The Fauna of British India Including Ceylon and Burma. Fishes – Vol. 1 and 2. William Dawson and Sons Ltd. London.

Gunther A (1861). List of the Cold Blooded Vertebrate Collected by B.H. Hodgson Esq. in Nepal. *Process. Zool. Soc. London*: 213-227.

Hamilton F (1822). An Account of the Fishes Found in River Ganges and its Branches. Edinburg and London.

Heckel JJ (1838). Fiche us Cashmir. Carl Friedherrn V. hugel Wein.

Hora SL (1922a). Notes on the Fishes in the Indian Museum. III. On Fishes Belonging to the Family Cobitidae from High Altitudes in Central Asia. Records of the Indian Museum: 24:63-83.

Hora SL (1922b). Notes on Fishes in Indian Museum IV. On Fishes Belonging to the Genus *Botia* Cyprinidae. Records of the Indian Museum. 24:313-321.

Hutchinson GE (1939). Ecological Observations on the Fishes of Kashmir and Indian Tibet. *Ecol. Mongr.* 92:147-181.

Jhingran VG and Sehgal KL (1978). Coldwater Fisheries of India. *Inland Fish Soc Barrackpore.*

Joshi BD and Kathait RS (1998). Limnological Characteristics of Three Tributaries of River Ganga between Dev Prayag and Rishikesh. *Him. J. Env. Zool.* 12:225-243.

Joshi BD, Pathak JK, Singh YN and Bisht RCS (1992a). On the Food Spectrum of the snow trout *Schizothorax richardsonii* and the mahseer *Tor tor* from river Bhagirathi in Garhwal Himalaya. *Him. J. Zool.* 6:152-157.

Joshi BD, Pathak JK, Singh YN., and Bisht RCS (1992b). A Study of Minor Limnobiotic Components of River Bhagirathi from Garhwal Himalaya. *Him. J. Env. Zool.* 6:158-163.

Joshi CB, Sehgal KL and Sunder S (1978). Observations on the Fishery Resources of the Hill Streams of Jammu Province with Special Reference to Mahseer and other Commercially Important Species. *Indian J. Fish.* 251/2:197-206.

Joshi CB (1988a). Development of Coldwater Fisheries in Kumaun Waters: Problems and Prospects. In: Perspectives in Aquatic Biology 1988 Proc. Nat. Sem. Ed. R.D. Khulbe. Papyrus Publishing House New Delhi.

Joshi CB (1988b). Mahseer Fishery of Some Hillstreams in Western Himalayas. Indian. *J. Fish.* 354:327-329.

Joshi BD and Singh R (1998). On Some Physico-Chemical Values of River Ganga between Devprayag and Rishikesh. *Him. J. Env. Zool.* 13:83-92.

Joshi BD and Singh R (1993). Studies on The Eco-biology of Selected Tributaries of River Ganga between Devprayag Rishikesh. Final Technical Report Submitted to G.B. Pant Inst. Himalayan Environment and Development Kosi Katarmal Almora pp. 134.

Joshi BD and Singh R (1999). On the Eco-Biology of Bhagirathi River in Garhwal Himalaya with a view to find out Remedial Measures for the Improvement of Riverine Eco-system and to Enhance Fisheries Potentials of the Region. Final Technical Report to Min. Env. and Forests. Government of India. New Delhi. pp. 165.

Kishore B. Bhatt J.P. Rawat V.S. and Nautiyal P. (1998). Stream Regulation: Variations in the Density of Benthic Macro Invertebrate Fauna of Ganga in Lateral Canal of Hardwar. *J. Hill Res.* 111:62:67.

Menon AGK (1949). Fishes of Kumaun Himalayas. *J. Bomb. Nat. Hist. Soc.* 483:535-542.

Menon AGK (1954). Fish Geography of the Himalayas. *Proc. Nat. Inst. Sci. India* 204: 467-493.

Menon AGK (1962). A Distributional List of Fishes of the Himalayas. *J. Zool. Soc. India* Calcutta 14:23-32.

Menon AGK (1974). A Check List of Fishes of Himalayan and Himalayan and Indo-Gangetic Plains. Spl. Pub. No. 1. pp. 136. *Ind. Fish. Soc.* India Barrackpore.

Menon AGK (1992). Fauna of India and Adjacent Countries. Pisces. Vol. IV. Part 2. Cobitidae. Zool. Survey. India Calcutta pp. 113.

Misra KS (1962). An Aid to the Identification of the Common Commercial Fishes of India and Pakistan. Records of Indian. Museum 57:1-320.

Nautiyal P (1995). Statistical Evaluation of Ecologically Different Glacier Fed Torrential Stenothermal GTS and Spring Fed Placid Eurythermal SPE Riverine Systems of the Himalayan Terrain Garhwal India. *J. Aqut. Biol. Fish.* 21-2:1-12.

Nautiyal P. Bhatt JP, Rawat VS, Kishore B, Nautiyal R and Singh HR (1988). Himalayan Masheer: Magnitude of Commercial Fishery in Garhwal Hills. Fish. Gen. Biodiversity Cons. Natcon Pub. 05:107-114.

Pant MC. (1970). Fish Fauna of Kumaun Hills. *Rec. Zool. Surv.* India 64 1-4:417-423.

Pathani SS (1994). Biology of *Tor* putitora Mahseer. In: Mahseer the Game Fish. ed. P. Nautiyal. Jagdamba Prakashan Dehradun 86-90.

Sehgal KL (1971). Fisheries Survey of Himachal Pradesh and Some Adjacent areas with Special Reference to Trout Mahseer and Allied Species. *J. Bom. Nat. Hist. Soc.* 70:458-474.

Sehgal KL (1983). Fishery Resources and their Management. In: Studies in Eco-development Himalayas Mountain and Men. 225-272. ed. Singh TV and Kaur J. Print House India Lucknow.

Sehgal KL (1990). Ecology Distribution and Abundance of Fish life in the North-western Himalayan Streams. pp. 287-299. In: Recent trends in Limnology Soc. Biosciences India. Ed Agarwal V.P.

Sehgal KL (1992). Review and Status of Cold water Fisheries Research in India. Spl. Publ. No. 3: pp. 60+X.N.R.C. on Coldwater Fisheries ICAR Haldwani.

Sehgal KL, Sunder S, Raina HS and Tyagi BC (1988). Twenty Five Years of Research on Coldwater Fisheries. *Spl. Sci. Rep.* 1.N.R.C.CW.F. pp. 60.

Singh HR and Kumar N (2000). Some Aspects of Ecology of Hill Streams: Stream Morphology Zonation Characteristics and Adaptive Features of Ichthyo-Fauna in Garhwal Himalaya. pp. 1-18. In: Modern Trends in Fish Biology Research. Ed. Duttamunshi JS Narendra Publ. House Delhi.

Sunder S, Bhagat MJ, Joshi CB and Ramakrishna KV (1978). Fishing Methods and Fish Catch Composition of Dal Lake Srinagar J and K during 1969-72. *J. Inland Fish. Soc.* India 10:9-18.

Tilak R. and Sinha NK (1975). A Study of the Fishes of the Subfamily Schizothoracinae Pisces Cyprinidae. On the Generic Status of *Schizothorax* Heckel 1838. *Annals Zool.* 32:290-297.

Zutshi DP and Khan MA (1978). On the Lake Typology of Kashmir. In: Environmental Physiology and Ecology of Plants. pp. 465-472. Ed. Sen DN and Bansal RP Published by B Singh and MP Singh Dehradun India.

Page 47-62

Fisheries and Aquaculture
Edited by: **Prof. (Mrs.) Neelima Gupta** and **Dr. D.K. Gupta**
Edition: **2015**
ISBN: 978-93-5056-736-4
Published by: **Discovery Publishing House Pvt. Ltd., New Delhi (India)**

3

Conservation of Fishery Resources for Food Security

Amita Saxena and **Paras Nath Jha**

Department of Fishery Biology, College of Fishery Science, G.B. Pant University of Agriculture and Technology, Pantnagar. Email: amitasaxena12@yahoo.co.in, parasincof@gmail.com

ABSTRACT

Indian fisheries are increasingly contributing to the nutritional security of the country with the present production of fish and shell fish from capture fisheries and aquaculture being around 8.0 million tonnes. Conservation and sustainable utilization of natural resources are issues receiving global attention after signing and convention on bio-diversity. Fish as a group, apart from its economic value from a bio-diversity viewpoint, has a highest diversity among all vertebrate taxa. It is one of the important food commodity having good nutritional profile specially protein and poly unsaturated fatty acid (PUFA). But now, at the present time due to some constraints like habitat alteration, over exploitation, illegal fishing, impact of exotic species, destruction, juvenile capture, indiscriminate fishing, and other anthropogenic effect, this resource is declining day-by-day. Therefore, some of the measures must be taken to conserve this resource for attaining food security and save this resource for future generations. The conservative measures include germplasm conservation, ranching, in-situ conservation, ex-situ conservation etc. The conservation of fisheries resource as a concept may sound simple but its realization and implementation is not an easy task. It is particularly so in a developing country like India with more than 120 crores of people, ongoing agriculture revolution, industrial modernization and where majority of the people are fish eaters and 14 million fishers and farmers earn their livelihood from fishing and allied sectors.

Keywords: Conservation, Fishery Resources, Food Security.

INTRODUCTION

Fishery Resources

With a long 8129 km. coastline, 0.5 million km^2 of continental shelf and 2.02 million km^2 of exclusive economic zone (EEZ), India is a major marine fish producer ranking seventh in the world. The warm, fertile inshore waters of India are among the most productive fishing grounds in the world, yielding shrimps, sardines, mackerels, Bombay ducks, carangids, croakers, soles, and a variety of other marine fish. Marine products are a major component of India's overseas trade. However, inland fisheries resources are equally rich and varied.

Fish Production

Fish and fisheries form important economic activities in India. The total fish production in the country increased sixfold from 0.75 million t in 1950-51 to 4.95t in 1994-95. During the same period, inland fish production increased from 0.22 million t to 2.09 million t registering a near tenfold increase. Over the last four and one-half decades, the annual growth rate in inland fisheries was 11 per cent and that of the marine segment was 9.0 per cent. The contribution from inland fisheries to national fish production has been consistently increasing. While in the 1950's it supplied less than one-half the volume of marine catch, it now contributes almost an equal quantity. Despite being a marine-fish producer traditionally, India is one of the few countries in the world which has substantially exploited its inland fisheries potential.

Inland Fisheries Resources

India's inland fisheries resources are as diverse as they are plentiful, comprising rivers, floodplains, estuaries, mangroves, estuarine impoundments, lagoons, upland lakes, reservoirs and ponds (Table 3.1). In India, inland fisheries is classified as follows: freshwater aquaculture, including the pond culture of carp; brackish water aquaculture, involving mostly shrimp culture; and capture fisheries in rivers, estuaries, lakes, reservoirs, etc.

Table 3.1: Fisheries resources

Marine Resources	
Indian Coastline	8129 km.
Continental shelf area	0.506 m. sq.km.
Exclusive Economic Zone	2.02 m.sq.kms.
Brackish water area	1.24 million ha.
Inland Resources	
Area under tanks and ponds	2.214 million ha.
Area available for fresh water fish culture	5.4 million ha.
Area of reservoirs	2.90 million ha.
Beels, Oxbow and lakes	0.82 million ha.
Lengths of rivers and canals	1,72,287 km.

Rivers

The country's major and minor rivers along with their tributaries, minor streams, creeks and all other microlotic systems have an estimated combined length of 45000 km. These along with the numerous man-made canals have a combined length of 0.17 million km. The Ganga river system and its tributaries have a combined length of 12,500 km., and the Brahmaputra is 4023 km., long. The peninsular rivers, Mahanadi, Godavari, Krishna and Cauvery, cover 6437 km., while the west-flowing Narmada and Tapti of Western Ghats have a combined length of 3380 km. The snow – and rain-fed Himalayan rivers are characterized by complicated flood regimes, a heavy silt load, marked seasonal variability in volume, course shifting and heavy bank erosion. In contrast, the rain-fed peninsular rivers are torrential and have well-defined stable courses, a lighter silt load and, except in the deltas, rocky terrain.

The catch from rivers does not contribute significantly to the total inland fish production in terms of volume, although a large number of traditional, artisanal fishers make a living on it. A substantial part of the Ganga and its tributaries flow through the Indo-Gangetic plains providing the richest source of freshwater capture fisheries in India. The Ganga is also the original habitat of the prized Indian major carp and a major source of riverine carp spawn, which meets 30 per cent of the carp seed requirements of the aquaculture sector.

Over the last few decades, marked alterations in the riverine systems have been detrimental to the fish stocks. The once remunerative capture fisheries no longer exists. Fish yield in middle stretches of the Ganga, which was 50.3 kg/ha/yr during the 1960's, declined to 20.0 kg/ha/yr in 1972 and 6.5 kg/ha in the mid 1980's. The average yield of Indian major carp declined from 13.3 to 4.6 kg during the same period. Fishing intensity along river courses varies from stretch to stretch owing to various factors such as:

- Seasonality of riverine fishing activity.
- Inconsistent catch composition.
- Conflicting multiple uses of river water.
- Aesthetic objections owing to nutrient loading and pollution.
- Lack of understanding of the fluvial system and unreliable database.
- Fragmentary and outmoded conservation measures.
- Lack of enforcement machinery.
- Inadequacy of infrastructure and supporting services.
- Defective marketing and distribution systems.
- Demand according to availability, affordability and palatability.
- Socio-economic and socio-cultural determinants.

Floodplain Lakes

The current yield of floodplain wetlands is not precisely known. Nonetheless, important scientific studies have been made on the limnology and productivity of these eco-systems and a production potential ranging from 1000 to 2000 kg/ha/yr has been estimated. They also provide the ideal location for pen and cage culture operations. Pen culture of major carp has indicated a production potential of up to 4 t/ha in six months according to the results in the Gandak basin. The rearing of *Clarias batrachus* and *Heteropneustes fossilis* in a weed-choked Assam *beel*, over a period of 90 days in 2 km^2 cages, obtained production results ranging from 0.190 kg to 4.8 kg.

Freshwater and Brackishwater Aquaculture

Ponds are among the most important inland fisheries resources of India, in terms of both surface area and the volume of fish produced. The country is believed to have a surface area of more than 2.21 million ha that can be developed for freshwater aquaculture, only a fraction of which is currently utilized. About 0.4 million ha are being supervised by government-sponsored aquaculture promotion agencies. Carp culture, traditionally restricted to the States of West Bengal, Bihar and Orissa, has recently spread to almost all the states of the country. Private fish farmers of the southern state of Andhra Pradesh have only recently been engaged in carp culture and have made great progress. The growth of brackishwater aquaculture has been most successful in the maritime states. Focusing on export-oriented shrimp culture, industrial giants of the corporate and multinational sectors are also involved.

Reservoir Fisheries

In India, reservoirs are considered the prime resource as regards capture fisheries and extensive aquaculture. The rivers, estuaries and other natural water bodies are threatened by increasing environmental degradation. With the great emphasis on conservation, there is little scope for a substantial increase in yields. The reservoirs, which already cover 3 million ha of surface area, are a growing resource with enormous potential for yield augmentation. The available estimates made by various agencies are conflicting and inaccurate. The study (Sugunan and Bhattacharya, 1995) estimated the combined surface area of all reservoirs, irrespective of size, as 31,35,366 ha. Enumeration of the medium and large reservoirs in India is a relatively easy task as there are fewer of them and the details are readily available from the irrigation, power and public works authorities. However, compilation of data on small reservoirs is a tedious task as they are ubiquitous and too numerous to count.

Conservation of Resources

Human use of natural resources has to be managed to provide maximum benefit to current generations while maintaining capacity to meet the needs of future generations. Conservation includes both the protection and rational use of natural resources.

Earth's natural resources are either nonrenewable, such as minerals, oil, gas, and coal, or renewable, such as: water, timber, fisheries, and agricultural crops. The combination of growing populations and increasing levels of resource consumption is degrading and depleting the natural resource base. The world's population stood at 850 million at the onset of the industrial age. The global population has grown to nearly seven times as large (6 billion), and the level of consumption of resources is far greater. This human pressure now exceeds the carrying capacity of many natural resources.

Nonrenewable resources, such as fossil fuels, are replaced over geologic time scales of tens of millions of years. Human societies will eventually use up all of the economically available stock of many nonrenewable resources, such as oil. Conservation entails actions to use these resources most efficiently and thereby extend their life as long as possible. By recycling aluminum, for example, the same piece of material is reused in a series of products, reducing the amount of aluminum ore that must be mined. Similarly, energy-efficient products help to conserve fossil fuels since the same energy services, such as lighting or transportation, can be attained with smaller amounts of fuel.

It may be expected that the biggest challenge of resource conservation would involve nonrenewable resources, since renewable resources can replenish themselves after harvesting. In fact, the opposite is the case. Historically, when nonrenewable resources have been depleted, new technologies have been developed that effectively substitute for the depleted resources. Indeed, new technologies have often reduced pressure on these resources even before they are fully depleted. Fiber optics, for example, has substituted for copper in many electrical applications, and it is anticipated that renewable sources of energy, such as photovoltaic cells, wind power, and hydropower, will ultimately take the place of fossil fuels when stocks are depleted. Renewable resources, in contrast, can be seriously depleted if they are subjected to excessive harvest or otherwise degraded, and no substitutes are available for, say, clean water or food products such as fish or agricultural crops. Moreover, when the misuse of biological resources causes the complete extinction of a species or the loss of a particular habitat, there can be no substitute for that diversity of life.

'Conservation' is sometimes used synonymously with 'protection.' More appropriately, however, it refers to the protection and sustainable use of resources. Critical elements of the effective conservation of natural resources include sustainable resource management, establishment of protected areas, and *ex-situ* (off-site) conservation.

Resource: Its Threats, Management and Conservation

Some of the most pressing resource conservation problems stem directly from the mismanagement of important biological resources. Many marine fisheries are being depleted, for example, because of significant overcapacity of fishing vessels and a failure of resource managers to closely regulate the harvest. In theory, a renewable resource stock could be harvested at its maximum sustainable yield and maintain constant average annual productivity in perpetuity. In practice, however, fishery harvest levels are often set too high and, in many regions, enforcement is weak, with the result that fish stocks are driven to low levels. A similar problem occurs in relation to the management of timber resources. Short-term economic incentives encourage cutting as many trees as quickly as possible.

A number of steps are being taken to improve resource conservation in managed eco-systems. *(i)* Considerable scientific research has been undertaken to better understand the natural variability and productivity of economically important resources. *(ii)* Many national and local governments have enacted regulations for resource management practices on public and private lands. *(iii)* In some of regions, programmes recently have been established either to involve local communities who have a greater incentive to manage for long-term production more directly in resource management decisions or to return to them resource ownership rights. *(iv)* Efforts are under way to manage resources on a regional or ecosystem scale using methods that have come to be known as ecosystem management or bioregional management. Since the actions taken in one location often influence species and processes in other locations, traditional resource conservation strategies were often focused too narrowly to succeed.

Protected Areas

One of the most effective strategies to protect species from extinction is the establishment of protected areas designed to maintain populations of a significant fraction of the native species in a region. Worldwide, 9832 protected areas, totaling more than 9.25 million square kilometers (24 million square miles), cover about 8 per cent of land on earth. Although these sites are not all managed exclusively for the conservation of species, they play an essential role in protecting species from extinction.

Many problems remain, however, in ensuring effective protected-area conservation networks. For example, several regions with important bio-diversity still lack effective protected-area networks. In addition, where protected areas have been designated, human and financial resources are not always available to effectively manage the areas. Particularly in developing countries, the establishment of protected areas has resulted in conflicts with local communities that had been dependent upon the areas for their livelihood. These challenges are now being addressed through international efforts, such as the International Convention on Biological Diversity, which aims to increase the financing available for protected areas and to integrate conservation and development needs.

Ex-situ Conservation

The most effective and efficient means for conserving biological resources is to prevent the loss of important habitats and to manage resources for their long-term productivity of goods and services. In many cases, effective conservation in the field is no longer possible. For example, some species have been so depleted that only a few individuals remain in their natural habitat. In these cases, there is no alternative to the *ex-situ* conservation of species and genetic resources in zoos, botanical gardens, and seed banks. *Ex-situ* collections play important conservation roles as well as serving in public education and research. Worldwide, zoos contain more than 3000 species of birds, 1000 species of mammals, and 1200 species of reptiles and botanic gardens are believed to hold nearly 80,000 species of plants. These collections hold many endangered species, some of which have breeding populations and thus could potentially be returned to the wild. Gene banks hold an important collection of the genetic diversity of crops and livestock.

Potential Effects of Climate Change

Higher temperatures reduce oxygen solubility in water but can raise the oxygen and food intake demand of fish as their metabolic rates are raised. Associated rises in gill ventilation rates can lead to increased uptake of aquatic pollutants, potentially rendering the flesh unfit for human consumption. Higher water temperatures can also favour the survival of parasites and bacteria. All these responses combine to potentially reduce fish survival, growth and reproductive success both in wild populations and aquaculture. Similarly, many species in temperate regions have characteristic temperature ranges in which they live and breed and rises in temperature may result in species being displaced to higher latitudes to be replaced by species preferring higher temperatures.

Hydrological Impact

In rivers, increasing flows during the flood season will translate to more extensive and prolonged floodplain inundation, potentially increasing overall system productivity including the fish component. Longer, more extensive floods are likely to provide greater and more prolonged feeding opportunities for fish. Improved growth can favour survival and reproductive potential (fecundity). Changes to the timing of flows also have the potential to disrupt spawning behaviour.

The dry season is a period of great stress to many river fish species arising from diminished feeding opportunities and water quality, and elevated risk of predation or capture. Fish survival during this period is therefore likely to be density-dependent. Increased precipitation and water availability during this period might favour fish survival and ultimately exploitable biomass, while drier conditions would have the converse effect.

The combination of reductions in river flow and sea level rise may change salinity profiles in river deltas and lead to greater upstream salinity intrusion. These changes may displace stenohaline (narrow salinity tolerance) species further upstream and increase the upstream range and biomass of euryhaline (wide salinity tolerance) species, including those that depend upon brackish water environments to complete their life cycles.

Perhaps the greatest impact will be in the conversion of snow – and glacier-fed rivers to rain-fed rivers as the permanent ice in many mountain regions is eroded. This will change the hydrological characteristics of such rivers fundamentally, altering their seasonality and the evenness of the food regimes.

Watershed, Basin Level Impacts

Careful consideration will have to be given to both planned and autonomous adaptive coping strategies pursued by the agricultural sector. Less predictable flooding patterns and reductions in dry season flows may force small-scale farmers to build makeshift levees to protect their crops from flood damage and to rely increasingly on surface water bodies to meet their irrigation needs. Planned adaptation may favour the construction of large-scale storage reservoirs, flood control embankments and irrigation schemes with an associated increase in withdrawal of water from the aquatic eco-systems, which impact negatively on the fisheries sector by obstructing fish migrations and diminishing dry season habitat availability and quality.

Basic Principles on Access to Waters and Resources

(i) ***Access to Community Waters***

(a) *The Principle of Equal Access*: The general rule is that Community fishing vessels have equal access to waters and resources in all Community waters.

(b) *Restrictions in the 12 Nautical Mile Zone*: This is an exception to the principle of equal access to Community waters that falls within 12 nautical miles from the baselines, where Member States may retain exclusive fishing rights. This derogation is based on preserving the most sensitive areas by limiting fishing effort and protecting traditional fishing activities on which the social and economic development of certain coastal communities depends. The measures establishing the conditions of access to waters and resources are adopted on the basis of the biological, socioeconomic and technical information available. A review of the current provisions is due to take place in 2012 (Article 17 of Regulation (EC) No. 2371/2002).

(c) *Other Access Restrictions beyond the 12 Nautical Mile Zone*: The Commission issued a communication in 2005 (COM (2005) 422) on the review of certain access restrictions in the common fisheries policy, referring to the Shetland Box and the Plaice Box. The communication is a response to the obligation to assess the justification for restrictions on access to waters and resources outside of the 12 nautical mile zone.

The Shetland Box was set up to control access to species which are of special importance in the region and which are biologically sensitive, while the Plaice Box was established to reduce the level of discards of flatfish, particularly plaice in North Sea fisheries.

According to the aforementioned communication, the Shetland Box will keep the restricted access measures for another three years, while no date has been set for the Plaice Box as there is uncertainty over the length and extent of the study needed.

(ii) ***Allocation of Resources and Sustainable Exploitation***

(a) *The Principle of Relative Stability:* Fishing opportunities are allocated among the Member States in such a way as to ensure the relative stability of the fishing activities of each Member State for each stock concerned. This principle of relative stability is based in particular on historical catch levels and implies the maintenance of a fixed percentage of authorized fishing effort for the main commercial species for each Member State. Fishing effort should be generally stable in the long-term, taking account of the preferences to be maintained for traditional fishing activities and regions that are most dependent on fishing.

(b) *Sustainable Exploitation:* Conserving resources by adjusting fishing capacity to catch possibilities is one of the priorities of the common fisheries policy (CFP). To achieve sustainable exploitation, fish stocks have to be managed applying the maximum sustainable yield (MSY). To this end, the CFP bases its decisions on the best scientific advice available and applies the precautionary approach, whereby the absence of sufficient scientific information should not be used as a reason for postponing or failing to take measures to conserve species on the brink of collapse. Sustainable exploitation also means to progressively implement the eco-system-based approach to fisheries management.

Fisheries Resource Conservation

(i) *Total Allowable Catches (TACs) and Effort Limitations*

(a) *Limiting Catches:* TACs, based on the scientific opinions of the International Council for the Exploration of the Sea (ICES) and the Scientific, Technical and Economic Committee on Fisheries (STECF), continue to be calculated annually so that they can be readjusted in accordance with the development of stocks. However, within the framework of the multiannual management of resources, they will be more stable and will enable fishermen to plan their activities better.

(b) *Limiting the Fishing Effort:* These measures may be applied as part of the plans for the recovery of stocks that are at risk. They will consist, for example, of an authorized number of fishing days per month. This number may vary according to the gear used, the fishing zone visited (according to the ICES divisions), the species targeted, and the state of the stock and possibly the power of the vessel. With a view to ensuring greater flexibility, the Member State may transfer these days among the various units of their fleet.

(c) *Technical Measures:* In general terms, they aim to prevent catches of juveniles, non-commercial species and other marine animals. They are determined in relation to the target species and associated species (in the case of mixed fisheries), the operating zone and the type of gear used. The most current types of technical measures are related to:

- fishing gear; the setting of minimum mesh size for nets, structure and number on board;
- the composition and limit of accidental catches of by-catches on board;
- the use of selective fishing gear to reduce the impact of fishing activities on marine eco-systems and non-target species;

- delimitations of zones and periods in which fishing activities are prohibited or restricted including for the protection of spawning and nursery areas; and
- setting a minimum size for species that may be retained on board and/or landed.

In the case of a serious threat to the conservation of living aquatic resources, or to the marine eco-system resulting from fishing activities and requiring immediate action, the Commission and the Member States (or the latter on their own initiative) may adopt emergency measures to protect fish stocks and to restore the balance of marine ecosystems that are in danger.

Alternatively, Member States may adopt conservation and management measures applicable to all fishing vessels within their 12 mile zone provided that these measures are not discriminatory and that consultations with the Commission, other concerned Member States and the relevant regional advisory council (RAC) have taken place.

Also, when these measures are no less stringent than Community legislation, Member States may apply them solely to fishing vessels flying their flag in waters under their sovereignty and jurisdiction.

Finally, it is worth mentioning that experimental fishing projects serve to promote conservation and the investigation of selective fishing techniques to be implemented.

(ii) ***Long-term Strategy for Fisheries Resources Management***

(a) *Multiannual Stock Management Plans:* Seek to maintain the volume of stocks within safe biological limits. These plans lay down maximum catches and a series of technical measures, taking into account the characteristics of each stock and fisheries (species targeted, gear used, state of stocks concerned) and the economic impact of the measures on the fisheries in question.

(b) *Multiannual Stock Recovery Plans:* Will be implemented for fish stocks that are in danger. They are based on

scientific advice and provide for limits on the fishing effort (that is, the number of days vessels are at sea). They ensure 'that the impact of fishing activities on marine eco-systems is kept at sustainable levels'.

(iii) Fleet Management

Fleet management is a way of adjusting fishing capacity in order to bring about a stable and enduring balance between such fishing capacity and their fishing opportunities. Some ways to achieve this are:

- fixing the number of vessels and type authorized to fish (*e.g.*, by fishing licences);
- fleet register as a means to control and monitor fishing capacity;
- entry exit schemes and overall capacity reduction;
- reduction of fishing effort;
- reference levels;
- member States' obligation to report on their fleet capacity;
- European Fisheries Fund (EFF) instruments to adjust fishing capacity.

Conclusions

Basic features of good Integrated Resource Management (IRM) include the formation of extensive partnerships and the close involvement of local interests. Fishery and aquaculture stakeholders, both public and private, may therefore pursue actions which aim to:

- Empower local interests to plan and to implement conservation of the environment for fisheries.
- Protect resources and environment for fisheries and aquaculture by actively seeking partnerships with relevant government and non-government organizations (including commercial entities) that also seek to manage resources and the environment.
- Promote capacity building on aspects of IRM.

IRM can begin with improved cross-sectoral co-operation among the agriculture, forestry and fisheries sub-sectors.

However, there may be a need for additional technical assistance and policy guidance on IRM for sustainable production of fish and other food in watershed areas. Such IRM efforts are often also required at international, especially regional levels, and further assistance may be necessary in regional decision-making for the transboundary management of shared river and lake basins.

REFERENCES

"Biography of Hugh Hammond Bennett". NRCS. http://www.nrcs.usda.gov/about/history/bennett.html. Retrieved 2008-01-10.

Cook Maurice. "Hugh Hammond Bennett: the Father of Soil Conservation". *Department of Soil Science, College of Agriculture and Life Sciences*. North Carolina State University. http://www.soil.ncsu.edu/about/century/hugh.html. Retrieved 30 September 2011.

Federal Crop Insurance Reform and Department of Agriculture Reorganization Act of 1994, 108 Stat. 3223, October 13, 1994.

NRCS. "National Conservation Practice Standards." National Handbook of Conservation Practices. Accessed 2009-06-05.

"Records of the Natural Resources Conservation Service". NARA. http://www.archives.gov/research/guide-fed-records/groups/114.html. Retrieved 2008-01-10.

Soil Conservation and Domestic Allotment Act., P.L. 74-46, 49 Stat. 163, 16 U.S.C. § 590(e), April 27, 1935.

SugunanVVand Bhattacharya B K (1995). Ecology and Fisheries of Beels in Assam. *CIFRI Bull. 104*, pp. 65.

U.S. Natural Resources Conservation Service (NRCS). Washington, DC. "Soil Survey Programmes." Accessed 2009-06-05.

Page 63-67

Fisheries and Aquaculture
Edited by: **Prof. (Mrs.) Neelima Gupta** and **Dr. D.K. Gupta**
Edition: **2015**
ISBN: 978-93-5056-736-4
Published by: **Discovery Publishing House Pvt. Ltd., New Delhi (India)**

4

Floodplain Wetland

An Important Resource of Fishery

Amita Saxena and **Paras Nath Jha**

Department of Fishery Biology, College of Fishery Science, G.B. Pant University of Agriculture and Technology, Pantnagar. Email: amitasaxena12@yahoo.co.in, parasincof@gmail.com

ABSTRACT

Wetlands are dynamic eco-systems and are among the most important natural resources on earth. On an account, roughly 12 per cent of the earth's surface is covered by wetlands; of this 15 per cent is under flood plain wetlands. This resource includes the flat lands bordering rivers and streams that are subjected to periodic or permanent flooding, which tend to be most expensive along the lower stretch of the river. The distribution of floodplain wetland in India is vast which are locally known as: jheel, maun, chaur, dhar, boar, beel etc., and are of different types like: Ox-bow lakes, open type floodplain wetlands, closed type floodplain wetlands etc. Floodplain wetlands are one of the important and potent resources of fish and fisheries. Not only it has importance in accordance to capture fisheries but is also significant from culture fisheries point of view. In many places, intensive culture is being practiced in floodplain wetland like Bihar, Uttar Pradesh,

Assam, West Bengal, Odisha and NE states. On the basis of fish production, we have to give more emphasis on good culture and management practices to take more and more production for sustaining this resource which could be a good option for enhancing livelihood and food security of people.

Keywords: Floodplain Wetlands, Fisheries.

INTRODUCTION

India is a South Asian country situated between the Himalayas in the north and the Indian Ocean in the south and is flanked on either side by Pakistan and Burma. India is a federal republic made up of 25 states and covers a total area of 3287728 km^2. One-half of India's national territory lies above the Tropic of Cancer and the rest is within the tropics. India's population of over 900 million is the second largest in the world and the population density is also very high with more than 70 per cent of the people living in rural areas. The economy is agriculture-based. Although rich in natural resources and self-sufficient in food grains, India has many unresolved problems relating to poverty, unemployment and malnutrition.

India is a land of diversity. The climate ranges from tropical heat in the south to temperate in the north. The landscape includes towering mountains, extensive alluvial plains, riverine wetlands, plateaus, deserts, coastal plains and deltas. The main soil types are alluvial, deep and medium black, red and yellow, laterite, saline and desert, and forest and hill. Almost all conceivable forms of vegetation, including tropical evergreen, littoral and swamp, tropical moist deciduous, tropical thorn, montane subtropical, Himalayan and Alpine are present in various parts of the country. The major physiographic divisions are the Himalayas, the Indo-Gangetic plains, the Vindhyas, the Satpuras, the Western Ghats, the Eastern Ghats, coastal plains, deltas and the riverine wetlands.

Floodplain Wetland Lakes

India has more than 200000 ha of floodplain lakes (locally called *mans, chaurs, beels, jheels,* and *pats*), especially in the States of Assam, Bihar, and West Bengal. These take the form of typical oxbow lakes, sloughs, meander scroll depressions, backswamps, residual channels or tectonic depressions, but it is very often difficult to establish their identity because of natural and man-made modifications. The evolution of river beds and the effects of extensive flood control and irrigation works have reduced the fish production levels of many of these lakes through siltation, habitat destruction, heavy weed infestation and isolation from seasonal floods and natural sources of fish stock. Heavy weed infestation, eutrophication and accumulation of bottom muck are the greatest problems, further aggravated by the indiscriminate killing of brood fish during recruitment phase.

The current yield of floodplain wetlands is not precisely known. Nevertheless, important scientific studies have been made on the limnology and productivity of these eco-systems and a production potential ranging from 1000 to 2000 kg/ha/yr has been estimated. They also provide an ideal location for pen and cage culture operations. Pen culture of major carp has indicated a production potential of up to 4 t/ha in six months according to the results obtained in a *man* in the Gandak basin. The rearing of *Clarias batrachus* and *Heteropneustes fossilis* in a weed-choked Assam *beel,* over a period of 90 days in 2 km^2 cages, obtained production results ranging from 0.190 kg to 4.8 kg.

Fishes Found in Flood Plain Wetlands

- Indian Major Carp: *Labeo rohita, L. calbasu, L. fimbriatus, Cirrhinus mrigala, Catla catla.*
- Mahseer: *Tor tor, T. putitora, T. khudree, Acrossocheilus hexagonolepis.*
- Minor Carp, Snow Trout and Peninsular Carp: *Cirrhinus cirrhosa, C. reba, Labeo kontius, L.bata, Puntius sarana, P. dubius, P. carnaticus, P. kolus, P. dobsoni, P. chagunio, Schizothorax plagiostomus, Thynnichthyes sandkhol, Osteobrama vigorsii.*
- Large Catfish: *Aorichthys aor, A. seenghala, Wallago attu, Pangasius pangasius, Silonia silondia, S. childrenii.*
- Featherback: *Notopterus notopterus, N. chitala.*

- Air-breathing Catfish: *Heteropneustes fossilis, Clarias batrachus.*
- Murrel: *Channa marulius, C. striatus, C. punctatus, C. gachua.*
- Weed Fish: *Ambassis nama, Esomus danrica, Aspidoparia morar, Amblypharyngodon mola, Puntius sophore, P. ticto, Oxygaster bacaila, Laubuca laubuca, Barilius barila, B. bola, Osteobrama cotio, Gadusia chapra.*
- Exotic Fish: *Oreochromis mossambicus, Hypophthalmichthys molitrix, Cyprinus carpio specularis, C. carpio communis, Gambusia affinis, Ctenopharyngodon idella.*

Floodplain wetlands are characteristic features along the rivers Ganga, Brahmaputra and Barak basin, especially along their middle and lower stretches in the eastern and north-eastern parts of India. Most of the tributaries of Ganga river support floodplain wetlands in Uttar Pradesh, Bihar and West Bengal. Similarly, tributaries of river Brahmaputra and Barak river basin also support floodplain wetlands in Assam, Meghalaya, Manipur, Mizoram, Nagaland and Tripura. Uttar Pradesh has a wetland spread area of nearly 1, 52,000 ha (Pathak *et al.* 2004). Floodplain wetlands covers an effective area of 42,000 ha area in West Bengal, which is about 22 per cent of total freshwater area of the state (Sugunan *et.al.* 2000). Assam has 1,392 floodplain wetlands spread over 1, 00,000 ha area. These include 322 wetlands along the river Barak which constitute 8,000 ha. (Sugunan and Bhattacharya, 2000) Floodplain wetlands cover an area of 40,000 ha in Bihar, mostly along northern part of the state. Manipur has a floodplain wetlands spread area of 16,500 ha (Sugunan *et.al.* 2000). In North Eastern Indian state of Assam, floodplain wetland fisheries following the history of traditional management and lessee based management approaches and the role of women especially fisherwomen in prevalent management regimes like co-operative and individual regimes are almost negligible and show *de facto* dominance of fishermen in decision-making. Community based fisheries management as new approach started in fisheries management of water bodies of Assam from 2007. Amguri-Bosapathar-herheri wetland was given under the control of fisheries department from revenue department in 2007-08 for intervention of community approach. Wetland development committee was formed of 402 members including 50 women of the households of three adjoining villages Amguri, Basapathar and Herheri for effective utilization of the natural fisheries resources, better price of the product and more market power for enhancement of livelihood in a sustainable manner by the landless, small and marginal wetland users. The executive committee was formed for running day-to-day business. In the executive committee, representation of women members is much larger than their representation in BDC. Women members are vice president, treasurer of the executive committee. In last two years with the involvement of both fishermen and women the productivity of this wetland has shown an upward trend and within three years it rose from 150 kg/ha/year to 800 kg/ha/year. The role of women is important in decision-making process of management in Amguri-Bosapathar-Herheri wetland in Golaghat district of Assam. Arunachal Pradesh constitutes around 2,500 ha of floodplain wetlands. The floodplain wetlands of Meghalaya and Tripura covers an area of 213 ha and 500 ha respectively (Sugunan *et.al.* 2000).

Summary

The floodplain wetlands are considered as biologically sensitive habitats as they play a vital role in the recruitment of fish populations in the riverine eco-systems and provide nursery grounds for commercially important fishes. They are extremely rich in plant nutrients, therefore have biological productivity. However, in many beels, the nutrients are usually locked up in the form of large aquatic plants like water hyacinth, and do not contribute significantly to the fish production.

REFERENCES

Pathak V, Tyagi R K and Singh B (2004). Ecological Status and Production Dynamics of Wetlands of Uttar Pradesh. *CIFRI Bull.* 131, pp. 44.

Sugunan V V and Bhattacharya B K (2000). Ecology and Fisheries of *Beels* in Assam. *CIFRI Bull.* 104, pp. 65.

Sugunan VV, Vinci G K, Bhattacharjya, BK and Hassan M A (2000). Ecology and Fisheries of *Beels* in West Bengal. *CIFRI Bull.* 103.

[II]

Fish Economics, Climatic Change and Remote Sensing

Page 71-84

Fisheries and Aquaculture
Edited by: **Prof. (Mrs.) Neelima Gupta** and **Dr. D.K. Gupta**
Edition: **2015**
ISBN: 978-93-5056-736-4
Published by: **Discovery Publishing House Pvt. Ltd., New Delhi (India)**

5

Ornamental Ichthyo-Resource

A Powerful Economic Engine

Alpana Vohra[1], Rakesh Kumar Gupta[2] and Kadambri Gupta[2]

Department of Zoology, GWC, Kathua. (Corresponding Author)[1]
Department of Zoology, University of Jammu, Jammu[2]. Email: alpnavohra 72@gmail.com

ABSTRACT

Human population over the world is exhibiting an unprecedented growth with an annual growth rate of 1.15 per cent, adding approximately 87 million individuals every year to the already explosive number of 6 billion. Job extending agencies are struggling hard to keep pace with this population explosion resulting in an ever increasing unemployment that acts as a compelling force to look for alternatives, particularly self-employable ones. The aquarium industry can prove to be an important and a fruitful project of entrepreneurship. Over the years, the ornamental fish production for the aquarium industry has risen as a multimillion dollar industry in various countries of the world. Though there is a vast potential offered by its rich diversity, India has yet to make its mark in the said industry. In terms of economic valuation, the global trade of ornamental fish is worth $282 million of which India's share is merely

0.4 per cent that amounts to about \$1.1 million. The present paper forms an eye opener to the fact that while some states of the country are way ahead in the field of ornamental fish trade, ours is still staggering behind with its dwindling populace of undermined ornamental ichthyo-diversity which otherwise could be a fertile field of entrepreneurship.

INTRODUCTION

Our nation is blessed with a rich bounty of ichthyo-fauna comprising approximately 2118 species (Basheer *et al.* 2001; Ingochouba, 2005). This vast diversity of fish fauna has been invariably used to meet the food requirements of the growing human population. Techniques like hybridization, induced breeding etc., have been used to optimize the yield resulting in a blue revolution. Presently, fisheries and aquaculture contribute 1.07 per cent to the National GDP and 5.30 per cent to agriculture and allied activities (FAO, 2010).

The beauteous ichthyo-diversity forms not only a source of food but their graceful display of acrobatics coupled with their vivid array of colours present an eye-cooling stimulus that produces a positive response by easing a tense mind.

Ever since humans began to marvel at splendors of this gift of nature, a new hobby came into being – the aquarium keeping. Human interest in this aspect of ichthyo-fauna soon gave rise to a booming industry worth 282 million US \$, of which, India's share is merely 0.4 per cent (Financial Express, 2010) in spite of the vast scope offered by its ichthyofauna to be used as aquarium fishes. The diversified Indian aquatic environment forms abode to about 600 fish species that have promising market as ornamental fish (Ingochouba, 2005). Workers like Sen (1985), Mercy (2004), Sinha (2005), Sharma *et al.* (2007), Biswas *et al.* (2008), Swain (2008) and Panigrahi *et al.* (2009) from different parts of the country have acknowledged the ornamental potential of these ichthyo-species thus paving way for trade of aquarium fishes in various parts of the country.

Indian exports rose from Rs. 24.8 m in 1998-99 to Rs. 61.0 m. in 2001-02 (Sunita, 2006). Though the export rose up to

Rs. 65 m in 2006-07, yet the growth was insignificant as compared to trade in food fishes which is about Rs. 8000 crore per annum (Financial Express, 2010). Swain *et al.* (2003), reported that the export of ornamental fishes from the country was mainly confined to fresh water varieties captured from wild (85%) and a few bred varieties of exotic species (15%).

Although India has plenty of water bodies right from Ladakh to Kanayakumari and from Kach in Gujrat to Sunderbans, rich in fish fauna, yet a capture based activity is not sustainable in the long run, there is a need to shift the focus from capture based to culture based activity with thrust on breeding and restocking of ornamental fishes.

Since the demand for good quality tropical ornamental fish far exceeds the supply, its culture and breeding has a major potential not only to earn a living by selling them in domestic market but also to earn profits by exporting them (Sunita, 2006). For instance, in local markets, *Daniorerio*is is sold at the rate of Rs. 6 while its value overseas is US $0.16/ pair. The cost of *D. dangilla* in local market is Rs. 12 while its overseas value is US $1.50/pair (Mahapatra and Vinod, 2009).

Though states like: Mumbai, Chennai, Kolkata, Andhra Pradesh, Orissa, Kerala, Assam and Chhattisgarh are way ahead in the field of ornamental fish industry, the state of Jammu and Kashmir is yet to make its mark in the said trade. This is despite the fact that the water bodies of the state harbor about 125 species of ichthyofauna (Jyoti *et al.* 2004). There are about 1248 lotic and lentic aquatics with a water spread of 39921.8 hectares. The length of 27781 km. of rivers/streams facilitates the farming of more than 40 million tons of food fishes. Due to the state government initiatives, the output of fish has increased in the past few years. Fish production went up from 1,35,011 quintal in 1990-91 to 1,88,510 quintal in 1998-99 (Statistical Digest of Jammu and Kashmir, 1999-2000).

Though the ichthyofauna is known to generate revenue for the state by way of food fish and game fish that attracts lots of tourists to the region, the ornamental value of the ichthyo-species of the state is yet to be explored and exploited for its money generating potential.

The present study, thus, intends to highlight the ornamental fishes of Jammu, a sub-tropical part of the state, and its suburbs so as to take the first step that shall lead to a journey towards achieving the goal of a full blooming ornamental-fish-industry in the state.

Jammu division of the state of Jammu and Kashmir is located in the Shiwalik range of the Himalaya between lat. 32°20′ and 33°10′ and long. 74°45′ and 75°55′ between an altitude of 300 meters and 4200 meters above Mean Sea Level (MSL).

One of the major landmarks of the region is Trikuta hills that shelter the world famous shrine of 'Mata Vaishno Devi'. The serpentine river Chenab or Chandrabhaga traverses through the middle. In the south flows another big river, Ravi that separates the Jammu region from the states like: Himachal Pradesh and Punjab. The province is also blessed with two important well sung lakes, Mansar and Surinsar and umpteen number of high altitude lakes besides a famous wet land Gharana. Apart from these water resources, there are about 227 rain fed pools (Dutta and Kaur, 2006).

Flowing through the heart of Jammu City is the river 'Tawi' (the west bank tributary of river Chenab) which is fed by a large number of seasonal and perennial tributaries called 'chos'. All these water bodies support a diversified fish fauna. About 103 species of ichthyo-fauna have been reported from Jammu (Dutta and Kaur, 2006).

Review of literature reveals that many of these fishes which have the potential to generate revenue (through ornamental fish trade) and do so in other parts of the country (as mentioned earlier) are acknowledged merely for their food value or as links in the food chain.

The piscine population is not only undervalued as mere food or forage fish but also face threat of depletion due to habitat destruction, over exploitation, deleterious means of fishing, pollution and introduction of exotic species, all of which are side effects of human population explosion (Vohra, 2011).

High rate of demographic pressure has adversely affected not only the bio-diversity in general and the fish fauna in particular but also has shown disastrous effects on the human population. The present day youth not only face unemployment but are also enveloped in a secluded and cocooned social networking like 'facebook' where virtual pet keeping is enjoyed in space only. Gone are the days of aesthetic hobbies.

Once ornamental fish industry blooms in the state, it shall not only open new avenues of employment/entrepreneurship for our youth but shall also popularize healthy hobbies. Thus inspired by the wonders the said industry can create in the region, at economic as well as social level, the present author undertook this study. This endeavour is a humble effort by the author that aims to serve the society in its own little way.

An extensive survey of the water bodies in and around Jammu city, located between $70^0$24′ and $75^0$18′E longitude and $30^0$50′ and $33^0$30′ N latitude at an elevation of 1073 feet, was conducted in order to prepare a checklist of fishes found to be of ornamental value and has been presented in the form of an inventory.

Collection and Identification of Fishes

Different collection sites (lentic and lotic) in and around Jammu *viz;* Gharana, Dablerh, Arnaia, Biaspur, Blah, Gror, Sehi (R.S. Pura), Tawi, Sari Rakwal, Ghou Manhasan, Chakraili, Marh, Flora were surveyed for presence of ichthyo-fauna of ornamental value and collection was made with help of drag and cast nets. Identification was done with help of Day (1958), Malhotra *et al.* (1975), Sterba (1989a, b) and Jayram (1999). For systematic arrangement of the fishes, classification followed by Jayaram (1999) was referred.

Criteria for Selection as Ornamental Fish

For the present study, small to medium sized fish specimens, ideal for keeping in aquaria were assessed for their potentiality as ornamental fishes. Basic parameters taken into consideration were:

1. Acceptance of captivity.
2. Ability to behold the onlooker (by means of colour, body contour, feeding tactics, behaviour).
3. Ability to survive on artificial feed.
4. Compatibility with other species.
5. Easy maintenance and longevity.

Observations

During the present investigation, 47 species of fishes belonging to 31 genera, 15 families under 7 orders possessing definite potential as aquarium fishes have been recorded from the various water bodies in and around Jammu city (as depicted in the Classificatory tree).

A glance at Table 5.1 clearly shows that Order Cypriniformes dominated the ichthyo-species of the region with 28 species under 3 families followed by Order Perciformes (7 species under 5 genera and 4 families), Order Siluriformes (6 species under 5 genera and 4 families), Order Synbranchiformes (3 species under 2 genera and 1 family) and Orders Beloniformes, Osteoglossiformes and Cyprinidontiformes each with 1 species under 1 genus and 1 family. The percentile distribution of these orders in the region is depicted in the pie-chart.

Table 5.1: Phylogenetic position of ornamental fishes of Jammu

S. No.	Orders	No. of Families	No. of Genera	No. of Species
1.	Cypriniformes	3	16	28
2.	Perciformes	4	5	7
3.	Sluriformes	4	5	6
4.	Synbranchiformes	1	2	3
5.	Beloniformes	1	1	1
6.	Osteoglossiformes	1	1	11
7.	Cyprinodontiformes	1	1	1
	Total	**15**	**31**	**47**

Beloniformes **Cyprinodontiformes** **Ostoeglossiformes**

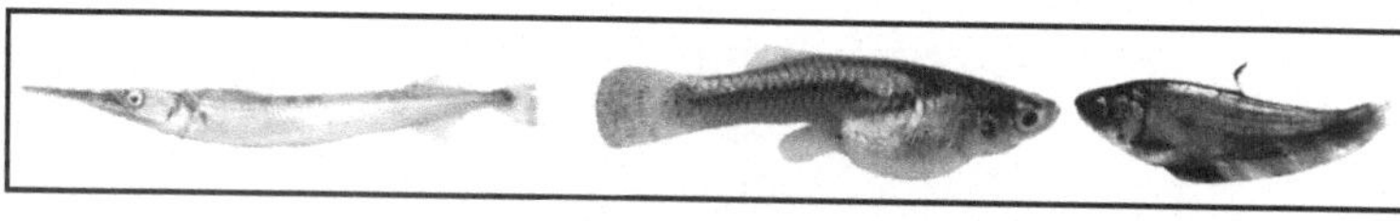

Synbranchiformes

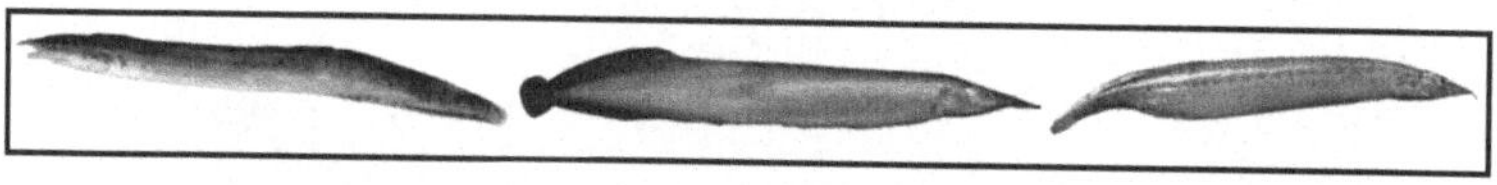

Perciformes

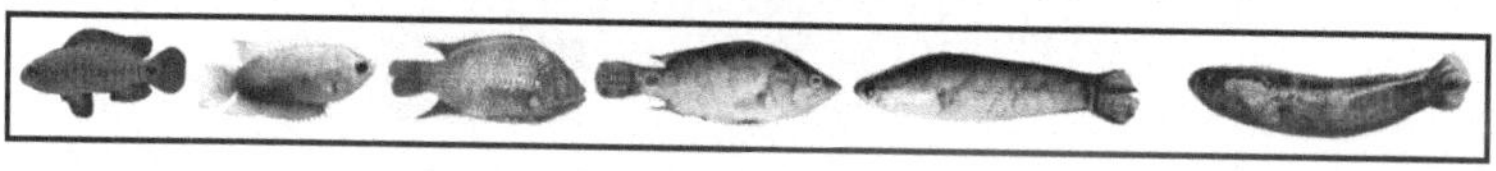

Siluriformes

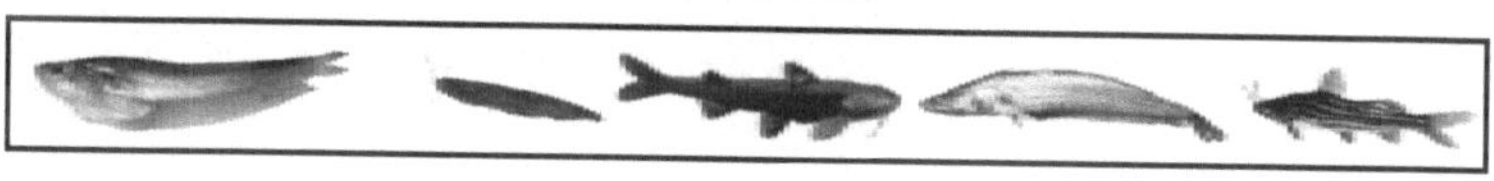

Cypriniformes

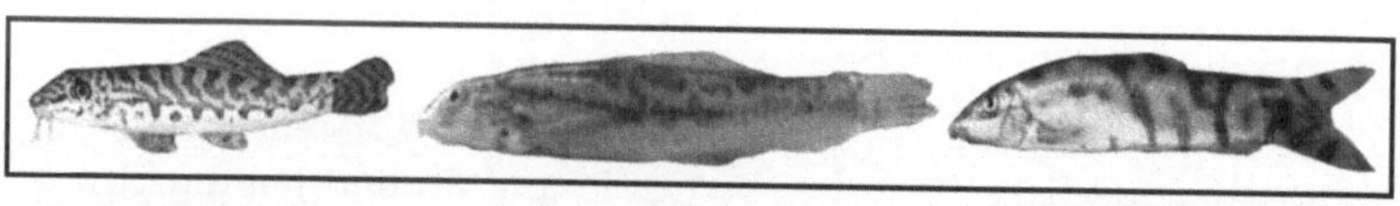

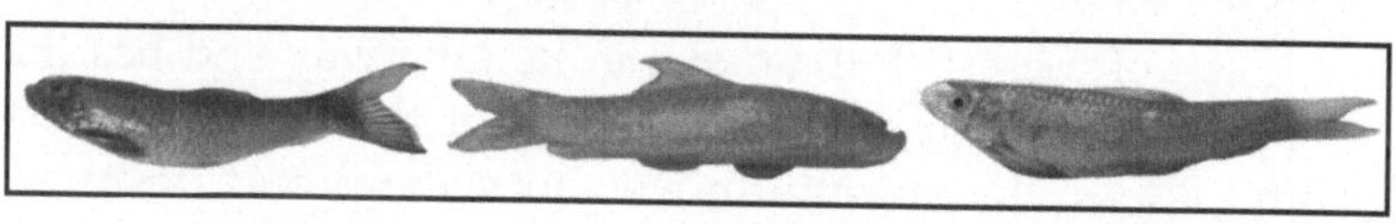

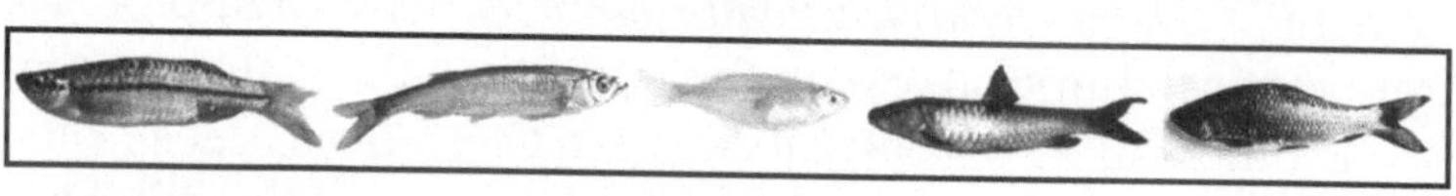

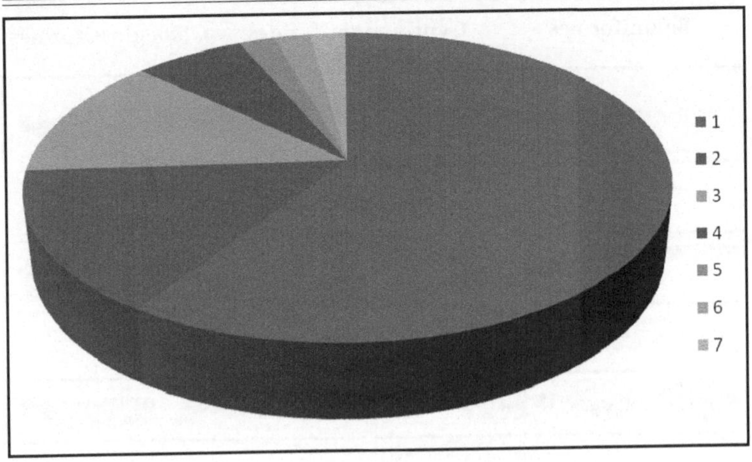

Key:

1	Cypriniformes	2	Perciformes
3	Siluriformes	4	Synbranchiformes
5	Beloniformes	6	Osteoglossiformes
7	Cyprinodontiformes		

Pie Chart depicting percentile availability of different orders of ornamental fishes in water bodies in and around Jammu city.

Each of these fish is unique in its own way and has the potential of driving away the stress of the beholder. The playful antics, the graceful movements, the proud postures, the hunting tactics, the coveted glances and the beautiful colors can easily enthrall any onlooker.

There are some fishes like: *Gambusia affinis, Brachy daniorerio, Danio devario, Esomus danricus, Rasbora* spp., *Chela* spp. that can impress one by their agility in the water column while others like *Lepidocephalusguntea, Glyptothorax cavia, Botia dayi, Nemacheilus botia* have the ability to behold the onlooker merely by their hide and seek among the aquarium accessories. It is quite obvious that it is not only the colour but various other diverse features by virtue of which many of our indigenous fish become worthy of the 'ornamental' tag.

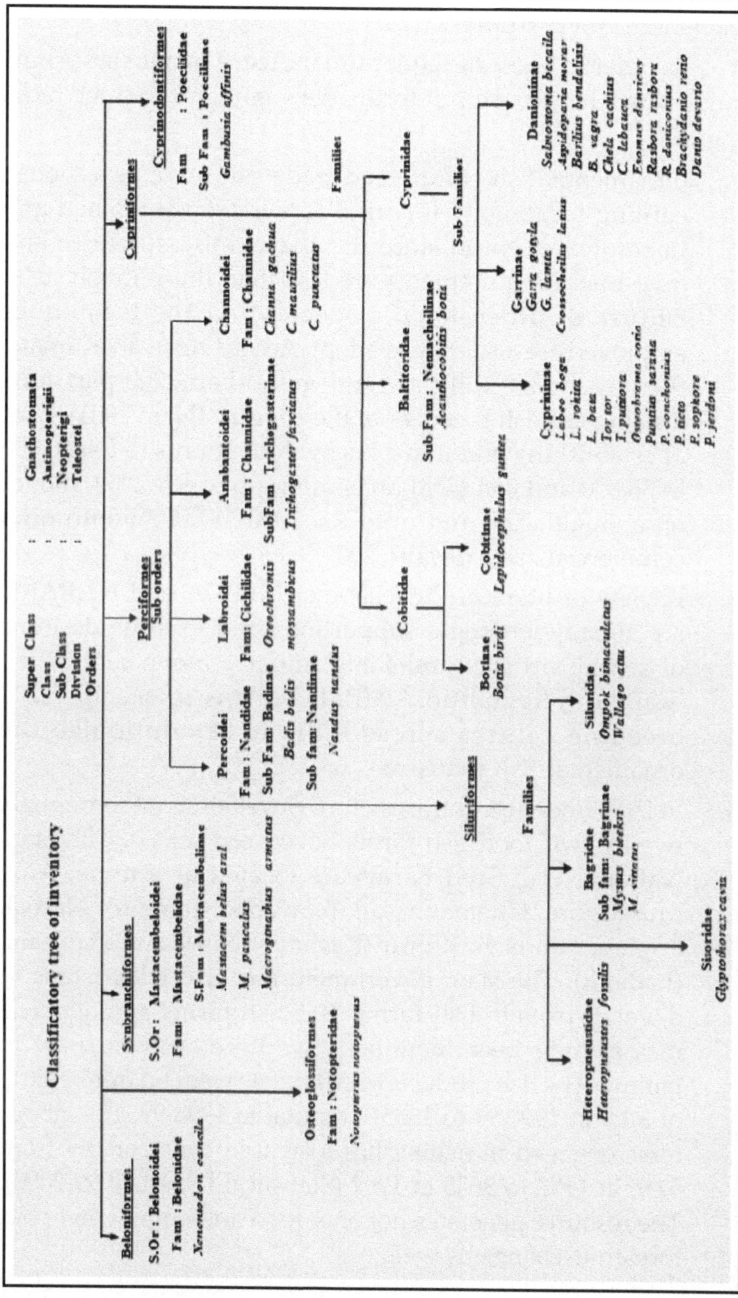

Classificatory tree of inventory

Facts and Suggestions

In order to boost the aquarium industry in our state, some suggestions have been put forth after highlighting some facts:

Facts

1. Ornamental fish culture and trade can serve as a money earning technology for rural farmers, farm-women and unemployed youth since the space, infra structure and investment requirements are less than those involved in culture of other aquatic species and the techniques employed are also easy to adopt. According to an estimate, there were 350 full time and more than 2000 part time ornamental fish breeders in the country (Nair, 2001). Cost of establishing a unit in a backyard amounts to Rs. 10,000 to 50,000 and can yield an earning up to Rs. 2000/month on a small scale and upto Rs. 5000-25,000/month on a commercial scale (Swain, 2008).
2. Review of literature reveals that MPEDA and NABARD are already lending a supporting hand to those desirous of setting up such units and under a movement called 'Rainbow Revolution' MPEDA plans to set up 7,200 breeding centres across India to revolutionize the ornamental fish industry.
3. In J&K, under the Infrastructure Development Programme, twenty two food fish farms have been set up. The State National Fish Seed Farms are located at Kathua, Anji, Muradpore, Ghomanhasan, Nowabad (Jammu), Narbal, Trigam, Pandach, Kohru (Kashmir), Shey and Damsana (Ladakh). The state government has also taken steps to develop private fish farms. 811 fish farms among rural masses have been identified, two-thirds of which are in Jammu. The fish production in the state went up from 135011 quintal in 1990-91 to 188510 quintal in 1998-99. The labour force engaged in fishing has increased considerably from 5446 in 1972 to 9655 in 1997 (Statistical Digest, 1999-2000). The resource generates not only food and employment but foreign exchange as well.

4. According to a report by Furi (2008) on a statement released by the Director of fisheries, Jammu, food fish production in the state head touched 19,000 tonnes and the department earned a revenue of Rs. 2.11 crores during 2006-07.
5. Since unit value of ornamental fish is more than food fish (MPEDA, 2008), one can easily imagine the financial gains that can be fetched through ornamental fish trade. Steps have already been initialized for utilization of ornamental fishes for enhancing revenue of our state by setting up India's largest and underground aquarium in Jammu. This serves as a major tourist attraction in the region.
6. Moreover, fish farms have been set up at Doomi village (Jammu) so that ornamental fishes could be cultured and traded (Kak, 2008). Recently, at Nowabad fish farm (Jammu), a batch of 39 woman trainee was introduced to undertake management, breeding and culture of ornamental fishes most suited to local environmental conditions.
7. Cost of establishment of a backyard fish hatchery unit for the culture was estimated to be Rs. 1 lakh. Materials required for the same would be provided on 50 per cent subsidy (Zee News.com, 2010).

In view of the above information, it would not be incorrect to mention, that Jammu has already taken initial steps towards establishment of ornamental fish industry in the state. But unfortunately none of the afore mentioned steps took into consideration the fate of the indigenous fish fauna that face depletion.

There are about 1248 lakes and water bodies in our state with a water spread of 39921.8 hectares harboring more than 125 species of fishes reported from the area (Statistical Digest, 1999-2000). More than 30 of these species are recognized as ornamental fishes internationally (Charak and Fayaz, 2006). This offers a good potential for ornamental fish trade but it is ironical that in our state these fishes are looked upon as link fish or as food for poor. In Kashmir valley, these are traded as sun dried fish.

Suggestions

1. Seminars and awareness programmes need to be held in order to make the masses aware of the richness of our water bodies with respect to ornamental fishes and their potential to generate revenue through trade at domestic, national and international level.
2. Training programmes, workshops may be held to educate people about culture of these fishes in captivity.
3. Vocational courses on 'Aquariology' can be devised to educate the students about the economic importance of ornamental fishes and the means to generate income via their culture and trade on a part-time or full-time basis. The aquarium industry deals not only with the living gems but also with aquarium accessories, feed manufacture etc. A know-how of the same can help in entrepreneurship and generation of many 'blue-collared jobs'.
4. At aquarium awareness centre, stress should be laid on spreading awareness about indigenous ornamental fishes.
5. Exhibitions can be held to glorify the splendours in an aquarium and instill in the minds of general public various benefits of not only possessing and maintaining an aquarium but also trading in ornamental fishes.
6. Agencies like: NABARD, MPEDA, and NFDB can give financial assistance for setting up of breeding units in rural as well as urban areas.
7. To generate interest and love for ornamental fish, the state fisheries department should essentially install aquaria at public places to enhance the vivacity of the locality.

It is sincerely hoped that the present paper has successfully highlighted the fact that the ornamental ichthyo-diversity can prove to be a powerful economic engine by offering a fertile field of entrepreneurship and contributing to rural development too as is done in Assam (Ingochouba, 2005) and West Bengal (Panigrahi *et al.* 2009).

It is, therefore, high time we realize the potential of our ichthyofauna, exploit them judicially and reap benefits before they end up either getting extinct or branded as patents at foreign hands.

REFERENCES

Basheer VS, Gopalakrishnan A, Lal K K and Ponnial A G (2001). Needs for Diversifying Research on New Aquaculture Species. NBFGR – NATP - Publication No. 3 Paper No. 23.

Biswas B K and Sugunan U U (2008). Fish Diversity of Brahmaputra River in Assam India. *J. Inland Fish Soc. India* 40 1: 23:31.

Charak K S and Fayaz F (2006). Status of Ornamental Fisheries in Jammu and Kashmir State. In: Fisheries and Aquaculture in Indus River Region. Ed. Kohli M. P. S. Indian Soc. Fisheries Professionals Mumbai. 157-160.

Day F (1958). The Fishes of India. A Natural History of the Fishes known to Inhabit the Seas and Fresh Waters of India Burma and Ceylon Vol. I and II. William Dawson and Sons Ltd. London.

Dutta S P S and Kaur H (2006). Ichthyo-fauna of Jammu District of Jammu Region J&K State India. In: Fisheries and Aquaculture in Indus River Region. Ed. Kohli M. P. S. Indian Soc. Fisheries Professionals Mumbai. 87-99.

FAO. 2010. FISHSTAT 2010.

Financial Express. (2010). MPEDA Hopes to Boost Ornamental Fish Exports to 50 mn. http://www.financialexpress.com/news.mpeda.hopes–to-boost–ornamental-fish-exports–to-50mn/311505/.

Ingochouba L (2005). Ornamental Fish Culture Project How and Where?. http://aquafind.com/articles/ornamental_fish_culture.php.

Jayaram K C (1999). The Freshwater Fishes of the Indian Region. Narendra Publishing House Delhi - 110 006 India.

Jyoti MK Sharma K K and Sharma S P (2004). 'Ecological Studies and Ichthyofauna of River Tawi.' In: 15th All India Congress of Zoology and National Symposium on 'Status of Coldwater Fisheries with Reference to Fragile Himalayan Aquatic Eco-system.' Oct-29-31 2004. Org. by University of Jammu Jammu and Zoological Society of India.

Kak M. L (2008). Bid to Promote Ornamental Fishes wwwtribuneindia.com/2008/20080312/ J&K. htm#13.

Mahapatra BK and Vinod K (2009). Biology and Culture of Indigenous Ornamental Danids of North-East India. 20th All India Congress of Zoology. 29-31.

Malhotra Y R and Jyoti M K (1975). An Identification of Fishes Found in Jammu Division of J&K State. Jammu Univ. Review 5: 50-66.

Mercy T V A (2004). Indigenous Ornamental Cyprinids of Western Ghats of India – Present Status and Future Prospects. 15th All India Congress of Zoology and National Symposium on "Status of Coldwater Fisheries with Reference to Fragile Himalayan Aquatic Eco-system." Oct 29-31 2004. University of Jammu. J&K.

MPEDA (2008). Indigenous Ornamental Fishes its Prospect in Assam. http://assam Agribusiness.nic.in/fish bullet/indigenous per cent 20 ornamental per cent fish.pdf.

Nair K S (2001). Status of Indian Ornamentals Fish Trade. Captive Breeding for Aquaculture and Fish Germplasm Conservation NBFGR-NATP. Publication No. 3. Paper No. 61.

Panigrahi A K Dutta S and Ghosh I. (2009). Selective Study on the Availability of Indigenous Fish Species Having Ornamental Value in some Districts of West Bengal. In: Advances in Aquatic Ecology Daya Publishing House. 77-81.

Sen T K (1985). The Fish Fauna of Assam and the Neighbouring Northeastern States of India. Records of Zoological Survey of India Occasional Paper No. 64: 1-216.

Sharma S Sharma P Siddiqui A and Belsare D K (2007). Fish Species Diversity of Sirpur Lake Indore M.P. India. *Him. J. Env. Zool.* 18 2: 349-352.

Sinha A (2005). Ornamental Fish Diversity of India. Aquatic Bio-diversity in India: The Present Scenario ed. D.R. Khanna A.K. Chopra and G. Prasad. Daya Publishing House New Delhi.

Statistical Digest. (1999-2000). Jammu and Kashmir Development Report.

Sterba G (1989a). Freshwater Fishes of the World: Vol. I. Cosmo Publications New Delhi. India.

Sterba G (1989b). Fresh Water Fishes of the World: Vol. II. Cosmo Publications New Delhi India.

Sunita. (2006). Studies on Breeding Performance and Larval Rearing of Goldfish *Carassius auratus* Linn.. M.Sc. Thesis. Department of Zoology and Fisheries Punjab Agricultural University.

Suri V (2008). J&K to have Fish Mandis soon. www.meri news.com/article/JK to have –fish mandis-soon/135003.shtml.

Swain S K (2008). 'Present Senario of Ornamental Fish farming and Trade' In: Applied Bio-informatics Statistics and Economics in Fisheries Research. eds. Ajit Kumar Roy and Niranjan Sarangi Pub: New India Publishing Agency New Delhi India. 165-184.

Swain S K, Jena J K and Ayyappan S (2003). Prospects of Export - Oriented Freshwater Ornamental Fish Culture in India. *Fishing Chimes* 22 10-11: 111-113.

Vohra A (2011). Studies on Breeding and Colouration Behaviour of Some Fresh Water Ornamental Fishes of Jammu. PhD., thesis University of Jammu.

Zee news.com (2010). J&K Women to Set-up Backyard Fish Hatcheries. www.zeenews.com/news 657766. html.

Page 85-100

Fisheries and Aquaculture
Edited by: **Prof. (Mrs.) Neelima Gupta** and **Dr. D.K. Gupta**
Edition: **2015**
ISBN: 978-93-5056-736-4
Published by: **Discovery Publishing House Pvt. Ltd., New Delhi (India)**

6

Climatic Changes and Chromatophore Diversity in Fishes

Amita Saxena and **Swati Sharma**

College of Fisheries,GB Pant University of Agriculture and Technology, Pantnagar - 263 145, India. E-mail: amitasaxena12@yahoo.co.in

ABSTRACT

Color change can serve a number of functions, and can be a singular aperiodic event or a rhythmic process driven by responses to environmental cues or endogenous rhythms. In invertebrates and poikilothermic vertebrates, color changes are effected by the chromatophores, stellate cells located in the hypodermis containing black (melanophores), red (erythrophores), yellow (xanthophores), or white (leucophores) pigment granules. Physiological color change results from migration of pigment granules into and out of dendritic cell processes and takes place over time scales of seconds to hours. Morphological color change, which consists of changes in the amount of pigment or number of chromatophores, takes place over longer time scales of days to weeks. Recent studies on the effects of climate on primary production are reviewed and the consequences for fisheries production are evaluated. Although our existing knowledge is in many respects incomplete, it nevertheless provides an adequate basis for improved management of ornamental fisheries and of marine ecosystems and for adapting to climate change. In order to adapt to changing climate, future monitoring and research must be closely linked to responsive, flexible and reflexive management systems.

INTRODUCTION

Ornamental fishes are characterized by a wide diversity of colours and colour patterns and success in the ornamental fish trade is very much dependent on the vibrant colour of the fish. Color is one of the major factors, which determines the price of aquarium fish in world market. Fish are colored in nature often show faded coloration under intensive culture conditions. Fish like other animals do not synthesize carotenoid and depend on dietary carotenoid content for the coloration. Hence, a direct relationship between carotenoids and using the natural carotenoids, pigmentation exists in them. An ornamental fish has more attractive colors and fins. Chromatophores are responsible for the attractive colour of ornamental fishes. Chromatophores, including melanophores, xanthophores, erythrophores, cyanophores, leucophores, and iridophores are color-related cells that are derived from the neural crest during embryonic development. Variations in pigments were studied by Amano and Isukula (1967). In lower vertebrates, these cells play a key role in the generation of the integument hue and patterns. Depending on the structural and chemical nature of their color-generating microstructures, chromatophores are grouped into two distinct sub-classes, light absorbing and light-reflecting. Melanophores (black/brown), xanthophores (yellow), erythrophores (red/orange), and cyanophores (blue) possess pigment vesicles that contain true pigments (biochromes) and are thus classified as light-absorbing chromatophores. Ultrastructural studies have revealed that the platelets in iridophores are arranged periodically in stacks. Hence, it is believed that structural colors are generated by multilayer interference phenomena via the selective reflection of light waves at which the wavelength satisfies the interference condition. On the other hand, light-reflecting and light scattering chromatophores are iridophores and leucophores, respectively. Iridophores are color-generating cells that reflect light using stacks of platelets made from guanine (Taylor, 1969). Ando and Hayano been (1987) conducted pigmentation maturation studies. Some work has done on aquarium and its management practices (Saxena, 1991). Data shows there are seasonal variations in gonadal cycle in relation to diet and health of ornamental fishes (Saxena, 1994). The basic requirements of ornamental fish culture and breeding facilities were discussed by Saxena (1994, 1995). Ornamental fisheries and its importance for rural and urban areas is not less than any employment source but it beautifies the cities also (Saxena, 1997a, b; 1998). In general, iridophores are thought to generate iridescent or metallic colors, whereas leucophores likely produce reflective white hues (Fujii, 2000). The orientation of the stack, thickness and tilt angle of the platelets, number of platelets in a stack, as well as thickness of the cytoplasm sheet interspacing the platelets play vital roles in the determination of perceived colors, either individually or collectively (Oshima and Nagaishi, 1992; Morrison *et al.* 1995; Goda and Fujii, 1998; Mäthger *et al.* 2003). The ornamental fisheries has great scope for employement generation for marketing of the bright coloration is very important (Saxena, 2004) and Uttarakhand hill areas economy must be related with ornamentation as there is small area for big ponds (Saxena, 2006 a,b). Ornamental fisheries is good for tourism in Uttarakhand state. Caretenoids play an important role for the development of colouration in fishes (Saxena and Verma, 2008).

Chromatophores are the pigments containing light reflecting organelle found in fishes and other animals. They are largely responsible for the generation of color in the skin. Carotenoids are synthesized only in plants but not in animals. Carotenoids are also responsible for coloration in plants. As they are not synthesized in animals, animals take them in their food and metabolize them. In fishes, carotenoids act as antioxidants and as feed meal ingredient it is used to enhance colouration in fishes. Thus it is necessary to study the biosynthesis and metabolism of carotenoids. In nature, more than 600 types of carotenoids have been determined. Carotenoids are localized in subcellular organelles (plastids), *i.e.*, chloroplasts and chromoplasts. In chloroplasts, the carotenoids are chiefly associated with proteins and serve as accessory pigments in photosynthesis, whereas in chromoplasts they are deposited in crystalline form or as oily droplets. Some of the carotenoids such as the xanthophylls are involved in photosynthesis by participating in energy transfer in the presence of chlorophyll in plants. The most abundant carotenoid is β-carotene, which accumulates as the end product in carotenogenic species. The anthropogenic climate change affects the marine eco-system . The impacts on fisheries are due to a variety of direct and indirect effects of a number of physical and chemical factors, which include temperature, winds, vertical mixing, salinity, oxygen, pH and others. The direct effects act on the physiology, development rates, reproduction, behaviour and survival of individuals and can in some cases be studied experimentally and in controlled conditions. Indirect effects act via eco-system processes and changes in the production of food or abundance of competitors, predators and pathogens.

Regulation of Carotenoid Biosynthesis

Carotenoid accumulation occurs in most plant tissues, including green shoots, flowers, fruits, seeds and roots. Although the contents and types of carotenoids of green tissues are relatively conserved across most plant species, the levels of carotenoids and their profiles in non-green tissues, such as: flowers, fruits and seeds, vary considerably, and are influenced by many factors, including the developmental stage, environment, stress or a combination of these. In general, the steady-state levels of carotenoids are determined by the rate of biosynthesis, storage capacity of the cell and the rate of catabolism and degradation. Combined, these factors have made the study of carotenoid regulation challenging. Here, we discuss only the regulation of carotenoid biosynthesis as determined by the main 'bottlenecks' in the biosynthesis pathway. We also briefly discuss how knowledge of these important steps has been used in the metabolic engineering of carotenoid biosynthesis in plants. The ability of the cell to sequester carotenoids and the rate of carotenoid catabolism will also be discussed as additional factors used to determine the levels of carotenoids.

Isopentenyl Pyrophosphate (IPP) Biosynthesis

The fact that the first reaction in the MEP pathway is catalyzed by the DXS enzyme makes it a presumptive regulatory step in carotenoid biosynthesis. The initial evidence in support of this came from results of over expressing and silencing of the *DXS* gene in *Arabidopsis* seedlings. Over expression of *DXS* was shown to result in up to 112-131 per cent increase in the total carotenoid content, whereas silencing of this gene reduced the carotenoid content by 75-87 per cent relative to the wild type control. In ripening tomato fruits, the abundance of *DXS* transcript was found to be developmentally regulated, and corresponded to changes in expression of *PSY* and accumulation of carotenoids. *DXS* has been exploited in biotechnological applications to improve the carotenoid content of crops. For example, its over expression in potato caused a~2-fold increase in tuber carotenoid content, with a 6 per cent 7-fold increase in phytoene content relative to the control.

Lycopene Biosynthesis

The first step in lycopene biosynthesis is catalyzed by phytoene desaturase (PDS). The promoter of the *Arabidopsis* *PDS* gene was found to have a regulatory region similar to that of the binding site of the RAP 2.2 transcription factor to the *PSY* promoter, and analysis showed that RAP 2.2 does indeed bind to the *PDS* promoter and affect carotenoid accumulation. Carotenoid isomerization catalyzed by CRTISO, which isomerizes *cis* bonds to all-*trans* lycopene, is another step with regulatory impact on carotenoid biosynthesis. Characterization of the *ccr1* locus of *Arabidopsis* revealed that it encodes a histone methyltransferase (SET DOMAIN GROUP, SDG8). This enzyme catalyzes the methylation of chromatin histones, and when the expression of *SDG8* gene was disrupted, it caused a reduction in the levels of *CRTISO* transcript and carotenoid content. In addition, *Arabidopsis* plants with reduced *SDG8* expression showed altered shoot and root branching, which were possibly caused by changes in levels of branch-inhibiting strigolocatone hormones that are derived from carotenoid catabolism products. This was the first report on epigenetic regulation of carotenoid biosynthesis; this breakthrough has the potential to open new avenues for engineering of carotenoids in plants.

Sequestration and Storage

In addition to the rate of carotenoid biosynthesis, other factors, such as sequestration and availability of storage compartments, play a significant role in determining levels of carotenoid accumulation. Even though carotenoid biosynthetic enzymes are nuclear-encoded, they are all located in the plastids, where carotenoids are synthesized and accumulated. In chloroplasts, most carotenoids accumulate in the form of chlorophyll–carotenoid–protein complexes in the thylakoid membranes associated with light-harvesting antenna. These complexes play an important role in stabilizing plant light–harvesting complexes (LHCs) and in assembling a functional photosystem II (PSII). Seed carotenoids are compartmentalized to elaioplasts (lipid–storing plastids), which use specialized lipoprotein-sequestering structures to store large quantities of carotenoids. In chromoplasts, significant amounts of carotenoids may be stored in membranes, oil bodies or other crystalline structures within the stroma. Reports in the literature have shown cases where enhanced carotenoid accumulation was accompanied by changes in the anatomical structure of plastids, resulting in enhanced ability to store carotenoids. For example, a mutation in *Brassica oleracea Orange (Or)* gene resulted in enhanced carotenoid content in the curds, but no significant change was detected in the expression of the major carotenogenic genes. Further analysis revealed changes in the thylakoid membranes of the plastids, thus allowing them to store large quantities of carotenoids. Over expression of *PSY* in *B. napus* seeds also resulted in increased carotenoid accumulation, and the plastids of transgenic seeds were found to have thread-like inclusion bodies, which were proposed to accumulate the excess carotenoids. In addition, changes in carotenoid accumulation during *B. napus* seed development, and those resulting from silencing of *ε-CYC*, did not correspond to changes in the expression of carotenogenic genes. The authors therefore suggested that enhanced carotenoid accumulation could be due to changes in the cell structure, thus allowing for storage of more carotenoids.

Catabolism and Degradation

A recent study revealed that carotenoids are constantly synthesized and degraded. This presumably maintains carotenoids at physiological levels, especially in green tissues, where a constant ratio of chlorophylls to carotenoids has to be maintained to ensure the integrity of the photosynthesis system. Carotenoid metabolism in animals takes place as a result of enzymes which catalyse three main types of reaction. These main reaction types are: *(i)* the substitution of carotenoid end groups (often s-end groups) by oxygen functions (-OH and -C=O); *(ii)* the alteration of end groups, *e.g.*, of to c, of to K, etc., and *(iii)* cleavage of the polyene chain to yield apocarotenoids and even the vitamins A (Davies, 1985). Perhaps all three main reaction types are represented in the formation of the oil droplet carotenoids. Carotenoid degradation by enzymatic oxidative cleavage produces an array of terpenoid products collectively known as apocarotenoids. These include abscisic acid and strigolactones, and other volatile and non-volatile compounds, which are well known in respective industries for their use as aromas, flavors and fragrances. Some apocarotenoids, *e.g.*, β-ionone, are also known to play a role in plant-insect interactions. In Arabidopsis, the gene family that encodes carotenoid cleavage enzymes is comprised of at least nine members. Four of these encode carotenoid cleavage dioxygenases (CCD), and the remaining five encode 9-*cis*-expoxycarotenoid dioxygenases (NCED), with many of these enzymes exhibiting substrate promiscuity *in vitro*. The functions of some of these enzymes have been reported to be associated with certain apocarotenoids in several plant species. For example, CCD7 and CCD8 act in a co-ordinated manner in strigolactone biosynthesis, CCD1 is involved in β-ionone biosynthesis, and NCED2, NCED3, NCED5, NCED6 and NCED9 are associated with abscisic acid production. In chrysanthemums, CCD activity is important for petal color, and elevated transcript levels of CmCCD4a is reported to play a role in the degradation of yellow carotenoid pigments, which resulted in flowers with white petals.

Types of Chromatophores

(a) Xanthophores and Erythrophores

Chromatophores that contain large amounts of yellow pteridine pigments are named xanthophores; those with a preponderance of red/orange carotenoids are termed erythrophores. Pteridine and carotenoid containing vesicles are sometimes found within the same cell, in which case the overall colour depends on the ratio of red and yellow pigments. Therefore, the distinction between these chromatophore types is not always clear. The capacity to generate pteridines from guanosine triphosphate is a feature common to most chromatophores, but xanthophores appear to have supplemental biochemical pathways that result in an excess accumulation of yellow pigment. In contrast, carotenoids are metabolised from the diet and transported to erythrophores. This was first demonstrated by rearing normally green frogs on a diet of carotene-restricted crickets. The absence of carotene in the frogs' diet meant the red/orange carotenoid colour 'filter' was not present in their erythrophores. This resulted in the frogs appearing blue in colour, instead of green.

(b) Iridophores and Leucophores

Iridophores, sometimes also called guanophores, are pigment cells that reflect light using plates of crystalline chemochromes made from guanine. When illuminated they generate iridescent colours because of the diffraction of light within the stacked plates. Orientation of the schemochrome determines the nature of the colour observed. By using biochromes as coloured filters, iridophores create an optical effect known as Tyndall or Rayleigh scattering, producing bright blue or green colours. A related type of chromatophore, the leucophore, is found in some fish, particularly in the tapetum lucidum. Like iridophores, they utilize crystalline purines (often guanine) to reflect light. Unlike iridophores, however, leucophores have more organized crystals which reduce diffraction. Given a source of white light, they produce a white shine. As with xanthophores and erythrophores, in fish the distinction between iridophores and leucophores is not always obvious, but generally iridophores are considered to generate iridescent or metallic colours while leucophores produce reflective white hues.

(c) Melanophores

Melanophores contain eumelanin, a type of melanin, that appears black or dark brown because of its light absorbing qualities. It is packaged in vesicles called melanosomes and distributed throughout the cell. Eumelanin is generated from tyrosine in a series of catalysed chemical reactions. It is a complex chemical containing units of dihydroxyindole and dihydroxyindole-2-carboxylic acid with some pyrrole rings. The key enzyme in melanin synthesis is tyrosinase. When this protein is defective, no melanin can be generated resulting in certain types of albinism. In some amphibian species there are other pigments packaged alongside eumelanin. For example, a novel deep (wine) red coloured pigment was identified in the melanophores of phyllomedusine frogs. This was subsequently identified as pterorhodin, a pteridine dimer that accumulates around eumelanin core, and it is also present in a variety of tree frog species from Australia and Papua New Guinea. While it is likely that other lesser studied species have complex melanophore pigments, it is nevertheless true that the majority of melanophores studied to date do contain eumelanin exclusively. Humans have only one class of pigment cell, the mammalian equivalent of melanophores, to generate skin, hair and eye colour. For this reason, and because the large number and contrasting colour of the cells usually make them very easy to visualise, melanophores are by far the most widely studied chromatophore. However, there are differences between the biology of melanophores and melanocytes. In addition to eumelanin, melanocytes can generate a yellow/red pigment called phaeomelanin.

(d) Cyanophores

In 1995 it was demonstrated that the vibrant blue colours in some types of mandarin fish are not generated by schemochromes. Instead, a cyan biochrome of unknown chemical nature is responsible. This pigment, found within vesicles in at least two species of callionymid fish, is highly unusual in the animal kingdom, as all other blue colourings thus far investigated are schemochromatic. Therefore a novel chromatophore type, the cyanophore, was proposed. Although they appear unusual in their taxonomic restriction, there may be cyanophores (as well as further unusual chromatophore types) in other fish and amphibians. For example, bright coloured chromatophores with undefined pigments have been observed in both poison dart frogs and glass frogs, and atypical dichromatic chromatophores, named *erythro-iridophores* have been described in *Pseudochromis diadema*. Fish chromatophores are mostly of dermal origin. These cells possess numerous granules in which pigments are stored. In some of these chromatophores pigment granules move out from the center resulting in increased coloration of animals; or they may aggregate in the cell center and the animal appears less coloured. Speed by which the granule moves varies from species to species.

Xanthophore Specification and Migration

Zebrafish xanthophore pigmentation first becomes apparent after 42 hours of development (high pec stage) in the dorsal head as a very pale cast of yellow (Kimmel *et al.* 1995). However, individual xanthophore cells are difficult to distinguish. After 3 days of development (protruding mouth stage), strong yellow xanthophore pigmentation is apparent in the entire dorsal half of the body in regions devoid of melanophores. Xanthophores become granular after 5 days of development and are now seen throughout the body, with greater numbers dorsally. Adult zebrafish have five alternating blue-black (melanophores and iridophores) and silvery-yellow (xanthophores and iridophores) stripes aligned parallel to the long axis of the body. This stripe pattern extends into the caudal and anal fins, but not into the dorsal and the paired lateral fins. Studies of adult pigmentation mutants revealed interactions between melanophores and iridophores in pigment pattern formation (Johnson *et al.* 1995). In contrast, little is known about the interaction of the xanthophores with other chromatophores. In *sal* and *pfe* mutant embryos a partial absence of xanthophores in the dorsal head becomes apparent after 4 days of development whereas melanophore and iridophore pigmentation appears normal. 1 day later, large areas devoid of granular xanthophores can be seen, and only a few individual yellow spots in the dorsal head are present. The overall number of xanthophores is reduced in *pfe* larva, as visualized by their fluorescence under UV light. In *sal* mutant larvae the number of xanthophores is strongly reduced in lateral and ventral regions, whereas many xanthophores remain dorsal to the neural tube. The strength of the defect in mutant larvae of both genes is dependent on the allele; weak alleles produce a slightly reduced number of xanthophores (data not shown), whereas in embryos with strong alleles only a very small number of xanthophores is detectable in the body. For the strong allele *pfetq 211*, we observed a slight reduction in the number of xanthophore cells, and also in heterozygous larvae (data not shown). Heterozygous adult fish carrying a mutation in *sal* or in *pfe* show irregular and interrupted melanophore stripes, thus indicating a defect in the formation or maintenance of the adult melanophore pattern. Xanthophores in the adult heterozygous fish are detectable at a slightly lower density (data not shown; Haffter, personal communication). The general appearance is slightly less yellow than wild type fish. We compared the dominant adult phenotypes to determine the relative strength of different alleles, which gave the same results as counting the xanthophore number in the larva Homozygous *sal* and *pfe* fish can be raised to adulthood. After 3 to 4 weeks of development these fish can be distinguished from wild type by a pigment pattern phenotype: the spotted melanophore stripe pigmentation (blue-black stripes) fades out towards the tail and shows a 'salt and pepper'-like appearance. This phenotype is very prominent in the adult fish, and no xanthophores are detectable in the body of embryos with the strong alleles. The weakest allele, *pfetg283a*, does not produce any obvious phenotype in the heterozygous or homozygous adults.

Pigment Pattern Formation is Different in the Larva and in the Adult

One surprising result of this study is the finding that most mutants with strongly reduced xanthophore pigmentation in the larva show no obvious xanthophore phenotype as adults (as observed under a dissecting microscope), indicating that larval and adult xanthophore pigmentation in the zebrafish require different genes. Xanthophores play an important role in pigment pattern formation in anal fin (Goodrich and Nichols, 1931; Goodrich *et al.* 1954). Mutations in only three genes (*salz*, *pfeffer* and *tartar*) cause adult phenotypes. Whereas xanthophores and melanophores are pale in *tar* homozygous adults, xanthophores are not detectable in *sal* and *pfe* homozygous adults. In *sandy* mutant larvae unpigmented melanophores form unpigmented gaps between pigmented xanthophores in the dorsal head. The observation of unpigmented spaces between melanophores and iridophores in *sal* and *pfe* larvae indicates that in the wildtype situation xanthophores fill the gaps between the melanophore and iridophore stripes. Whereas xanthophores are apparently not required for the proper formation of the larval melanophore stripes, they have an important function in adult pigment pattern formation. Partial absence of xanthophores in *sal* and *pfe* heterozygous adult fish leads to irregular blue-black stripes, and a 'salt and pepper' pattern of melanophore pigmentation fading out towards the tail. A similar but stronger phenotype can be observed in homozygous mutant fish. The correlation of a reduced number of xanthophores with an irregular melanophore pattern in the adult is in agreement with earlier findings, which indicated that the xanthophores play an important role in pigment pattern formation in the body (Epperlein and Löfberg, 1984). The correlation between xanthophore and melanophore pattern can also be seen in adult zebrafish that are mutant for *leopard*, where the number of xanthophores in the anal fin is reduced and the melanophore pigment pattern is disrupted as well. A similar influence on the adult melanophore pigment pattern by iridophores has been found (Johnson *et al.*, 1995). In mutants where the number of iridophores is reduced (*transparent, rose, shady*), the melanophore pattern in the adult body is disrupted (Haffter, 1996). Again this influence is restricted to the adult pigment pattern and has no effect on larval pigment pattern formation. At present it is unclear whether xanthophores have a function in the initiation or in the maintenance of the melanophore stripes. A more detailed analysis of the transition from the larval to the adult pigment pattern in these mutants is required to address this point.

Fish species are expected to shrink in size by up to 24 per cent because of global warming. Researchers modelled the impact of rising temperatures on more than 600 species between 2001 and 2050. Warmer waters could decrease ocean oxygen levels and significantly reduce fish body weight. The scientists argue that failure to control greenhouse gas emissions will have a greater impact on marine eco-systems than previously thought. Previous research has suggested that changing ocean temperatures would impact both the distribution and the reproductive abilities of many species of fish. This new work suggests that fish size would also be heavily impacted. The researchers built a model to see how fish would react to lower levels of oxygen in the water. They used data from one of the higher emissions scenarios developed by the Intergovernmental Panel on Climate Change (IPCC). Climate change has both direct and indirect impacts on fish stocks. Direct effects act on physiology and behaviour and alter growth, reproductive capacity, mortality and distribution. Indirect effects alter the productivity, structure and composition of the marine eco-systems on which fish depend for food. However many other factors, including fishing, biological interactions and non-climatic environmental factors can also have similar effects. When a change is ascribed to climate these other factors should also be evaluated and the degree of confidence in the ascription should be given. *Calanus finmarchicus* has declined throughout much of the North Atlantic since 1958 due to warming and changes in the extent of cold, deepwater masses in which the species overwinters (Beaugrand *et al.* 2002). Changes in all of these since 1958 resulted in increased survival and good recruitment of cod throughout the 1960s and 1970s and then a progressive decline over the past 30 years (Beaugrand *et al.* 2003). In the North Sea it has been largely replaced by a southern congener *C. helgolandicus* but there have also been substantial changes in phenology, which affect trophic interactions, food web structure and eco-system functioning (Edwards and Richardson, 2004). This has consequences for plankton predator species, including fish, whose life cycles are synchronised to the seasonal production of particular prey species. The survival of young cod in the North Sea appears to depend on the abundance, seasonal timing and size composition of their prey. Although the processes can as yet only be sketched, rather than unequivocally determined, there is good evidence that climate changes related to the North Atlantic Oscillation (NAO) are behind many of the observed changes in plankton production, phenology and fisheries. For example, the decline of the European cod stocks due to overfishing has been exacerbated by climate induced changes in plankton production and these stocks are no longer able to provide as much surplus for the fishery as in the 1960s and 1970s. As the stocks of cod have declined, they have become more sensitive to the effects of the climate indicator (the NAO), due to shrinkage of the age distribution and geographic extent (Brander, 2005; Planque *et al.* 2010).

REFRENCES

Amano A and Isukula CA (1967). Pigments in Fishes. *J. Fish Biol.* 14: 23-29.

Ando and Hatano (1987). Metabolic Pathways of Carotenoid in Chum Salmon *Oncorhynchus Keta* during Spawning Migration. Comp. Biochem. *Physiol.* 87B: 411-416.

Beaugrand G, Brander KM, Lindley JA, Souissi S and Reid PC (2003). Plankton Effect on Cod Recruitment in the North Sea. *Nature* 426: 661-664.

Beaugrand G, Reid PC, Ibanez F, Lindley JA and Edwards M (2002). Reorganization of North Atlantic Marine Copepod Bio-diversity and Climate. *Science.* 296: 1692-1694.

Brander KM (2005). Cod Recruitment is Strongly Affected by Climate when Stock Biomass is Low. ICES *J. Marine Sci.* 62: 339-343.

Davies B H (1985). Carotenoid Metabolism in Animals a Bio-chemist's View. *Pure and Appld. Chem.* Vol. 57, No. 5 pp. 679-684.

Edwards M and Richardson AJ (2004). Impact of Climate Change on Marine Pelagic Phenology and Trophic Mismatch. *Nature.* 430: 881-884.

Epperlein HH and Löfberg J (1984). Xanthophores in Chromatophore Groups of the Premigratory Neural Crest Initiate the Pigment Pattern of the Axolotl Larva. *Wilhelm Roux's Arch. Dev. Biol.* 193: 357-369.

Fujii R (2000). The Regulation of Motile Activity in Fish Chromatophores. Pigment Cell Res. 13: 300-319.

Goda M and Fujii R (1998). The Blue Coloration of the Common Surgeonfish *Paracanthurus Hepatus* – II. Color Revelation and Color Changes. *Zool. Sci.* 15: 323-333.

Goodrich HB and Nichols R (1931). The Development and the 398 Regeneration of the Colour Pattern in *Brachidanio Rerio. J. Morph. Physiol.* 52: 513-518.

Goodrich H B, Marzullo CM and Brownson WH (1954). An Analysis of the Formation of Colour Patterns in two Fresh-Water Fish. *J. Exp. Zool.* 125: 487-505.

Haffter P, Granato M, Brand M, Mullins MC, Hammerschmidt M, Kane D A, Odenthal J, van Eeden FJM, Jiang YJ, Heisenberg CP, Kelsh RN, Furutani-Seiki M, Vogelsang E, Beuchle D, Schach U, Fabian C and Nüsslein-Volhard C (1996). The Identification of Genes with Unique and Essential Functions in the Development of the Zebrafish *Danio Rerio. Development* 123: 1-36.

Hannoufa A and Hossain Z (2011). *Agriculture and Agri-Food Canada 1391.*

Johnson SL, Africa D, Walker C and Weston JA (1995). Genetic Control of Adult Pigment Stripe Development in Zebrafish. *Dev. Biol.* 167: 27-33.

Kimmel CB, Ballard WW, Kimmel SR, Ullmann B and Schilling TF (1995). Stages of Embryonic Development of the Zebrafish. *Dev. Dynam.* 203: 253-310.

Mäthger LM, Land MF, Siebeck UE and Marshall NJ (2003). Rapid Colour Changes in Multilayer Reflecting Stripes in the Paradise Whiptail *Pentapodus Paradiseus*. *J. Exp. Biol.* 206: 3607-3613.

Morrison RL, Matthew SR and Frost-Mason SK (1995). Cellular Basis of Color Differences in Three Morphs of the Lizard *Sceloporus Undulatus Erythrocheilus*. Copeia 1995 397-408.

Oshima N and Nagaishi H (1992). Study of the Motile Mechanism in Neon Tetra *Paracheirodon Innesi* Iridophores. *Comp. Biochem. Physiol. Part A. Physiology* 102: 2 273-278.

Planque B, Fromentin JM, Cury P, Drinkwater K, Jennings S, Perry RI and Kifani S (2010). How does Fishing alter Marine Populations and Eco-systems Sensitivity to Climate? *J. Mari. Syst.* 79 403-417.

Saxena A (1991). An Aquarium Indian Farmers Digest XXIV 9-10 41-43.

Saxena A (1994). Health and Colouration of Fishes. International Symposium on Aquatic Animal Health California U.S.A. 16-17 Sept.

Saxena A (1995). Prospects of Ornamental Fishes in India. Workshop on Recent trends in Aquaculture Lecture 20 July-2 Aug. FRTC GBPUAT Pantnagar.

Saxena A (1997). Ornamental Fisheries Marteque 97 Les-Trois Ilets Martiques FWI 4-9 May.

Saxena A (1998). Ornamental Fish Production. National Symposium on Sustainable Aquaculture Delhi Feb. 20-21.

Saxena A (2004). Scope of Ornamental Fisheries in Hill States 15th AIMZSI Jammu University Jammu. Oct. 27-29.

Saxena A (2006a.) Ornamental Fisheries a Promising Enterprise for Unemployed Youth Key Note Address Souvenir UGC Sponsored National Symposium or Application and Recent Advance in life Sciences November-17 Meerut-38-44.

Saxena A (2006b.) A Text-book of Biochemistry Discovery Publishing House New Delhi.

Saxena and Verma VK (2008.) Importance of Carotenoids in Fishs. 4th International Congress on Aquaculture Fishery Technology and Environment Management 21-22 Nov Athens Greece 27. *Aqua Medit.* 2008 ISBN 978-960-87795-2-5.

Taylor JD (1969). The Effects of Intermedin on the Ultrastructure of Amphibian Iridophores. *Gen. Comp. Endocrinol.* 12: 405-416.

Page 101-107

Fisheries and Aquaculture
Edited by: **Prof. (Mrs.) Neelima Gupta** and **Dr. D.K. Gupta**
Edition: **2015**
ISBN: 978-93-5056-736-4
Published by: **Discovery Publishing House Pvt. Ltd., New Delhi (India)**

7

Applications of GIS and Remote sensing in Fisheries

Prabjeet Singh[1], **Amita Saxena**[1] and **Ajeet Singh Nain**[2]

Department of Fishery Biology, College of Fisheries, GB Pant University of Agriculture and Technology, Pantnagar.[1]
Department of Agrometerology, College of Agriculture, GB Pant University of Agriculture and Technology, Pantnagar.[2] Email: amitasaxena12@yahoo.co.in

ABSTRACT

Fish stocks are an important high-protein food source for mankind, yet world fisheries are under increasing pressure factors related to the growth of the human population, including overfishing, global climate change, pollution, and habitat degradation. About 40 years ago, ocean productivity began declining, having reached Maximum Sustainable Yield. Conventional approaches of sampling the ocean using research vessels are limited in both time and space scales of coverage, making it difficult to study the entire eco-system. Since the advent of satellite remote sensing, especially remote sensing of ocean color and temperature, it has become possible to sample the global ocean on synoptic scales and with acceptable temporal resolutions. For example, satellite data on chlorophyll concentrations and sea surface temperature (SST) have been used to delineate regions, or ecological provinces, in the ocean with similar physical and biological forcing. Applications of remote sensing

(RS) in aquaculture include several aspects such as: land/water use pattern, suitability classification and resource use zoning. Collectively RS and GIS can be served as an analytical and predicting tool for planning of aquaculture development and to test the consequence of various development decisions before their use in the landscape. Both GIS and remote sensing technology are also used to define geographic framework, specify environmental constraints and identify resource limitations.

INTRODUCTION

Remote sensing is the science and art of obtaining information about an object through the analysis of data acquired by a device that is not in contact with the object. Remotely sensed data can be of many forms, including variations in force distribution, acoustic wave distribution or electromagnetic energy distributions and can be obtained from a variety of platforms, including satellite, airplanes, remotely pilot vehicles and handheld radiometers. They may be gathered by different devices, including sensors, film camera, digital cameras and video recorders. Our eyes acquire data on variations in electromagnetic radiations. Instruments capable of measuring electromagnetic radiation are called sensors.

Fish stocks are an important high-protein food source for mankind, yet world fisheries are under increasing pressure factors related to the growth of the human population, including overfishing, global climate change, pollution, and habitat degradation. About 40 years ago, ocean productivity began declining, having reached Maximum Sustainable Yield. Nearly 80 per cent of the world fish stocks are now either fully exploited or overexploited. Moreover, world demand for seafood has been rising everywhere, both in developed countries due to increasing standards of living, as well as less-developed countries whose population keeps growing rapidly. Sustainable use of marine resources requires effective monitoring and management of entire ecosystems, not just exploited fish stocks. Conventional approaches of sampling the ocean using research vessels are limited in both time and space scales of coverage, making it difficult to study the entire eco-system. Since the advent of satellite remote sensing, especially remote sensing of ocean color and temperature, it has become possible to sample the global ocean on synoptic scales and with acceptable temporal resolutions. For example, satellite data on chlorophyll concentrations and sea surface temperature (SST) have been used to delineate regions, or ecological provinces, in the ocean with similar physical and biological forcing. These ecological provinces are not fixed in time or space, but vary seasonally and inter-annually. The instantaneous boundaries of these ecological provinces can contribute to our understanding of eco-system characteristics and can highlight the changes that happen due to short–and long-term environmental variations which can frequently be observed in satellite derived patterns of ocean temperature and productivity. These changes can affect the recruitment, survival, condition, distribution patterns and migration of fish stocks.

Stages in Remote Sensing

1. Requirement of an energy source (Sun is the main source of energy during day time.)
2. Energy interaction with the atmosphere.
3. Interaction with the target.
4. Recording of energy by sensor.
5. Data transmission and processing.
6. Image processing and analysis.
7. Application.

Advantages of Remote Sensing

The major advantages of remote sensing over ground based methods are:

- *Synoptic View*: It facilitates the study of various features of earth surface in their spatial relation to each other and helps to delineate the required features and phenomenon.
- *Accessibility*: It makes it possible to gather information about inaccessible areas where it is not possible to gather information through ground surveys.
- *Time*: These techniques save time and efforts as information about large area can be gathered quickly.

- *Multidisciplinary Applications*: Remote sensing data are useful to different disciplines such as geology, fisheries, forestry, land use etc.

Applications of Remote Sensing in Fisheries

1. Remote sensing data help in regular management of water resources.
2. Remote sensing techniques are useful in finding different types of bio-resources.
3. Remote sensing plays potential role in both rapid and comprehensive EIA.
4. For detection and monitoring of the water pollution, remote sensing proves useful.
5. Remote sensing is applicable in acquiring information regarding offshore engineering activities, fisheries surveillance, ocean features, coastal regions and storm forecast operations.
6. Remotely sensed data provides the necessary spatial data on suspended sediments, dissolved organic matter, phytoplankton, algal blooms and oil slicks etc., which will be useful in management of fish stocks, monitor the water quality and natural water pollution such as oil or algal blooms, which are harmful to aquatic life.
7. Remote sensing techniques are giving necessary data needed for monitoring changes on coastal erosion, shoreline monitoring and management, loss of natural habitat, sea level rise, wetland mapping urbanization, sewage disposal and aquatic population etc.
8. Remote sensing is very useful in identifying Potential Fishing Zones (PFZ). This data is very useful for fishermen because they come to know likely occurrence of fish shoals which helps them for getting more catch.
9. Continuous monitoring of land use or land cover with remote sensing imageries have been of immense use in providing information on temporal and spatial changes in areas under aquaculture, mangrove areas, coral reef mapping and other land use patterns.

10. Specific conditions and processes affecting fish populations may often be deduced from measurements made by remote sensors. Remote sensors can provide a range of indices of eco-system status, including a compact description of the pelagic ecosystem at a given time and place.
11. Acoustic techniques are widely used for detecting fish schools in coastal and deep ocean waters. The advantages of sonar methods include their ability to provide better high-resolution data on fish abundance and distribution than can be obtained with typical trawl surveys.

Geographical Information System (GIS)

GIS may be defined as the integration of computer hard and software with spatially referred digital data so that storage, retrieval, manipulation, analysis of all forms of geographically referenced information can be displayed. GIS is a computer assisted system that can input, store, retrieve, analyze and display geographically referenced information useful for decision-making. Therefore, a GIS can combine geographic and other types of data to generate maps and reports, enabling users to collect, manage, and interpret location-based information in a planned and systematic way. In short, a GIS can be defined as a computer system capable of assembling, storing, manipulating, and displaying geographically referenced data.

Advantages of GIS

- It helps the planners in efficient and cost effective decision-making based on multiple scenarios available.
- GIS allows integration of all types of data together based on geographical and locational components of data.
- GIS is application oriented.
- Frequent revision of digitized GIS data is possible.
- Changes over time can easily and rapidly monitored through GIS.
- GIS technology enables high quality output.

- Spatial patterns and processes can be effectively described and explained by GIS.

Applications of GIS in Fisheries

- Identification of suitable sites for freshwater and brackish water aquaculture.
- Management of marine fisheries and coastal regulation zone.
- Study of land-use pattern including mangroves and forest cover of a particular area.
- Planning for water body resource zonation and mapping of aquatic species.
- Fish disease modeling and management.
- Study of temporal/spatial changes in fish production and consumption.
- Environmental Impact Assessment.
- Distribution of different fish species in relation to physical habitat characteristics.

REFERENCES

Bandelj, V., Curiel, D., Lek, S., Rismondo, A., Solidoro, C., (2009). Modelling Spatial Distribution of Hard Bottom Benthic Communities and their Functional Response to Environmental Parameters. Ecol. Model. 220, 2838-2850.

Bartholdy, J., Folving, S., (1986). Sediment Classification and Surface Type Mapping in the Danish Wadden sea by Remote-Sensing. Neth. J. Sea Res. 20, 337-345.

Blaschke, T., Strobl, J., (2001). What's Wrong with Pixels? Some Recent Development Interfacing Remote Sensing and GIS. In: Proceedings of GIS – Zeitschrift fur Geoinformation Systeme, Heidelberg, Germany, pp. 12-17, 6.

Flanders, D., Hall-Beyer, M., Pereverzoff, J., (2003). Preliminary Evaluation of eCognition Object-based Software for Cut Block Delineation and Feature Extraction. Can.J. Remote Sens. 29, 441-452.

Folk, R.L., (1968). A Review of Grain size Parameters. Sedimentology 6, 73-93.

Fulton, J.W., Wagner, C.R., Rogers, M.E., Zimmerman, G.F., (2010). Hydraulic Modeling of Mussel Habitat at a Bridge-Replacement Site, Allegheny River, Pennsylvania, USA. Ecol. Model. 221, 540-554.

Yoo, J.W., Hwang, I.S., Hong, J.S., (2007). Inference Models for Tidal Flat Elevation and Sediment Grain Size: A Preliminary Approach on Tidal Flat Macrobenthic Community. Ocean Sci. J. 42, 69-79.

Ysebaert, T., Meire, P., Coosen, J., Essink, K., (1998). Zonation of Intertidal Macrobenthos in the Estuaries of Schelde and Ems. Aquat. Ecol. 32, 53-71.

Zomer, R.J., Trabucco, A., Ustin, S.L., (2009). Building Spectral Libraries for Wetlands Land Cover Classification and Hyperspectral Remote Sensing. J. Environ. Manage. 90, 2170-2177.

[III]
Fish Biology and Haematology

Page 111-117

Fisheries and Aquaculture
Edited by: **Prof. (Mrs.) Neelima Gupta** and **Dr. D.K. Gupta**
Edition: **2015**
ISBN: 978-93-5056-736-4
Published by: **Discovery Publishing House Pvt. Ltd., New Delhi (India)**

8

Adaptive Modifications in Paired Fin Epidermis of the Hill-Stream Fish *Homeloptera brucei* (Gray 1830) of Kumaun Himalaya

A SEM Investigation

Hoshiyar Singh*, Ila Bisht and **S.K. Agarwal**

Department of Zoology, S.S.J. Campus Almora, Kumaun University Nainital - 263 002, India. *E-mail: singh.hoshiyar320@gmail.com

ABSTRACT

Surface architecture of paired fins of **Homeloptera brucei**, *adapted to life in fast flowing streams has been examined. Epidermis is differentiated into smooth and rough in both the fins. Rough epidermis covering ventral surface is mainly composed of epithelial cells which are thrown into elongated curved spine unculi in pectoral fin and stout and blunt unculi in pelvic fin. The smooth epidermis covering the remaining parts of the fins is equipped with epithelial cells, mucous cells secreting mucus which cause a weak adhesion and prepares the substratum for subsequent action of the unculi. A dense network of microridges in the epithelial cells could be interpreted as a means to retain more mucus of the surface of epithelial cells.*

Keyword: Paired Fins, Ultrastructure, SEM.

INTRODUCTION

Many teleost fishes are reported to inhabit the sub Himalayan streams and rivers of India. These mountain streams are perennial shallow water bodies characterized by low temperature, high turbulent current and sandy rocky substratum (Nag and Bhattacharjee, 2002). To thrive successfully against the action of strong water currents, many hill stream fishes demonstrate several unique adaptive modifications. In some hill-stream fishes an unusual form of adhesive organ is present in pectoral and pelvic fins. The present study was aimed to examine the surface architecture of adhesive structures that are located at pectoral and pelvic fins of *Homeloptera brucei* Gray, 1830 by scanning electron microscopy.

Materials and Methods

Live adult specimens of *H. brucei* were collected from west Ramganga River at Chaukhutiya, district Almora. Water current was very fast having velocity 1.5-2.5 m/sec. in west Ramganga (Bhatt and Pathak, 1991). Specimens were maintained in laboratory at 25±2^{0}C. The fishes were cold anesthetized following Mittal and Whitear (1978) for SEM preparation of paired fins. Tissues were excised and rinsed in 70 per cent ethanol and one change saline solution to remove debris and fixed in 3 per cent Glutaraldehyde in 0.1M phosphate buffer at pH. 7.4 over night at 4^{0}C in a refrigerator. The tissues were washed 2-3 changes in phosphate buffer and dehydrated in ascending series of ice cold acetone (30%, 50%, 70%, 90% and 100% 20-30min. each) and critical point dried, using critical point dryer (BIO-RAD England) with liquid carbon dioxide as the transitional fluid. Tissues were glued to stubs, using conductive silver preparation (Eltecks, Corporation, India) coated with gold using a sputter coater (JFC 1600) and examined in a scanning electron microscope (JEOL, JSM-6610 LV). The results were recorded using computer.

Results

The pectoral and pelvic fins of *H. brucei* are unusually large expanded, fan shape in appearance and posteriorly directed. These fins are situated on the under surface of the body and are placed horizontally on the side of the body. The paired fins become flat and broad on the ventral surface (Fig. 8.1). In *H. brucei,* ventral epidermis is much thick at rays than that of interrays region (hinge region) in between first four anterior rays of pectoral and two rays of pelvic fins and adjacent anterior first eight rays in pectoral fins and three rays of pelvic fins. The epidermis covering entire length of first 7-8 anterior rays of pectoral fin and first 1-3 anterior rays of pelvic fin shows remarkable modifications from epidermis of rest of parts of fins (Bisht *et al.* 2008). The epidermis is differentiated into rough and smooth in both the fins. The epidermal cells of the ray region are thrown into numerous spine like structures, the unculi (Fig. 8.2). The unculi are numerous, long, curved and backwardly directed in the ray region of pectoral fin (Fig. 8.3). On the other hand, the cells that line the interray region are apparently devoid of these unculi. In pelvic fins the unculi of the ray region are stout, that often have slightly curved apical ends could serve as pegs or anchors. (Fig.8.4)

On the dorsal surface, epidermis is smooth in both the fins. In smooth epidermis, epithelial cells are characterized with microridges, these are filamentous (Fig. 8.5). Interspersed between the epithelial cells, mucous cells apparatus are distinguished.

It is interesting to note that a large number of well protruded tubercles appearing to be cleaved in the centre are present in between the epithelial cells (Fig. 8.6). The density of these tubercles is, however, much greater in the dorsal surface than that of ventral surface. Roberts (1982) also described large numbers of such tubercles in Ostariophysean fishes. They are well developed in the dorsal surface of the paired fins in sexually mature males and poorly developed or absent in females.

Discussion

In the present study, we have shown the surface feature of adhesive devices existing in pectoral and pelvic fins of *H.brucei*. In teleosts, fins have been employed for various

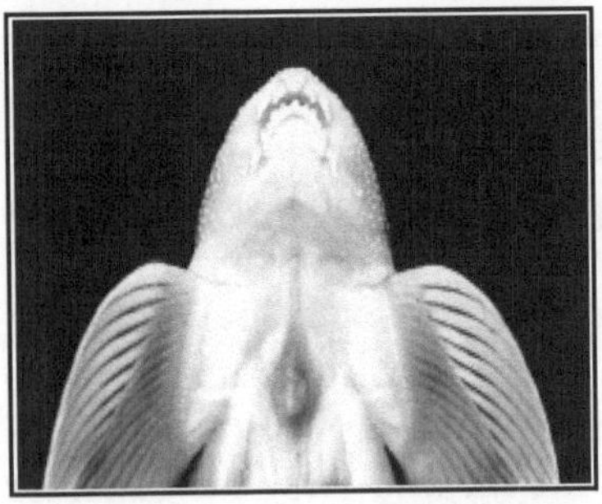

Fig. 8.1: Ventral View of *Homeloptera Brucei* Showing Flat and Broad Fins

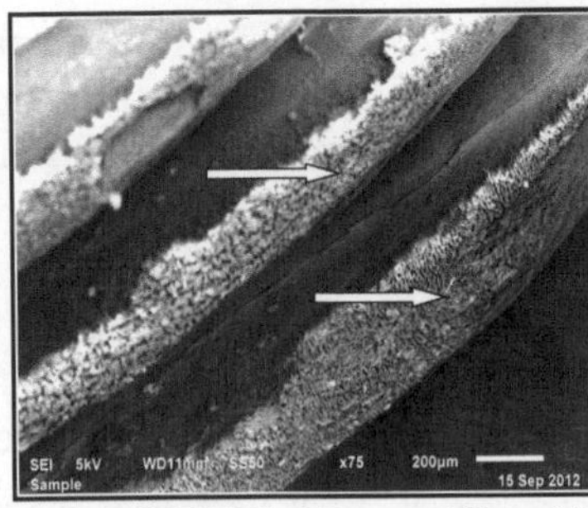

Fig. 8.2: SEMPH of Pectoral Fin of *H. Brucei* Showing Numerous Unculi at the Surface Epithelium of First Three Fin Rays (Scale bar-200μm).

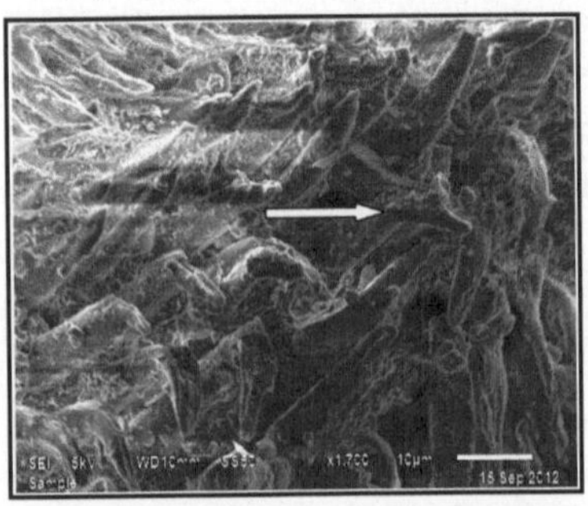

Fig. 8.3: SEMPH of Pectoral Fin of *H.brucei* Showing Long Curved Unculi (scale bar-10μm)

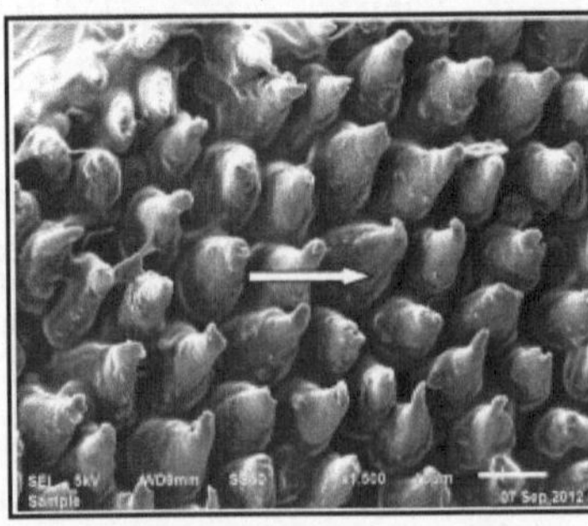

Fig. 8.4: SEMPH of Pelvic Fin of *H. Brucei* Showing Unculi at the Ray Region (scale bar-10μm)

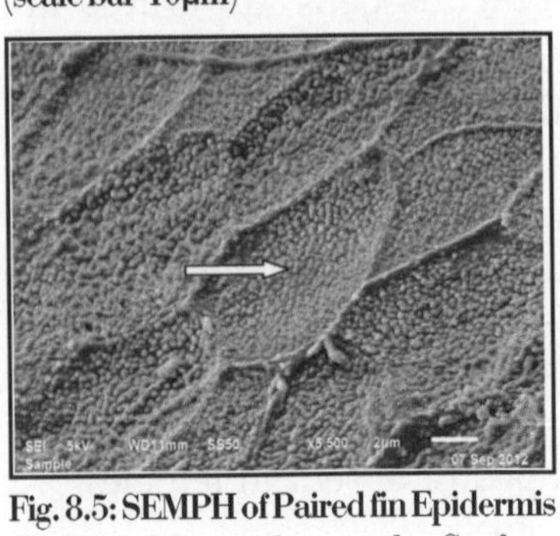

Fig. 8.5: SEMPH of Paired fin Epidermis Showing Microridges at the Surface Epithelium of the Dorsal Surface (scale bar-2μm)

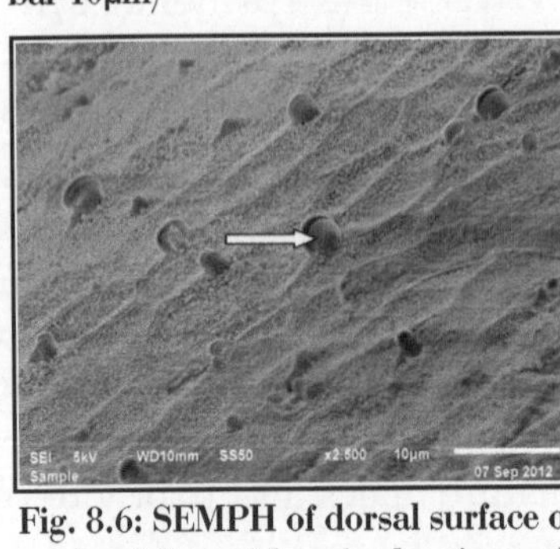

Fig. 8.6: SEMPH of dorsal surface of pectoral fin epidermis showing well protruded tubercles in between epithelial cells (scale bar-10μm)

SEMPH: Scanning Electron Microphotograph

functions in addition to swimming. In flying fish, *Exocoetus volitans* the modified pectoral fins are used for gliding for a considerable distance above the water surface and in the sucking fish *Remora remora* the first dorsal fin is utilized for adhesion (Migdalski and Fichter, 1983). In several genera of mountain stream fishes (*Pseudecheneis sp., Glyptothorax* sp. and *Homeloptera* sp.), the expanded pectoral and pelvic fins are used for swimming against the strong water current. At rest, however, these fins are involved in adhesion (Hora, 1930). The outer rays of these fins are generally modified and employed for adhesion. This change seems to have been brought about by two reasons, first it allows the ventral surface of the body to be firmly applied to rocks and second, to enable the fins to act as organs of attachment. The epidermis undergoes remarkable modifications to achieve the function of adhesion. The epidermis covering the outer rays is characterized by the presence of unculi, whereas the inter ray region is devoid of unculi. These ultra structural features allow us to speculate about the mechanism in the process of adhesion by the paired fins in this teleost. The long backwardly directed and numerous uncular projections of pectoral fin are deeply penetrated into the substratum by anchoring to the organic growth on the submerged rocks and prevent the fish from being washed away in high velocity of water current.

In pelvic fins, the number of unculi is less but stout in comparison to pectoral fins indicating that the frictional force becomes reduced in the posterior region of the fish. Similar spine like projections were observed on the adhesive apparatus of *Glyptothorax* sp. (Horra, 1922), *Glyptothorax pectinopterus* (Lal, *et al*. 1966, Das and Nag, 2004) and in several hill-stream fishes (Saxena, 1959; Saxena and Chandy, 1966).

The smooth epidermis covering the remaining parts of the paired fins, both on dorsal and ventral surfaces in this fish is equipped with epithelial cells and mucous cells. These cells may act as macrophages, playing an important role in preventing the colonization by parasites, fungi and bacteria over the fin surface. The surface epithelial cells here are in contrast, non-keratinized and metabolically inactive (Joshi, 2011).

The microridges of epithelial cells are organized in different ways to form intricate patterns and are thought to be involved in various functions; *e.g.*, absorptive or secretory activities, to aid in laminar flow, holding mucus secretion to the cell surface, to provide reserve surface area for stretching or distortion, to facilitate the spread of mucus away from the mucous cells, to provide mechanical protection and to enhance mechanical flexibility (Whitear, 1990; Olson, 1995). The mucus secretion from the mucous cells causes a weak adhesion and prepares the substratum for subsequent action of the unculi. In addition, the mucus seems to afford protection to the unculi from abrasion during adhesion.

REFERENCES

Bhatt S D and Pathak J K (1991). Streams of Great Mountain Are: Physiography and Physiochemistry. In: Ecology of the Mountain Water; Ashish Publ. House N. Delhi., pp. 43-58.

Bisht I, Joshi S C and Agarwal S K (2008). Comparative Study of Paired Fin Epidermis of Hill-Steam Fishes: Histochemical and Biostatistical Analysis; J. *Exp. Zool.* India., 11: 1: 241-249.

Das D and Nag T C (2004). Adhesion by Paired Pectoral and Pelvic Fin in a Mountain Stream Cat Fish. *Pseudecheneis Sulcatus* (Teleost: Sisoridae): A Scanning Electron Microscope Study; *Environmental Biology of Fishes*. pp. 71 1-5.

Hora S L (1922). Structural Modifications in the Fish of Mountain Torrents; *Res. Ind. Mus.*, 24: 31-36.

Hora S L (1930). Ecology, Bionomics and Evolution of the Torrential Fauna with Special Reference to the Organs of Attachment; Phill. Trans. Roy. Soc. London. 218: 171-282.

Joshi S C (2011). Adaptive Modifications in the Epidermis of Certain Hill-Stream Fishes of Kumaun Region: A Scanning Electron Microscope Investigation, Ph.D. Thesis. Kumaun University Nainital.

Lal M B, Bhatnagar A N, Uniyal J D (1966). Adaptive Modification of a Hill-Stream Fish, *Glyptothorax Pectinopterus* (Mc. Clelland); *Proc. Nat. Acad. Sci.* India. 36, 109-116.

Migdalski E C and Fichter G S (1983). Fichter The Fresh and Saltwater Fishes of the World; Greenwhich House, New York. pp. 316.

Mittal A K and Whitear M A (1978). Notes on Cold Anaesthesia of Poikilotherms; *J. Fish. Biol.* 13: 519-520.

Nag T C and Bhattacharjee J (2002). Retinal Cytoarchitecture in Some Mountain Stream Teleosts of *India. Environ. Biol. Fish.* 63: 435-449.

Olson K R (1995). Scanning Electron Microscopy of Fish Gill, In: Datta Munshi, J S and H M Dutta (eds), Fish. Morphology: Horizon of New Research; Oxford and IBH Publishing Co. Pvt. Ltd. New Delhi. pp. 31-45.

Robert T R (1982). Unculi Horny Projections Arising from Single Cell, an Adaptive Feature of the Epidermis of Ostariophysean fish. *Zool. Scrpt.* 11: 55-76.

Saxena S C (1959). Adhesive Apparatus of a Hill-Stream Cyprinid Fish *Garra mullya* (Sykes). *Proc. Natn. Acad. Sci. India.* 25: 205-214.

Saxena S C and Chandy B (1966). Adhesive Apparatus in Certain Hill-Stream Fishes; *J. Zool.* London. 148: 315-340.

Whitear M (1990). Causative Aspects of Microridges on the Surface of Fish Epithelia; J. Submicrosc. *Cytol. Pathol.* 22: 211-220.

Page 118-123

Fisheries and Aquaculture
Edited by: **Prof. (Mrs.) Neelima Gupta** and **Dr. D.K. Gupta**
Edition: **2015**
ISBN: 978-93-5056-736-4
Published by: **Discovery Publishing House Pvt. Ltd., New Delhi (India)**

9

Toxic Effect of Profenofos on Haematology of *Channa triatus*

Kumari Minoo and **D.N Sadhu**

Department of Zoology, Chas Mahila College, University
Department of Zoology, Vinoba Bhave University, Hazaribag. Email: kumariminoo 77@gmail.com

ABSTRACT

The aim of the present experimental endeavour was to evaluate stress symptoms on exposure of sub-lethal concentration of 16.5 ppm of Profenofos (an organophosphate composition of (0-(4-bromo-2-chlorophenyl) 0-ethyl s-propyl phosphorothioate) in blood of Channa striatus for a long-term duration. The effect of the chemical on various blood parameters was observed for different time periods. The effect of 4 to 24 days Profenofos showed a significant decrease in the haemoglobin (Hb) per cent count from 9.2 to 5.5 per cent, R.B.C count 2.80 to 1.15 ($10^6/mm^3$), WBC Count decreased from 6700 to 2800 ($10^3/mm^3$) Lymphocytes from 90 per cent to 50 per cent, Heterophils 6.1 per cent to 26 per cent, Monocytes decreased from 3 to 1.1 per cent, Eosinophils increased from 0.9 to 3.5 per cent, Packed cell volume (%) increased from 27.6 per cent to 16.5 per cent after 24 days exposure. Mean corpuscular volume (MCV) increased from 98.571 to 143.487 (cμ) Mean Corpuscular Haemoglobin (MCH) increased from 32.85 to 47.82 (μg). Necessary preventive measures are suggested to save the aquatic biota in general and fish wealth in particular.

Keywords: *Channa triatus, Blood, Profenofos, Organophosphorus, PPM.*

INTRODUCTION

Indiscriminate use of various agricultural chemicals, especially synthetic insecticides and pesticides, to boost up crop production, is now considered as a causative factor for the contamination of water media (Gaufin, 1967, Konar and Ghosh, 1977, Anees 1978).

Blood parameters have been used as sensitive indicators of stress in fish exposed to different water pollutants and toxicants, such as metals, biocides, pesticides, chemicals industrial effluents, etc. A number of deformities in the adult fishes has been reported earlier in such fishes like: *Colisa fascitus. Oreochromis mossambicus* to sub lethal concentration of lead, copper and zinc which produce haemolytic anemia due to lyses of erythrocytes together concomitant decrease in Hb per cent, RBC count and PCV per cent value (Haley and Weiser (1985), Benarjy and Nath (1990), Svobodova, *et al.* (1996).

Material and Methods

Haematological effects of Profenofos were estimated by blood-profiling of *Channa triatus*. Blood was collected from heart using EDTA (Ethylene diamin tetra acetate) in plastic tubes. Haemocytometer was used for estimating blood cell counts. Ganti fluid was used as a diluting fluid (Iodine Crystal 0.3, Potassium iodide 0.4 gms. Sodium citrate 2.0 gms and distilled water 100 ml). Due to this fluid, red blood cells are stained brown. Therefore it is easy to count them on a faint yellow back ground. Cells are not clumped and cell setting in the counting chamber is quick.

WBC count: The diluting fluid of leucocytes are glacial acetic acid 2 ml 1 per cent acid 2 ml 1 per cent, aqueous solution of gentian violet 1 ml, distilled water 100 ml.

Haemoglobin estimation (Hb); Haemoglobinometer was used for haemoglobin estimation PCV (Packed cell volume), MCV (Mean Corpuscular Volume) was estimated by centrifuging heparinized blood in a capillary tube.

Other parameters were calculated as follows:

$$\text{MCV} = \frac{\text{PCV}}{\text{RBC in millions}} \times 10 \text{ cubic microns}$$

Mean corpuscular haemoglobin (MCH)

$$MCH = \frac{\text{Hb in gms/100 ml}}{\text{RBC in millions}} \times 10 \text{ micro grams}$$

MCHC (Mean corpuscular haemoglobin concentration)

$$MCHC = \frac{\text{Hb in gms/100 ml 100}}{\text{PCV}}$$

Table 9.1: Impact of exposure of 15.5 ppm of Profenofos on haematological parameters of *Channa striatus*

Parameters	Control	4 Days	8 Days	16 Days	24 Days
Hb%	9.00	8	7.5	7	6.7
RBC (*10^6/mm^3	2.81	1.71	1.52	1.40	1.20
WBC (*10^3/mm)^3	6700	4200	4000	3800	3000
Lymphocytes (%)	90	72	69	62	55
Heterophils (%)	6.1	45	35	30	28.5
Monocytes (%)	3	2.5	2.3	1.5	1.2
Eosinophils (%)	0.9	1	1	1	2.5
PCV (%)	27	24	21.6	20.4	19.5
MCV (cμ)	95.405	138.728	142.105	145.714	162.5
MCH (μμ g)	23.02	46.78	47.36	48.57	54.16
MCHC (%)	33.33	33.33	3.33	33.33	33.33

Table 9.2: Impact of exposure of 16.5 ppm of profenofos on haematologcal parameters of *Channa striatus*

Parameters	Control	4 Days	8 Days	16 Days	24 Days
Hb(%)	9.2	7.5	6.9	6.3	5.5
RBC (*10^6/mm^3)	2.80	1.69	1.50	1.35	1.15
WBC (*10^3/mm^3)	6700	4000	3500	3000	28000
Lymphocytes (%)	90	70	61	52	50
Heterophils (%)	6.1	40	31	28	26
Monocyte (%)	3	2.1	2	1.5	1.1
Eosinophils (%)	0.9	1	1	1	3.5
PVC (%)	27.6	22.5	20.7	18.9	16.5
MCV (cμ)	98.571	133.136	138	140	143.487
MCH (μμg)	32.85	44.37	46	44.44	47.82
MCHC (%)	33.33	33.33	33.33	31.74	33.33

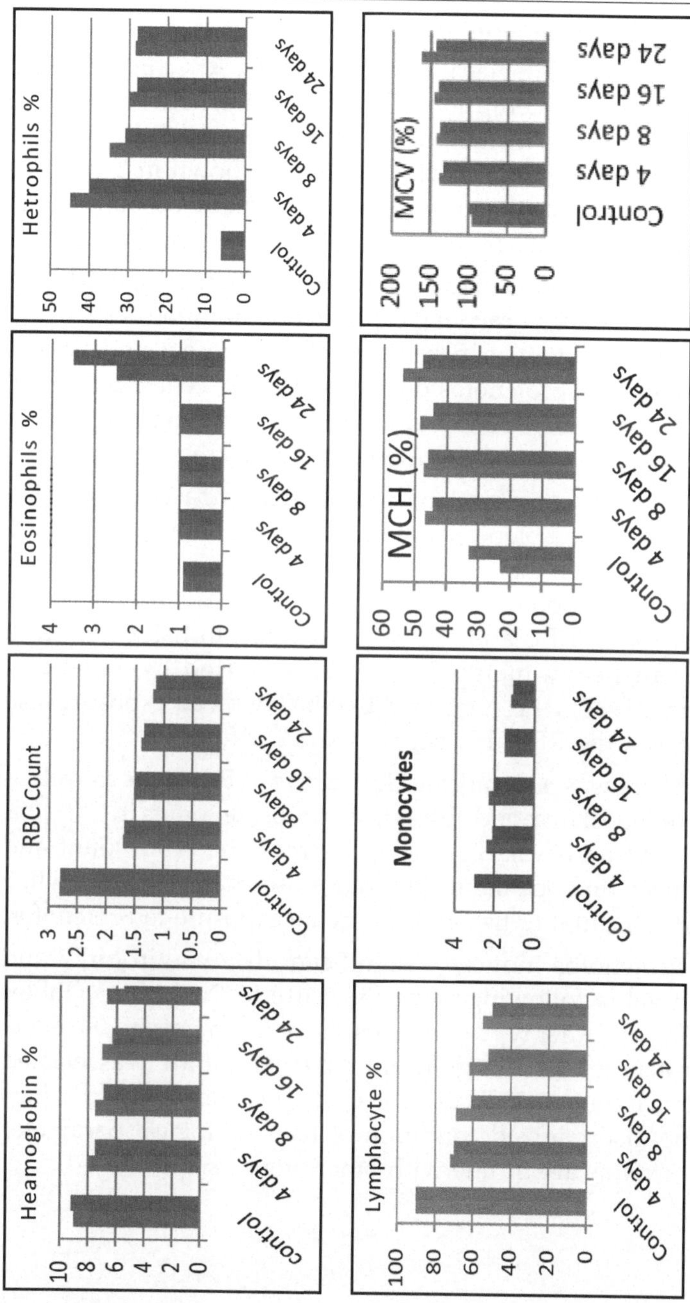

Fig.9.1: *Haematological Parameters of Channa triatus Exposed to 15.5 and 16.5 ppm of Profenofos*

Result and Discussion

The haematologiacal parameters (Hb, RBC, Eosinophils, Lymphocytes, Heterophils, PCV, Monocytes, MCH and MCV) showed changes in their values when exposed to 15.5 and 16.5 ppm of profenofos. The values are shown in Tables 9.1 and 9.2. These results indicated fluctuation blood parameters and they even caused death of fish.

Detailed studies show many disorders or changes in blood circulation, oxygen carrying capacity and immune system and due to this, mortality of fish increased. The present study shows that impact of profenofos decreased Hb per cent, RBC count, WBC count, PCV, MCV, and MCHC per cent value in *Channa striatus* thereby increasing mortality rate increased in fish.

Many investigators have reported the impact of insecticide and toxicides on blood parameters of fishes. Impact of organo phosphorous on *Clarias gariepinus* show decreased erythrocyte count, haemoglobin, WBC Count and PCV (Adedeji *et al.* 2007) Reduction of RBC and Hb per cent count in fish exposed to different heavy metals have been reported by, Goel and Sharma (1987) who suggested that heavy metal exposure also decreased the RBC, Hb per cent and PCV(%).

There was a significant decrease in WBC count as well as in both the relative and absolute lymphocyte counts in *C striatus* (Table 9.1 and 9.2). Significant decrease of WBC count and absolute lymphopenia and granulocytosis characterize the white blood cell count of fish after the acute exposure to Profenofos.

Profenofos induced a significant decrease in MCV and MCH value following acute exposure to Profenofos (Tables 9.1, 9.2). Another type of haematological response to the effect of profenofos was a significant increment of MCV associated with increment of PCV value in *C. striatus* The present findings on the disorganized condition of haematological parameter of *C. striatus* are in line with other workers.

REFFERENCES

Adedeji, Olufemi B, Adetola O, Olanike K A and Amuel A A (2007). Acute Toxicity of Diazion to the African Catfish *Clarias*. *Afr. J Biotechnol.* 75: 651, 654.

Anees MA (1978). Haematological Abnormalities in a Fresh Water Teleost, *Channa punctatus* Bloch, Exposed to Sub Lethal and Chronic Level of the Organophosphorus Insecticide. *Int J. Ecol. Envron. Sci.* 453: 351-356.

Benargy G and Nath R (1990). Haematological Changes Induced by an Insecticide in a Fresh Water Fish *Clarias batrachus* Linnaeus. *Trop. Fresh Water Biol.* 2: 197-202.

Gaufin RF (1967). Accumulation of DDT by Aquatic Indicator Organism. Thesis, University of Utah, p. 230.

Goel KA and Sharma SD (1987). Some Haematological Characteristics of *Clarias batrachus* under Metallic Effect of Arsenic. *Comp. Physiol. Ecol.* 12: 63-66.

Haley PJ and Weiser MG (1985). Erythrocyte Volume Distribution in Rainbow Trout. *Am.J. Vet Res.* 46: 2210-2212.

Konar SK and Ghosh BB (1977). Hazards of Water Pollution by Pesticide. Symp. Envirron. *Poll. Toxicol.* pp. 84-93.

Svobodova ZD Pravada and Palackova J(1996). Uniform Methods of Haematological Examination of Fish. *Vodary Environ Sci.* 453: 351-356.

Page 124-134

Fisheries and Aquaculture
Edited by: **Prof. (Mrs.) Neelima Gupta** and **Dr. D.K. Gupta**
Edition: **2015**
ISBN: 978-93-5056-736-4
Published by: **Discovery Publishing House Pvt. Ltd., New Delhi (India)**

10

Effects of Sodium-Heparin and Di-potassium EDTA on the Hematological Parameters and Blood Cell Morphology of Freshwater Snowtrout, *Schizothorax plagiostomus* Heckel

Aamir Maqbool and **Imtiaz Ahmed**

DST, Sponsored Fish Nutrition Research Laboratory, P.G. Department of Zoology, University of Kashmir, Hazratbal, Srinagar 190006, Jammu and Kashmir, India. Email: *aamir.aquaculture@yahoo.co.in

ABSTRACT

The aim of the present study was to evaluate the effects of two commonly used anticoagulants i.e., sodium-heparin and di-potassium EDTA with a concentration of 20 I.U/ml and 1.0mg/ml on the hematological parameters and blood cell morphology of the freshwater teleost, Schizothorax plagiostomus Heckel. Twenty fishes weighing 340 ± 25.4g and average length 32 ± 2.8 cm were used for blood sampling. Blood cell counts and haematocrit was done within one hour of sampling. Samples collected with K_2EDTA showed an increased haematocrit. Red blood cell counts were lower in K_2EDTA samples as compared to heparin samples while WBC counts and haemoglobin concentrations did not differ significantly ($p>0.05$)*. Mean corpuscular haemoglobin (MCH) and mean corpuscular volume (MCV) increased in K_2EDTA sample, while a significant decrease*

($p<0.05$) was observed in mean corpuscular haemoglobin concentration (MCHC). Blood smears were prepared from fresh sample and stained with Leishman-Giemsa cocktail stain. Cell morphometric analysis showed an increase in the RBC area in the K_2EDTA sample as compared to heparinized sample. However, no significant difference ($p>0.05$) was observed in WBC and thrombocyte area of K_2EDTA and heparinized sample. The present study suggests the use of Na-heparin as a preferred anticoagulant for routine hematological analysis of fish blood.

Keywords: Sodium-Heparin, Di-potassium EDTA, Hematological analysis, Cell Morphology.

INTRODUCTION

Hematological study of fish has assumed greater significance due to increasing emphasis on fish culture and greater awareness of the pollution of natural fresh water resources. The knowledge of hematological characteristics is a valuable diagnostic tool to evaluating fish health (Satheeshkumar *et al.* 2010) and can be used as an effective and sensitive index to monitor physiological and pathological changes in fishes (Blaxhall 1972; Smit *et al.* 1977 and Kori-Siakpere *et al.* 2005). Hematological parameters of fish are closely related to the response of fish to environmental and biological factors (Fernandes and Mazon 2003). Hematological parameters can be of great importance to aquaculturists serving as indicators of the physiological status and helping to prevent and control pathologies related to stress (Aldrin *et al.* 1982). Therefore, analysis of blood indices is a valuable guide to assessing the condition of the fish, as it provides a reliable index of their physiological condition and is important in fish aquaculture (Alyakrinskyaya and Dolgova 1984). Many of the clinical tools used to evaluate mammalian health are not developed for use in fishes. Fish haematology has revealed that interpretation of blood parameters is quite difficult, since variations in the blood are caused by internal and external factors.

Fish blood contains a large number of thrombocytes due to which it clots quickly, and samples almost always require anticoagulant treatment. Blood cells of various animals show different reactions to various anticoagulants (Witeska and Wargocka, 2011). In fish hematology, the most commonly used anticoagulants are different salts of heparin and EDTA (Walencik and Witeska 2007). The mode of action of EDTA is by binding calcium ions, which are essential in the coagulation cascade and for cell-to-cell interaction. Due to this property, EDTA salt is used as a blood anticoagulant because it chelates calcium ions which promote blood clotting (Jain, 1993). Heparin binds to and accelerates the activity of antithrombin III, which inhibits the action of thrombin and other proteases necessary for coagulation (Harr *et al.* 2005). Some authors consider EDTA salts the most appropriate for fish blood analyses (Blaxhall 1972; Blaxhall and Daisley 1973), while others recommend heparin (Hesser 1960; Hattingh and Smith 1976; Mainwaring and Rowley 1985; Svobodova *et al.* 1991; Walencik and Witeska 2007 and Ishikawa *et al.* 2010). However, varying results of hematological parameters have been reported on both the anticoagulants in different fish species. Therefore, the aim of the present study was to compare the values of basic hematological parameters and blood cell morphology of *Schizothorax plagiostomus* blood collected on two anticoagulants: sodium-heparin and Na_2EDTA to evaluate their usefulness for routine fish blood analysis.

Material and Methods

Experimental Fish

Adult specimens of *Schizothorax plagiostomus* used in this study were obtained from a local fish farm. Twenty fishes weighing 340 ± 25.4 g and average length 32 ± 2.8 cm were kept in fish tanks (1.22 m × 0.91 m × 0.91 m; water volume = 600 L) at 18.6 ± 1.6^0 C, D.O 6.5mgL ± 1 and pH 7.1-7.6 with 12:12 h photoperiod, fitted with a continuous water flow-through system. Fishes were acclimated to the laboratory conditions for 2 weeks and during this period, were fed to apparent satiation on commercial pelleted diet at 09:00 and 17:00 h.

Anticoagulants Used

Dry salts of Na-Heparin and K_2EDTA (Loba Chemie, India) were dissolved in Phosphate buffer saline (PBS, pH 6.8) to get a final concentration of 20 I.U of Na-Heparin per 25µL and 1.0 mg of K_2EDTA per 25µL.

Blood Sampling

Fishes were carefully netted minimizing the stress and placed in a fish trough. They were positioned ventral side up (with gill region submerged) so that the blood could be easily drawn from the caudal vein, with the whole sampling event usually taking less than 2 min. All blood samples (3 ml from each fish) were collected from the caudal vein using a chilled needle with a 3 ml syringe without any anticoagulant. Blood smears were quickly made on the spot and then the blood sample was transferred (1 ml each) to sterilized blood collection tubes, containing the respective anticoagulant (20 I.U Na-Heparin and 1.0 mg K_2EDTA). Blood vials were kept in an ice-bath until further analysis.

Hematological Analysis

Total erythrocyte count (RBC) and total leucocyte count (WBC)

Total RBC and WBC counts were measured as follows: 20µl of blood sample was taken from a well mixed blood with a micro pipette (Thermo Scientific, Finland) and diluted with Natt and Herrick's (1952) diluent (1:200). The diluted sample was placed in a Neubauer hemocytometer (Marienfeld-SupeRior, Lauda-Königshofen, Germany) and the blood cells were counted using a microscope (Magnus, MLX-Tr).

Haemoglobin (Hb)

Haemoglobin content of blood was estimated by the method of Drabkin (1946). 20 µl of blood was mixed with 5 ml of Drabkin's reagent (Loba Chemie, India) and left to stand for at least 15 minutes. Haemoglobin concentration was determined by measuring the absorbance at 540 nm and compared to that of haemoglobin standard (Ranbaxy India). Prior to reading the absorbance, hemoglobin test samples were centrifuged to remove dispersed nuclear material.

Haematocrit (HCT)

Haematocrit or packed cell volume (PCV) was determined on the basis of sedimentation of blood. Heparinised blood (50μl) was taken in a micro hematocrit capillary (Na-heparinised) and centrifuged in a micro centrifuge (REMI RM-12C BL, India) spun in at 12,000 rpm for 5 min to obtain haematocrit value. The haematocrit was measured using a haematocrit reader (REMI India) and reported as percentage (Del Rio-Zaragoza *et al.* 2008).

The following indices: mean corpuscular volume (MCV), mean corpuscular hemoglobin (MCH) and mean corpuscular hemoglobin concentration (MCHC) were calculated by standard formulas with data of HCT, RBC and Hb.

Blood Cell Morphology

For each blood sample, two blood smears were prepared on microscope slides. The smear was left to air-dry, fixed in 100 per cent methanol for 5-8 min and stained. The smears were stained by Garbyal's cocktail stain (Garbyal *et al.* 2006) and examined under a compound light microscope (Magnus MLX-Tr, India) at 1000x magnification. Cell morphometric analysis was done with Image analysis software (Image Pro-premier 9.0, Media Cybernetics, Inc.) calibrated to a stage micrometer.

Statistical Analysis

Hematological indicators were summarized as mean ± standard deviation (SD) and differences between Na-heparin and K_2EDTA anticoagulated blood samples were statistically analyzed using the Student's *t* test. Results were considered significant at $p<0.05$. Statistical analyses were carried out using SPSS version 20.

Results

Haematological Parameters

Table 10.1 shows the hematological parameters of the blood samples treated with Na-Heparin (20 I.U/ml of blood) and K_2EDTA (1.0mg/ml of blood). Haematocrit values in all K_2EDTA treated samples were significantly higher ($p<0.05$)

and much more variable compared to those of heparin collected samples. Significant ($p<0.05$) differences were found in total RBC counts between blood samples obtained with K_2EDTA and those obtained with Na-Heparin. Mean corpuscular haemoglobin (MCH) and mean corpuscular volume (MCV) increased in K_2EDTA sample, while a significant decrease ($p<0.05$) was found in mean corpuscular haemoglobin concentration (MCHC). Haemoglobin concentration, total WBC counts and leucocyte morphology did not differ significantly ($p>0.05$) in the samples treated with Na-heparin and K_2-EDTA.

Table 10.1: Hematological parameters of *Schizothorax plagiostomus* (n=20) treated with anticoagulant sodium-heparin (20 I.U/ml of blood) and di-potassium-EDTA (1.0mg/ml of blood)

Anticoagulant	HCT (%)	Hb (gdl^{-1})	RBC ($x10^6$/ mm3)	WBC ($x10^3$/ mm3)	MCV (fl)	MCH (pg)	MCHC (gdl^{-1})
Na-Heparin	31.40[a] ± 4.11	11.23[a] ± 0.96	1.83[a] ± 0.06	13.03[a] ± 3.81	185.2[a] ± 9.54	62.86[a] ± 5.57	35.91[a] ± 2.13
K_2EDTA	38.89[b] ± 5.45	10.95[a] ± 1.15	1.56[b] ± 0.11	12.61[a] ± 4.03	237.23[b] ± 13.63	74.50[b] ± 6.14	29.71[b] ± 1.03

HCT, Haematocrit; Hb, Haemoglobin concentration; RBC, Red blood cell count; WBC, White blood cell count; MCV, Mean corpuscular volume; MCH, Mean corpuscular haemoglobin; MCHC, Mean corpuscular haemoglobin concentration. Values are mean ± SD. Means with different superscripts are significantly different ($p<0.05$).

Cell Morphometric Analysis

Blood cells were identified and characterized by light microscopy and the results of cell dimensions were tabulated (Table 10.2). Analysis of blood smears revealed that in heparinized samples, most of the erythrocytes were normal and intact, while in all K_2EDTA samples, erythrocytes showed considerable swelling leading to significant enlargement ($p<0.05$) compared to normal erythrocytes (Table 10.2). RBC's of K_2EDTA collected sample showed an increase in the total erythrocyte area as well as nucleus area. No morphological changes were found in the leucocytes in K_2EDTA and Na-Heparin anticoagulated blood.

Table 10.2: Erythrocyte dimensions and area of *Schizothorax plagiostomus* (N=100)

Anticoagulant	EL (µm)	EW (µm)	EA (µm²)	NL (µm)	NW (µm)	NA (µm²)
No anticoagulant	15.02[a] ± 0.99	7.67[a] ± 0.65	98.26[a] ± 10.57	6.73[a] ± 0.45	3.53[a] ± 0.36	18.68[a] ± 3.51
Na-Heparin	15.43[a] ± 0.80	7.85[a] ± 0.51	102.11[a] ± 12.85	6.81[a] ± 0.44	3.59[a] ± 0.35	20.32[a] ± 3.64
K_2-EDTA	16.48[b] ± 0.89	8.45[b] ± 0.42	128.69[b] ± 12.07	7.69[b] ± 0.37	4.10[b] ± 0.39	26.85[b] ± 4.88

EL, Erythrocyte length; EW, Erythrocyte width; EA, Erythrocyte area; NL, Nuclear length; NW, Nuclear width; NA, Nuclear area.

Values are mean ± SD. Means with different superscripts are significantly different ($p<0.05$).

Discussion

The results obtained show that the values of some hematological parameters and morphology of red blood cells were significantly affected by K_2EDTA, which included swelling of RBC, elevated haematocrit and low RBC counts. Similar observations were reported byWalencik and Witeska (2007) and Ishikawa and Hisano (2010). Elevated haematocrit levels in K_2EDTA samples observed in the present study could be related to erythrocyte swelling. This might have been caused by an increase in pCO_2 and acidification due to treatment with acidic EDTA salt (Smit *et al.* 1977). Similar phenomenon was observed by Blaxhall (1973), Hattingh (1975), Korcock *et al.* (1988) Walencik and Witeska (2007) and Witeska and Wargocka (2011). Mainwaring and Rowley (1985) reported distortion of erythrocyte shape followed by lysis, when blood of *Blennius pholis* was incubated for 20 min with 10 mg/mL of EDTA. Hattingh (1975) compared the effects of heparin and EDTA on haematocrit of five species of fish and found that EDTA had a tendency to increase PCV in fish, and in some species induced haemolysis, while heparin produced very little change in erythrocyte volume and PCV values. According to Jain (1993) EDTA sequesters Ca^{2+} ions responsible for the activation of Na^{+} and K^{+} ions on the cell membrane, allowing the free entry of water into the cell, promoting-swelling and its consequent lysis. Heparin is known to cause little alteration in corpuscular size and is considered to be a more suitable anticoagulant, because varying the concentration has little effect on the PCV values (Pennock and Jones 1966; Dubin *et al.* 1976). In the present study, Na-Heparin caused insignificant alteration in RBC size, which was also observed by Walencik and Witeska (2007) and Witeska and Wargocka (2011) in common carp.

Low RBC count in K_2EDTA sample in the present study could be due to the haemolytic action of EDTA. Haemolysis of fish erythrocytes in blood treated with EDTA was observed by Van Vliet *et al.* (1985) in tilapia and by Walenick and Witeska (2007) in common carp that lead to low RBC counts. Hemolysis in EDTA anticoagulated samples of rainbow trout blood was also reported by Korcock *et al.* (1988). Witeska and Wargocka (2011) observed gradual destruction of erythrocytes in Na_2EDTA samples, where Na_2EDTA caused cell swelling, followed by disintegration of the outer membranes of erythrocytes, which resulted in release of the nucleus. Haemolytic action of EDTA can be attributed to the adverse effect of Na_2EDTA on erythrocyte membrane structure, permeability, and stability, which is probably related to decalcination induced by the chelating action of the anticoagulant (Blaxhall 1972; Hattingh 1975). EDTA increases the osmotic fragility of erythrocytes, making them susceptible to lysis. Van Vliet *et al.* (1985) and Walencik and Witeska (2007) reported hemolysis in *Cyprinus carpio* blood collected with EDTA. This was probably due to the chelation of Ca^{2+} ions that play a key role in cell membrane permeability and stability (Walencik and Witeska, 2007). Increased osmotic fragility in the blood samples treated with EDTA was observed by Walencik and Witeska (2007) in common carp and Mafuvadze and Erlwanger (2007) in ostritches and which eventually lead to a decrease in the RBC count.

In the present study, no significant effects by Na-heparin and K_2EDTA were observed on the total leucocyte count and cell morphology which was also observed by Mainwaring and Rowley (1985) in *Blennius pholis* Adeyemo *et al.* (2009) in African catfish.

Conclusions

On the basis of above findings, it is concluded that Na-Heparin is the preferable anticoagulant for blood sampling in fish as it imparts minimum changes to hematological parameters while, K_2EDTA significantly affects the hematological parameters and alters the shape and size of blood cells.

REFERENCES

Adeyemo O K, Wilagwe O O and Ajani F (2009). Comparative Assessment of Sodium EDTA and Heparin as Anticoagulants for the Evaluation of Haematological Parameters in Cultured and Feral African Catfish (*Clarias gariepinus*); *Braz. J. Aquat. Sci. Technol.* 13: 19-24.

Aldrin J F, Messager J L and Baudin-Laurencin F (1982). La Biochimie Clinique en Aquaculture. Interet et Perspective; *Cnexo Actes Colloq.* 14: 219-326.

Alyakrinskyaya I O and Dolgova S N (1984) Hematological Features of Young Sturgeons; *Vopr. Ikhtiol.* 4: 135-139.

Blaxhall P C (1972). Haematological Assessment of the Health of Freshwater Fish; *J. Fish Biol.* 4: 593-604.

Blaxhall P C (1973). Error in Haematocrit Value Produced by Inadequate Concentration of Ethylenediamine Tetra-Acetate; *J. Fish. Biol.* 5: 767-769.

Blaxhall P C and Daisley K W (1973). Routine Hematological Methods for use in Fish Blood; *J. Fish Biol.* 5: 771-781.

Del Rio-Zaragoza O B, Hernández-Rodríguez M and Bückle-Ramirez L F (2008). Thermal Stress Effect on Tilapia *Oreochromis mossambicus* (Pisces: Cichlidae) Blood Parameters; *Mar. Freshwater Behav. Physiol.* 41: 135-145.

Drabkin D L (1946). Spectrometric Studies, XIV - The Crystallographic and Optimal Properties of the Hemoglobin of Man in Comparison with Those of other Species; *J. Biol. Chem.* 164: 703-723.

Dubin S, Piszczek J, Beard R and Schmukler R (1976). Effects of Anticoagulants on Packed cell Volume Measurement. *Lab. Anim. Sci.* 2:6 586-591.

Fernandes M N, Mazon A F (2003). Environmental Pollution and Fish gill Morphology; In: Val AL, Kapoor BG (eds) *Fish Adaptation*. Science, Enfield, pp. 203-231.

Garbyal R S, Agarwal N and Kumar P (2006). Leishman-Giemsa Cocktail: An Effective Romanowsky Stain for Air-Dried Cytologic Smears. Acta. Cytol. 50: 403-406.

Harr K E, Raskin R E and Heard D J (2005). Temporal Effects of 3 Commonly used Anticoagulants on Hematological and Biochemical Variables in Blood Samples from Macaws and Burmese Pythons; *Vet. Clin. Path.* 34: 383-388.

Hattingh J (1975). Heparin and Ethylenediamine Tetra-Acetate as Anticoagulants for Fish Blood; *Pflugers Arch.* 355: 347-352.

Hattingh J and Smith EM (1976). Anticoagulants for Avian and Reptilian Blood: Heparin and EDTA; *Pflugers Arch.* 363: 267-269.

Hesser E F (1960). Methods for Routine Fish Hematology; *Prog. Fish-Cult.* 22: 164-171.

Ishikawa M M, de Pádua S B, Jerônimo G T, Satake F, Martins M L and Hisano H (2010). Heparin and Na_2 EDTA as Anticoagulants for Hybrid Surubim Catfish (*Pseudoplatystoma reticulatum* x *P. corruscans*): Efficacy and Hematological Changes.*Ciência Rural.* 40: 1557-1561.

Jain N C (1993). Coagulation and its Disorders; In: Jain NC (Ed.) *Essentials of Veterinary Hematology*. Philadelphia, Lea and Febiger. pp. 82-104.

Korcock D E, Houston A H and Gray J D (1988). Effects of Sampling Conditions on Selected Blood Variables of Rainbow Trout, *Salmo gairdneri* Richardson; *J. Fish Biol.* 33: 319-330.

Kori-Siakpere O, Ake J E G and Idoge E (2005). Haematological Characteristics of the African Snakehead, *Parachacnna obscura; Afr J Biotechnol* 4: 527-530.

Mafuvadze B and Erlwanger K H (2007). Effect of EDTA, Heparin and Storage on the Erythrocyte Osmotic Fragility, Plasma Osmolality and Haematocrit of Adult Ostriches (*Struthio camelus*); *Vet. Arhiv.* 77: 427-434.

Mainwaring G and Rowley A F (1985). The Effect of Anticoagulants on *Blennius pholis* L. Leucocytes; *Comp. Biochem. Physiol.* 80: 85-91.

Natt M P and Herrick C A (1952). New Blood Diluent for Counting the Erythrocytes and Leucocytes of the Chicken; *Poult. Sci.* 31: 735-738.

Pennock C and Jones K (1966). Effect of Ethylene-diamine-tetra-acetic (Dipotassium Salt) and Heparin on the Estimation of Packed Cell Volume; *J. Clin. Pathol.* 19: 196-199.

Satheeshkumar P, Ananthan G and Senthilkumar D, Khan A B and Jeevanantham K (2010). Comparative Investigation on Haematological and Biochemical Studies on Wild Marine Teleost Fishes from Vellar Estuary, Southeast Coast of India. *Comp. Clin. Path.* 21: 275-281.

Smit G L, Hattingh J and Schoonbee H B (1977). Observations on Some Effects of Disodium Ethylenediamine Tetra-acetate and Heparin on Fish Blood; *Comp Biochem Physiol.* 57 35-38.

Svobodova Z, Prada D and Palackova J. (1991). Unified Methods of Haematological Examination of Fish. Res Inst Fish Cult Hydrobiol, Vodany, Czechoslovakia. pp. 31.

Van Vliet K J, Smit G L, Pieterse J J, Schoonbee H J and van Vuren J H J (1985). The Effects of Generally used Anticoagulants on the Haemolysis of Fish Erythrocytes; *Water SA.* 2: 87-92.

Walencik J and Witeska M (2007). The Effects of Anticoagulants on Hematological Indices and Blood Cell Morphology of Common carp (*Cyprinus carpio* L.); *Comp Biochem Physiol.* 146 331-335.

Witeska M and Wargocka W (2011). Disodium EDTA used as Anticoagulant Causes Hemolysis in Common Carp Blood; *Turk. J. Vet. Anim. Sci.* 35: 99-104.

Page 135-140

Fisheries and Aquaculture
Edited by: **Prof. (Mrs.) Neelima Gupta** and **Dr. D.K. Gupta**
Edition: **2015**
ISBN: 978-93-5056-736-4
Published by: **Discovery Publishing House Pvt. Ltd., New Delhi (India)**

11

Alteration in Lactic Acid Dehydrogenase Enzyme Activity in the Blood of *Colisa fasciatus* Induced by Azodyes

Poonam Gupta

Department of Zoology, D.A.K. College, Moradabad. E-mail: poonamgupta 2909@gmail.com

ABSTRACT

The present study is an attempt to evaluate the toxic affects of two azodyes Metanil yellow (4-aniline azo benzene – m – sulfonic acid) and Bismark brown (2, 4 – diamino 3′ amino azo benzene) on Lactic dehydrogenase activity in the blood of Colisa fasciatus. An increased lactic dehydrogenase activity in the blood was observed at both acute (48 hrs and 96 hrs) and chronic (15 days and 30 days) exposures. The results were statistically highly significant (P<0.01).

Keywords: Colisa fasciatus, Lactic Dehydrogenase, Metanil Yellow, Bismark Brown, Lactic Dehydrogenase.

INTRODUCTION

The preservation of the natural water reservoirs both fresh and marine is of great concern as the pesticides and the trade effluents are discharged into them. In India, principal trade effluents discharged from textile, paper pulp industries, sugar factories, distillaries and tanneries contain chemicals such as: phenols, detergents, heavy metals, dyes etc. These chemicals not only affect the quality of drinking water for men and his domestic animals but also adversely affect the inhabiting flora and fauna including fish. These chemicals may sometimes cause a huge mortification in fish population and degrade its food quality.

Dyes (nonazo and azo) constitute important water pollutants (Klien 1962). The dyes, specially azodyes discharged in inland water, render tremendous chemico azo stress on fish with the result that a large number of fishes are subjected to mortification. *Colisa fasciatus* is a common larvivorous fish of South East Asia. This fish is used for biological control of mosquito larvae and is also eaten by poor people specially in villages. The aim of this study is to examine the toxic effects of dyes on fishes.

Material and Methods

Live specimens of *Colisa fasciatus* were collected from local fresh water resources and acclimatized under laboratory conditions for a minimum period of seven days before experimentation. Visibly healthy fishes were selected and treated with 0.1 per cent $KMnO_4$ solution and divided into five batches. One batch was kept in water and was used as control. The remaining four batches were kept in acute and chronic concentrations of metanil yellow and four batches in bismark brown. Water was replaced periodically and black paper was used to prevent any possible photo-oxidation of the dyes. The fishes of all batches were sacrificed at 48 hrs., and 96 hrs. (acute exposure) and 15 days and 30 days (chronic exposure). The blood was collected from the caudal vein and was allowed to clot at room temperature and then centrifuged at 2000 rpm. The 't' test of Fisher (1963) was used to calculate the significance of data.

Results

The present study reveals a significant increase in the lactic dehydrogenase activity in the blood of *Colisa fasciatus* under the stress of metanil yellow and bismark brown. The increase was 12.11 per cent, 24.99 per cent, 46.02 per cent and 104.27 per cent in response to metanil yellow and 16.61 per cent, 26.48 per cent, 49.61 per cent and 108.34 per cent in response to bismark brown upon acute (T1 and T2) and chronic (T3 and T4) exposures respectively. All the elevations are statistically highly significant ($P<0.01$) (Table 11.1).

Discussion

Lactic dehydrogenase is an enzyme which is considered most important in tissue respiration. LDH enzyme is used in interconversion of pyruvic acid to lactic acid. It acts as a pivotal enzyme between the glycolytic pathway and tricarboxylic acid cycle.

An increased enzymatic activity was reported by Goel *et al.* (1983) in the liver of *Clarias batrachus* in response to congo red and bismark brown intoxication . Increased LDH activity was found in liver, kidney and gills of *Clarias batrachus* under the stress of congo red and bismark brown by Awasthi (1984). Elevated LDH activity was reported by Gupta (1986) in liver, kidney and blood of *Heteropneustes fossilis* when exposed to zinc and metanil yellow. Sastry and Shukla (1988) found increase in muscle LDH activity in *Heteropneustes fossilis* due to zinc and chromium intoxication. Increased LDH activity was seen in brain, liver, gills and intestine of *Colisa fasciatus* after chrysophenine-G and direct deep black exposure by Sharma and Gupta (1989). Increase in LDH activity after 96 hrs., exposure at 16°C water temperature in muscles, liver gonadal and nervous tissues of *Colisa fasciatus* when exposed to cypermethrin was reported by Singh *et al.* (2010). Phillip *et al.* (1995) found increased LDH activity in different tissues in *Labeo rohita* when exposed to cypermethrin.

However, a decreased LDH activity was observed by Tripathi and Verma (2004) in brain, liver and skeletal muscles of *Clarias batrachus* after 21 days exposure of endosulfan. Kumari *et al.* (2011) reported decrease in LDH activity in muscles, liver, brain and blood of *Labeo rohita* due to exposure of hexavalent chromium. Yadav *et al.* (2003) also found 30 per cent decrease in muscles, 77 per cent decrease in liver and 77 per cent to 91 per cent decrease in gonads in LDH activity in *Channa punctatus* when treated with stem bark extract of *Croton tiglium* of family Euphorbiaceae. Osman *et al.* (2010) found increased LDH activity in *Clarias gariepinus* collected from six sites along the river Nile. Osman *et. al.* (2013) also reported increased LDH activity in gills, kidney, intestine, brain and liver of *Channa striatus* after 15 days exposure of cypermethrin while Suneetha (2012) reported decrease in LDH activity following sublethal and lethal exposures of endosulfan and fenvalerate in brain, gills kidney, liver and muscles after 24 hrs., and 15 days exposure to *Labeo rohita.*

Lactic dehydrogenase catalyses the conversion of pyruvic acid to lactic acid under anaerobic conditions. The increase in activity of LDH indicates increased anaerobic catabolism of substrate rather than its entering the oxidative breakdown cycle. This also indicates the physiological stress that the fish is facing on exposure to metanil yellow and bismark brown. The diversion towards anaerobiosis might be expected since in stress conditions some extra amount of energy is needed to mitigate the stress and the evaluated glycolysis.

Table 11.1: Alteration in the activity of lactic dehydrogenase (LDH) induced by 4'AASA and DAAB in the blood of *Colisa fasciatus*. Values are mean + S.E. of nine observations each

		Acute Exposure		Chronic Exposure	
DYES	C	T1	T2	T3	T4
4'AASA	120.36 + 0.27	134.940 + 0.002 (12.11%)	150.44 + 0.06 (24.99%)	175.76 + 0.87 (46.04%)	245.86 +0.77 (104.27%)
DAAB	120.36 + 0.27	140.36 + 0.29 (16.61%)	152.24 +0.22 (26.48%)	180.08 + 0.001 (49.61%)	250.76 + 0.06 (108.34%)

4'AASA – Metanil Yellow C – Control T1 – 48 hrs. T2 – 96 hrs.
DAAB – Bismark Brown T3 – 15 days T4 – 30 days

REFERENCES

Awasthi A K (1984). Histopathology and Biochemistry of a Few Tissues of *Clarias batrachus* Exposed to Amino Azodyes. Ph.D. Thesis, Meerut University, Meerut.

Fisher RA (1963). Statistical Methods for Research Workers. 13th Edition, Oliver and Boyd, London. pp. 119.

Goel KA, Garg V K, Awasthi A K and Tyagi S K (1983). Some Oxidases in the Liver Intestine and Gills of *Clarias batrachus* under the Chemico Azostress of Congo Red and Bismark Brown dyes. 53rd Annual Session of National Academy of Science, 45.

Gupta K (1986). Ph.D. Thesis, Meerut University, Meerut.

Klein L O (1962). In: River Pollution, Causes and Effects, Butterworths, London, p. 33.

Kumari K, Nitish R and Sinha RC (2011). Multiple Biomarker Response in the Fish *Labeo rohita* due to Hexavalent Chromium. 2nd National Conference on Biotechnology and Food Science. IPCBEE, Volume 7 (2011) IACSIT Press, Singapore.

Osman AGM, Abd-El-Baset M. Abd El Raheen, Khalid Y. Abuel, Ali G GadEl – Rab (2010). Enzymatic and Histopathologic Biomarkers as Indicators of Aquatic Pollution in Fishes. *Natural Science*, 2(11): 1302-1311.

Osman AMD, Mastan S A and Rabia BS (2013). Effect of Cypermethrinon Dehydrogenase (LDH) Activity in Various Organ Tissues of *Channa triatus* (Bloch). *Research Journal of Biotechnology*, 8(1): 59.

Phillip GH, Reddy P M. and Sridevi G, (1995). Cypermethrin – Induced *in vivo* Alterations in the Carbohydrate Metabolism of Fresh Water Fish *Labeo rohita*. *Ecotoxicology and Environmental Safety*. 31(2): 173-178.

Sastry K V and Shukla V (1988). Acute and Chronic Toxicity of some Heavy Metals to *Heteropneustes Fossilis*. In: Threatened Habitat, Agrawal VP and Chaturvedi LD (eds). *Society of Biosciences*. pp. 321-334.

Sharma D and Gupta RC, (1989). Impact of Dyes on Lactic Dehydrogenase Activity in a few Fresh Water Teleost *Colisa fasciatus*. *National Development and Natural Resource Conservation*. 73-80.

Singh S K, Singh SK and Yadav RP (2010). Toxicological and Biochemical Alterations of Cypermethrin (Synthetic Pyrethroids) against Fresh Water Teleost fish *Colisa fasciatus* in Different Seasons. *World Journal of Zoology* 5(1): 25-32.

Suneetha K. (2012). Effects of Endosulfan and Fenvalerate on Carbohydrate Metabolism of a Fresh Water Fish *Labeo rohita*. *International Journal of Pharmacy and Pharmaceutical Sciences*, 4(1): 975-1491.

Tripathi G.and Verma P (2004): Endosulfan Mediated Biochemical Changes in the Fresh Water Fish *Clarias Batrachus*. *Biomedical and Environmental Science*, 17: 47-56.

Yadav R P, Singh D, Singh SK and Singh A. (2003). Metabolic Changes in Fresh Water Fish *Channa punctatus* due to Stem Bark Extract of *Croton tiglium*. *Pakistan Journal of Biological Sciences* 6 (14): 1223-1228.

[IV]

FISH DISEASES AND HEALTH

Page 143-156

Fisheries and Aquaculture
Edited by: **Prof. (Mrs.) Neelima Gupta** and **Dr. D.K. Gupta**
Edition: **2015**
ISBN: 978-93-5056-736-4
Published by: **Discovery Publishing House Pvt. Ltd., New Delhi (India)**

12

Fish Diseases in India, their Causes and Control Measures
A Review

Bashir Ahmad Sheikh* Tanveer A. Sofi and **Fayaz Ahmad**

Post-Graduate Department of Zoology, University of Kashmir, Srinagar - 190 006. Email: bashirzoology@gmail.com

ABSTRACT

Until few years from now, diseases were not considered to be a serious problem in our country, as economic losses in fish culture was not known. Recent incidences of Epizootic Ulcerative Syndrome (EUS) in various Southeast Asian countries as well as in our own have focused tremendous attention on the threat the disease epidemics hold for the farmers. Economic losses of the order of US $10 million in Thailand and over $3 million in Bangladesh are lessons enough to realize their importance. Since seasonality of many fish diseases is well known in our country, experienced farmers prevent simultaneous occurrence of stressful conditions and pathogenic organisms. The recent trend on vaccination programme in fry and fingerlings will set the aquaculture programme of the country in a smoother pathway. Researchers have already developed vaccines against bacterial diseases like: Aeromoniasis and Vibriosis. Some more vaccines against some of the potential bacterial diseases like: Pseudomoniasis and

Edwardsiellosis might bring about revolutionary changes in Indian aquaculture, for which efforts are already on in some pioneer research institutes of the country. Control of EUS by application of a specific medicine developed by the scientists of the country is an achievement in itself. Several such developmental activities in health management and disease control programme will give a new dimension to the aquaculture industry.

Keywords: Disease, Epizootic Ulcerative Syndrome, Fish, Vaccine, Aquaculture.

INTRODUCTION

In recent years, intensive fish culture is being practiced in the brackish water, coastal water and freshwater impoundments of India. Recent techniques of intensive and super intensive fish culture involve high rates of stocking and supplementary feeding which has substantially enhanced the incidence of diseases in fishes in our country.

In the first two decades of post-independence, a lot of interest was paid to Inland fisheries and considerable amount of attention was paid to diseases in cultivable fishes in various states. Fishes suffer from a wide variety of diseases of infectious and non-infectious etiology in their natural environment. Adequate literature is available on fish mortalities due to bacteria, parasites, fungus, nutritional deficiencies, metabolic disorders and faulty environmental conditions like: oxygen deficiency, high or very low water temperature, chemical pollutants, overcrowding, malnutrition, algal blooms etc.

In India, traditional aquaculture has in recent years turned into a science based economic and commercial activity involving heavy inputs, and therefore diseases of all kinds are now known to occur on an increasingly larger scale. However, fish mortality is not the only criterion to evaluate the effect of fish disease. Even the morbidity, which leads to weight losses and poor growth in surviving fish, contributes substantial losses to the farmers. Since the last decade, there is an increased realization of the necessity to avoid infectious agents in order to maintain healthy stocks for enhancing production.

Bacterial Diseases

Innumerable diseases are caused in fishes due to bacterial pathogens and several of them are reported in Indian literature. They occur in nursery, rearing and grow out ponds causing serious concern to fish farmers. Some of them often wipe out the entire population of fish. Some of the important bacterial pathogens are: *Aeromonas hydrophila, A. salmonicida, Pseudomonas fluorescens, Pseudomonas putrefaciens, Flexibacter columnaris, Edwardsiella tarda, Vibrio alginolyticus* and *V. parahaemolyticus* which have been identified as most commonly encountered agents in fish diseases. Symptomatology, clinical pathology, microbiology and anatomic pathology have been carefully correlated to arrive at the diagnosis of the diseases caused by these organisms.

Hora and Pillay (1962) and Gopalakrishnan (1963) have reported fin-rot both in young and adult fishes. They have inferred that the disease is contagious and is capable of causing immense damage. However, none of them could attribute any particular pathogen for the disease. Recently, scientists at CIFA have reported that the fin and tail rot in young fish are due to a mixed infection of *A. hydrophila* and *P. fluorescens*. Earlier workers suggested some control measures like bath treatment in 1: 2000 copper sulphate for 1-2 minutes or painting of concentrated copper sulphate solution in the affected fish (Pal and Ghosh, 1975).

Dropsy is another important fish disease in India where rohu, catla and mrigal are affected mostly in the late winter. Several workers have reported occurrence of the disease in composite fish culture ponds (Pal and Tripathi, 1978). The epidermis and body cavities get filled with fluid and scales protrude out from their pockets leading to severe anaemic condition. Pal and Tripathi (1978) although did not isolate the causative agent, could treat the affected fishes fully using terramycin in the feed. Kumar *et al.* (1986a) revealed a mixed infection of *A. hydrophila* and myxosporidian parasite in case of infectious dropsy in *Catla catla*. Histopathological changes in cases of dropsy have been described by these workers.

Mukherjee *et al.* (1992) have attributed cases of dropsy of *A. hydrophila* in conjunction with malnutrition.

Another bacterial disease in the epidemic form has been studied by Gopalkrishnan (1961), and Kamaraiah *et al.* (1977), the causative organism of which is identified as *A. liquifaciens* infecting the eyes of *C. catla*. The corneas of the eye gets vascularized leading to opacity and complete necrosis resulting in the death of the fish. Gopalakrishnan and Gupta (1960) have noted that optic nerves and brain are the primary sites of infection. Corneal opacity in silver carp (*Hypophthalmichthys molitrix* val.) due to Gram positive bacterium, *Staphylococcus aureus* was reported by Shah and Tyagi (1986). Jhingran (1991) also could observe similar eye disease in epidemic form in *Channa marulius* and attributed it to the same type of organisms. Mukherjee *et al.* (1992) have recorded a mass mortality in silver carps in a government farm and isolated *Staphylococcus aureus* from the affected eyes of diseased fish. Chloromycetin bath @ g 8-10 mg/litre of water has been found effective in controlling the disease at an early stage by some pioneer workers. Disinfecting the environment with $KMno_4$ a dose of 0.10 ppm followed by liming @ 300 ppm check the disease as reported by Kamaraiah *et al.* (1977).

Myxobacterial organisms have been attributed to a condition known as gill hyperplasia syndrome in common carp (*Cyprinus carpio*) as reported by Kumar *et al.* (1986 b). The infectious nature of the disease has been proved by transmitting the disease in Asiatic major carp species through contact. These workers have conducted some antibiotic therapy, but could not succeed in getting any significant result.

Ulcerative disease in *Catla* has been reported by many workers where bilateral ulcerations of the opercula and the head are observed. In several cases, the ulcerations have been reported to have penetrated the opercular bones and cranium. Gopalakrishnan (1963) and Karunasagar *et al.* (1986) have investigated several such outbreaks. Kumar *et al.* (1987a,b) studied this condition in composite fish culture ponds. In most of the cases *A. hydrophila* could be isolated, although several other bacterial forms were also present as secondary invaders. Mukherjee *et al.* (1991) have reported the role of *A. hydrophila* in ulcerative disease of fish and identified the biochemical differences among the various strains of these organisms. Nayak and Mukherjee (1994) made a detailed study of the biochemical properties of these organisms and drew antibiograms on the basis of the antibiotic sensitivity tests.

In a recent study, these workers have elucidated the role of *A. hydrophila* in dropsy, fin and tail rot and more elaborately in epizootic ulcerative syndrome. It is beyond doubt that in the ulcerative disease of fish, these organisms might be playing an important role not only in necrotizing the muscle tissue but also damaging the internal organs *viz;* kidney, liver and spleen. Another disease of similar nature causing external lesions over the surface of the body has been described by Kumar *et al.* (1986b). The causative organism has been identified as *Flexibacter columnaris.* Topical application of potassium permanganate or short bath in 500 ppm of $KMno_4$ has been found to be very effective in completely curing the disease.

A septicaemic disease called Edwardsiellosis was reported by Kumar (1989) affecting brood fish population. *Edwardsiella tarda* was isolated from the diseased fish showing anaemia, cutaneous lesions and gas filled abscesses in the muscle. Although the mortality was not too high, but the morbidity has been reported to be extreme. Large-scale mortality in the spawn of Indian major carps has been reported by Mukherjee *et al.* (1994) in an organized hatchery. *E. tarda* could be isolated from the disease affected spawn. The young ones showed anatomical deformities and greyish white discolouration of the body within 48 hours post-hatching and died within 72 hours. Although treatment with lodophor has been found to be effective, water quality improvement in the hatchery is the most essential component for keeping this disease away.

Epizootic Ulcerative Syndrome (EUS) is hitting the headline of the country since the last six years and has become a matter of tremendous concern not only among the fishermen and fish farmers, but also among general public, entrepreneurs, administrators and planners. Initially the epizootic was mainly reported from the North Eastern States of the country in the year 1988. Gradually, it has spread throughout the country. At the moment it has engulfed the entire length and breadth of the country barring only few states like the Punjab, Jammu and Kashmir, Himachal Pradesh and Gujarat. Mukherjee (1994) has reported this not only in the freshwater fishes, but also brackishwater fishes in Orissa, Kerala, Karnataka and Goa. One common feature of the disease is that it initially affects the bottom dwelling species like: murrels followed by catfishes and weed fishes. Sub-sequently other fishes including Indian major carps are affected. Although the extent of economic loss has not been properly quantified, loss incurred by the fisheries sector due to this particular disease runs to several crores of rupees.

The lesions start as small grain to pea-sized haemorrhagic spots over the body, which ultimately turn into big ulcers of the size of a coin with greyish slimy central necrotic area surrounded by a zone of hyperemia. The disease affects the fish to such an extent that they start rotting while still alive and eventually die.

A number of bacteria *viz; Aeromunas hydrophila. A. punctata, Flavohaclerium* sp., *Pseudomonas* sp., *E. tarda, V. parahaemolyticus* and *Streptococcus* sp., have been isolated from the affected specimens (Kumar, 1989). Histopathological studies revealed complete loss of epidermis in the ulcerative area of the skin where the dermis and hypodermis showed characteristic granulomatous changes (Dey, 1989), Gill tissue showed hyperplasia of the secondary lamellar epithelium, fusion of lamella and clubbing of gill tips. Haemopoietic tissue of the kidney showed proliferation of macrophages.

Besides bacteria, virus, fungus and parasites were also reported to be associated with epizootic ulcerative syndrome (Dey, 1989; Kumar *et al.* 1989).

Several methods have been tried or are being tried to control the disease. Many antibiotics, sulfonamides, chemicals, herbal preparations etc., have been advocated as preventive and curative measures. Lime was accepted widely among the fish farmers of the country until the formulation of a medicine by the scientists of CIFA. Marked improvement of the ulcerative condition is noticed within 7 days of application of the medicine and the ulcers are healed up within 10-14 days. The medicine acts as a preventive also. Records reveal that there is no recurrence of the disease for at least eleven months in the ponds where the medicine is applied. The cost of application is only Rs. 260/- (Approx. $ 8 US) for one Ha-m water body.

Protozoan Diseases

Myxosporidia are one of the most important group of pathogen capable of producing diseases in fish causing heavy loss in the juvenile. Several species of this pathogen have been reported from various parts of the country (Chaudhuri and Chakravarty 1970, Karuchandani, 1970; Senappa and Manohar, 1980; Sanaullah and Ahmad, 1980; Ahmad 1982; Dey *et al* 1988). These workers have reported great problems and heavy losses in intensive fish culture and fish seed rearing due to emaciation and asphyxiation. *Myxobolus* cysts of varying sizes have been reported on the gills and kidney of *Catla catla*. Larger cysts are located at the distal end of the gill filament where as smaller ones are seen at the proximal end. Infection damages the respiratory surface of the gill and excretory tubules of the kidney. Diagnosis of the disease can be made on the basis of gross appearance of the pin head sized greyish cysts and large number of myxosporidian spores under the microscope.

The other groups of protozoa infecting fish belong to Ciliophora. The carp fry and fingerlings sometime carry heavy infection of the gills and skin with *Trichodina indica*. In heavy infection, there is excessive mucus secretion on the gills which hampers respiration and the fish start surfacing. Some species of *Trichodina* occur inside the urinary bladder. Under the microscope they appear as circular transparent organisms with an internal disc-like structure. Fish affected with trichodiniasis eventually turn sluggish, lose weight and become moribund. There may be excessive mucus secretions and epidermal necrosis. A short bath in 2-3 per cent salt solution for 5 minutes can control the infection effectively.

Whirling disease in *Cirrhinus mrigala* (Ham) observed by Maheswari (1986) has been attributed to a protozoan parasite *Myxosoma cerebralis.* The gross changes are characterized by deformed spinal column as reported in European and American salmonids suffering from whirling disease. Ichthyophthiriasis or 'white spot' disease has been reported by Gopalakrishnan (1963, 1964) causing large scale mortality in nursery and rearing ponds in different parts of the country. The fish disease unit of CIFA has also similar observations in carp nursery ponds. Presence of numerous pinhead shaped white spots on the skin, fins and gills are the common diagnostic features. On microscopic examination, these spots look like blisters or nodules. Fingerlings of *Labeo bala* and C. *mrigala* have been experimentally infected with this parasite, but use of chemotherapy has not produced any encouraging results.

Helminthic Parasites

Fishes are infected on their gills and skin by many species of monogenetic and digenetic trematodes and cestodes. The important monogenetic species are: *Gyrodactylus* and *Dactylogyrus.* They remain attached to the skin or gills by the help of anchors which causes wounds. Their presence cause hypersecretion of mucous and haemorrhage from blood capillaries. These wounds later get infected with pathogenic bacteria and fungi. Alternate bath in 1: 2000 acetic acid solution followed by bath in 2 per cent sodium chloride solution has been found effective. Some workers have advocated dip treatment in 5 per cent salt solution followed by bath in 1:5000 formalin.

The digenetic trematode generally infects the alimentary canal but is rarely harmful. However, in the metacercarial stage they are harmful as they get encysted in any part of the body, *i.e.,* skin, muscle, abdominal cavity, liver, eyes and brain. In these cases fish serve as intermediate host while the final host is generally a fish-eating bird. In many carp fingerlings the 'black spot disease' is due to metacercaria of Diplostomatidae. This was first reported by Ganapati and Rao (1962) in *Catla* and silver carp are the most susceptible species.

Cestodes are also internal parasites in alimentary canal. Their larval forms are more harmful than the adults. They are found more in catfishes than in carps. The infected fish show softening of the muscle tissue probably due to accumulation of water. In case of heavy infestation, the abdomen bursts resulting in death of the fish. Bose and Sinha (1985) described histopathological changes in cases of intestinal cestodes in *Clarias batrachus.*

Acanthocephala have been recorded from major carps and catfishes in India, but the life history or biology of the parasite has not been studied in detail. The parasite causes lesions in the intestinal wall by its proboscis.

Crustacean Parasites

Parasitic Copepoda are external parasites infecting skin or gills or buccopharyngeal cavity. Amongst them species of two genera *Lernea* and *Ergasilus* are reported from Indian carps. *Lernea* is reported to infect fingerlings and adults of major carps especially *Catla*. The parasite penetrates the muscles and reaches the blood vessels as it feeds on the host's blood. The fish thus become anaemic and weak. Gopalakrishnan (1966) was of the opinion that larger number of these parasites may cause serious problems while a few may not cause any harm.

Ergasilus sp infect the gill lamellae. They attach themselves to the gill by the help of their hook-like second antenna. Due to this, there are wounds and haemorrhages in the gill tissue. There are no reports in India where mortality of fish has taken place due to *Ergasilus* infection.

Heavy mortality due to Argulosis or fish lice infestation has been reported in Indian major carps. Several species of *Argulus* have been reported to infect cultured fishes. These parasites inhabit the skin, fins and gills of the host and cause extensive pathological lesions in the skin showing circular haemorrhagic patches which become ulcerated. Mucous cells proliferate and copious mucous is produced. These lesions promote secondary infections like: fungi and bacteria. Rohu has been observed to be the most susceptible species among the Indian carps.

Histopathological changes in rohu naturally parasitized by *Argulus* spp., have been described by Dey (1989). Skin from the parasitized areas showed epithelial degeneration, oedema and hyperplasia of dense connective tissue. Kidneys exhibited marked glomerular changes tubular degeneration and necrosis. In the liver, increased sinusoidal spaces and focal necrotic areas were also noticed. Gill lamellae showed hypertrophy and hyperplasia in many areas resulting in the fusion of secondary lamellae, Kumar, *et al.* (1987b) advised weekly applications of malathion @ 0.25 ppm for three consecutive doses. They also reported that bath in potassium permanganate @ 500 ppm/ minute once a week with the combination of malathion treatment is helpful for eradication of the parasite.

Fungal Diseases

Gopalakrishnan (1966) observed *Saprolegnia parasitica* in the fry and fingerlings of major carps. The disease in fish is characterized by a white to brown cotton like growth consisting of colonies of mycelium and filaments which appear as small to large patches on various parts of the body like: fins, gills, mouth, eyes or muscle. Shrivastava and Shrivastava (1977a) identified this infection in *Channa punctata* and opined that the infection starts due to netting injury and over-crowding or lesions caused by other diseases. Jhingran (1991) reported that saprolegnia often infects the fertilized eggs. They attack the dead eggs first and then spread to the viable living eggs resulting in their spoilage. Shrivastava and Shrivastava (1977b) reported infection of *Cirrhina mrigala* with *Aphanomyces pisci* where the scales became black and later fell off. The hyphae of this species were not visible like those *Saprolegnia.* The author in the year 1982 reported other species of fungus, *i.e., Achlya urion* and *Dictynchus anomalous.*

Jhingran and Pullin (1988) reported branchiomyces infection causing gill rot' in fish. They opined that these pathogens invade the blood vessels of gills causing necrosis of the surrounding tissues also.

Apart from these, *Aspergillus flavus, A. ochraceous* and *Fesiformis momiliforme* have been reported from some of the EUS affected specimens (Mishra, 1992) at CIFA.

Many workers have recommended several treatment measures to counter fungal infection in fish which include dip treatment in 3 per cent common salt solution or 1:2000 copper sulphate solution or 1:1000 potassium permanganate solution for 5-10 minutes. A flush treatment for 1 hour in malachite green (0.1 ppm) is found to be quite effective in curbing fungal infection.

REFERENCES

Ahmed AT A (1982). Skin Myxoboliasis of Major Carp *Labeo rohita* in Bangladesh. *Fish Health News* 24: 1-11.

Bose K C and Sinha A K (1985). Histopathology *of Clarias batrachus* L Attributable to the Intestinal Cestode *Lytocestus Indicus* Moghi. *Proc. Nat. Acad. Sci. India.* 5313 3: 226.

Chaudhuri S R and Chakravarty N M (1970). Studies on the Myxosporidia Protozoa: Sporozoa from the Food Fishes of Bengal. Three New Species from *Ophiocephalus punctatus. Acta Protozool.* 167: 173.

Dey RK (1989). Histopathology of Argulosis in the Indian Major Carp *Labeo rohita* Hamilton. *Proc. Natl. Sem. on Forty Years of Aquaculture in India:* 7-9 Nov.

Dey R K, Kumar D and Mishra B K (1988). Tissue Level Reactions in the Indian Major Carp *Catla catla* Ham. Due to *Myxobolus* sp. Infection. *Asian Fisheries Sciences* 1:117-122.

Ganapati P N and Rao K M (1962). Ecological and Life History Studies on a Strigeid Metacercaria Trematode Diplostomatidae from Freshwater Fishes of Andhra Pradesh. *Parasitology* 52: 519-525.

Gopalakrishnan V (1961a). Observations on Infectious Dropsy of Indian Major Carps and Its Experimental Induction. *J. Scien. Ind. Res.* 357:58.

Gopalakrishnan V (1961b). Observations on a New Epidermical Eye Disease Affecting the Indian Carp *Catla catla* Ham. *Indian. J. Fish.* 8: 222-232.

Gopalakrishnan V (1963). Controlling Pests and Diseases of Cultured Fishes. *Indian Livestk.* 11: 51-54.

Gopalakrishnan V (1964). Recent Development in the Prevention and Control of Parasites of Fishes Cultured in Indian Waters *Proc. Zool. Soc Calcutta* 17: 95-100.

Gopalakrishnan V (1966). Diseases and Parasites of Fishes in Warm Water Pond in Asia and the Far East. *FAO. World Symp. on Warm-Water Fish Pond Culture Rome 18-25 May.*

Gopalkrishnan V and Gupta P D (1960). An Eye Disease Which Causes Mortality of the *Catla catla* Ham. *Curr. Sci.* 296:240.

Hora S L and Pillay T V R (1962). Handbook on Fish Culture in the Indo-Pacific Region. FAO Fish. *Biol. Tech. Paper* 14: 204.

Jhingran V G (1991). Text-book of Fish and Fisheries of India Third Edition. Hindustan Publishing Corporation India. Delhi 1991.

Jhingran V G and Pullin RVS (1985); Revised (1988). A Hatchery Manual for the Common Chinese and Indian Major Carps. Asian Development Bank and International Centre for Living Aquatic Resources Management Manila. p. 191.

Kamaraiah P, Murgesan VK and Dehadrai P V (1971). A New Record of a Bacterium Causing Eye Disease and Mortality in *Channa maruatius* Ham.. *J. Inland Fish. India* 9: 214-15.

Karamchandani S J (1970). A New Species of *Myxobolus* from the Gill Cavity of Labeo bata Ham. *J. Indian. Fish. Soc. India.* 2: 170-171.

Karunasagar I, Manzoor P KM, Jeyasekaran G and Karunasagar I (1986). Ulcerative form of *Aeromonas hydrophila* Infection *of Catla Catla. Current Science* 5523: 94-95.

Kumar D (1989). Epizootic Ulcerative Syndrome Outbreak in India. Summer Inst. on Fish Dis. Dia. and Health Mgmt. In: Fresh water. *Aqua. Syst.* 5-24 June CIFA.

Kumar D, Mishra BK and Dey R K (1986a). Dropsy *of Catla catla* Ham. Caused by a mixed Infection of *Aeromonas hydrophila* and Myxosporidian sp. *Aquaculture Hungarica Szarvas* 107-112.

Kumar D, Dey R K and Kumar K (1986b). Preliminary Observations of Gill Hyperplasia in Common Carp *Cyprinus carpio* L. Abst. In the *Proc. of International Symp. on Ichthyology'* Held at Dubronik Yugoslavia Sept. 1986.

Kumar D, Dey RK, Mishra B K and Kumar K (1989). Observation on Some Cases of Ulcerative Disease in Indian Major Carp *Catla catla* Hamilton *Proc. Nat. Sem. on Forty Years of Freshwater Aquaculture in India'* 7-9 Nov. 1989 pp. 6.

Kumar D, Dey RK, Mishra BK and Kumar K (1987a). Ulcerative Disease in *Catla catla* Ham. Research Highlights in the First Indian Fisheries Forum Dec. 6-10 Mangalore India.

Kumar D, Dey RK, Mishra BK and Kumar K (1987b). Observations on the Efficacy of Malathion and Potassium Permanganate Combination Treatment in Combating Acute Argulosis. Abstract. *Publ. Proc. of Nat. Seminar on Fish Aqua. in India* Held at Nagarjuna University. A.P. 27-30 Dec. 1987.

Meshwari S C (1986). Occurrence of Whirling Disease in *Cirrhina mrigala* in Wardha. *J. Bombay Nat. Hist. Soc.* 83 (3:) 673.

Mishra B K (1992). Annual Report CIFA Kausalyaganga Bhubaneswar.

Mukherjee SC (1992). Dropsy Due to *A. hydrophila* in Conjunction with Malnutrition in Fishes. Annual Report CIFA.

Mukherjee SC, Sahu BB, Gayatri M and Patnaik P (1994). Mass Mortality in Rohu Spawn Due to Edwarsiellosis. Nat. Sem. on Aqua. Anin. Hlth. at Univ. of Kerala Tiruvanathapuram 15-17 March 1995.

Mukherjee S C Chandra S and Kausalay N (1991). Studies on Biochemical Differences among Isolates of *Aeromonas hydrophila* Obtained from Ulcerative Disease Affected Fishes. Proc. Nat. Symp. on New Horizons in Fresh. *(Aquaculture)* 23-25 Jan. 1991.

Mukherjee SC Chandra S, Dey RK and Gayatri M (1991). Role of *aeromonas hydrophila* in fish Disease. Compnd. Annual Conf. of Indian Assoc. Vet. Pathologist Ranchi 24-26 Aug. 1991 pp. 21.

Mukherjee SC (1992). Mass Mortality of Silver Carp due to *Staphylococcus* Aureus. Annual Report CIFA.

Mukherjee S C (1994). Epizootic Ulcerative Syndrome in India. Man. Train. *Prog. on Fish. Dis. Diag. And Cont.* pp. 5-13.

Mukherjee T K, Geeta S, Rohani A and Phang SM (1992). A Study on Integrated Duck Fish and Goat Fish Production Systems. In: *Proceedings of the FAO/IPT International Workshop on Integrated Livestock Fish Production.* Food and Agriculture Organization Rome pp. 41-48.

Nayak H K and Mukherjee S C (1994). Drug Resistance *of Aeromonas hydrophila* Strains Isolated from Freshwater and Brackish Water Fishes. *Fishing Chimes* Sept. 1994 pp. 41-42.

Pal RN and Ghosh AK (1975). An Effective Method of Controlling Tail and Fin rot in Indian Major Carps. *J. Inland Fish. Soc.* 7: 98-99.

Pal RN and Tripathi SD (1970). Use of Terramycin for Fish Diseases in Carp and Catfish Culture in Indian Waters. *J. Inland Fish. Soc.* 10: 166-68.

Senappa D and Manohar L (1980). *Myxobolus vanivilasac* n.sp. Parasitic in *Cirrhina mrigala. Proc. Indian. Acad. Sci.* 89: 485-491.

Senaullah M and Ahmed ATT (1980). Gill Myxoboliasis of Major Carp Bangladesh. *J. Fish. Dis.* 3: 349-354.

Shah KL and Tyagi SC (1986). An Eye Disease in Silver Carp *Hypophthalmichlhys molitrtx* Held in Tropical Ponds Associated the Bacterium *Staphylococcus aureus.* Aquaculture 551: 1-4.

Shrivastava GC and Shrivastava RC (1977a). Host Range of *Seprolegnia ferox* Gnith Thuret on Certain Freshwater Teleost *Curr. Sci.* 46-47.

Shrivastava GC and Shrivastava RC (1977b). Ability of Saprolegniasis Fungi to Parasities *Colisa fasciatus* BL Geobios. 4: 29-31.

Page 157-169

Fisheries and Aquaculture
Edited by: **Prof. (Mrs.) Neelima Gupta** and **Dr. D.K. Gupta**
Edition: **2015**
ISBN: 978-93-5056-736-4
Published by: **Discovery Publishing House Pvt. Ltd., New Delhi (India)**

13

Infection Level of *Pomphorhynchus kashmirensis* in *Schizothorax niger*, from River Sindh (in Kashmir) Relative to Season, Sex, Length and Condition Factor

Ibraq Khurshid and **Fayaz Ahmad**

Post-Graduate Department of Zoology, University of Kashmir, Srinagar - 190 006, Kashmir. Email: kibraq@yahoo.com

ABSTRACT

Pomphorhynchus kashmirensis Kaw, 1941, an acanthocephalan helminth parasite of fishes causes great economic loss in fisheries production. For understanding the seasonal variation, parasitological investigation was carried out in Schizothorax niger Heckel, 1838 from September, 2011 to August, 2012. Overall, this study revealed definite seasonality of infection ($p<0.05$), with greater infection in summer (prevalence = 50.00%) and lesser in winter (prevalence= 5.26%). Gender was not an important factor influencing the prevalence of Pomphorhynchus kashmirensis. A strong positive correlation (Pearson's correlation, $r = 0.9$; $p = 0.038$) between total length of S. niger and number was observed. Prevalence and mean abundance were positively and significantly correlated with water temperature ($r=0.7$, $p<0.01$ and $r=0.9$, $p<0.01$, respectively). Thus seasonal dynamics, total length and weight of the host significantly influenced Pomphorhynchus infection. The above findings will be useful in *devising appropriate strategies for control of Pomphorhynchus kashmirensis in fish in Kashmir valley as well as in similar climatic zones of other parts of the world. Also, information from this study will be used to assess the spread and extent of Pomphorhynchus kashmirensis which is a potential threat to the indigenous fish fauna of Kashmir waters including river Sindh.*

Keywords: River Sindh, Parasite; *Pomphorhynchus kashmirensis*, Fish, *Schizothorax niger*, Kashmir.

INTRODUCTION

Monticelli (1905) proposed genus *Pomphorhynchus* for such species of *Echinorhynchus* which had a bulla at the anterior end of neck. Linstov (1908) confirmed the validity of *Pomphorhynchus* and added *P. perforator* to the genus. Meyer (1933) placed *Pomphorhynchus* under his new sub-family *Pomphorhynchinae* Kaw (1941) made the first report of Pomphorhynchus from Indian region and described *P. kashmirensis* from *Nemachilus kashmirensis,* a fresh water fish in Kashmir. Kaw (1951) described an encysted juvenile of *Pomphorhynchus* sp., from the intestinal wall of *Botia birdi.* Mature form of *P. kawi* was described by Fotedar *et al.* 1970 from the intestine of *Botia birdi,* which was found to be quite distinct from the juvenile encysted form described earlier by Kaw (1951) from the same host. Fotedar and Dhar (1977) described five new species of genus *P. orientalis* from *S. niger, P. jammuensis* from *Orienus plagiostomum, P. megacanthus* from *Cyprinus carpio spicularis, P. oreini* from *Oreinus sinuatus* and *P. tori* from *Tor tor. P. jammuensis* was described from Jammu and the other four species from Kashmir.

Methodology

Study Area

The valley of Kashmir is situated in the middle of the Himalayas between the northwest and southeast (33° 012-35° 002 N latitude and 73° 482-75°302 E longitude) at an altitude ≥1,500 m above sea level. River Sindh (34° 07′ 40″ to 34° 27′ 46″ N latitude and 74° 40′ 37″ to 75° 35′ 15″ E longitude.) which is situated in the northwest of Srinagar city at an elevation of

1583 m was selected for the present endeavour in view of its socio-economic importance including its role as a source of fish production. The river comes under mountain valley climate with a conspicuous cold season from October to March (average temperature 7.5°C), and warm summers (average temperature 19.8°C). January is the coldest month ("2°C to-3°C), and July the warmest (30-35°C). The average annual rainfall is 551 mm. Most of the rainfall is in the form of snow (January-March). Three sites were selected for the present study-Wayil, Shallabugh and Shadipora differing in pollution levels Wayil being less polluted and Shadipora being highly polluted while Shallabugh is moderately polluted.

Water Sampling

The physico-chemical characteristics of water were analysed as per the methods described by the Council for Scientific and Industrial Research (CSIR, 1974), Mackereth *et al.* (1978) and the American Public Health Association (APHA 1998). Water temperature, conductivity and transparency were recorded on the spot, whereas samples were fixed at the sampling site in accordance with the azide modification of the Winkler method (APHA 1998) for the estimation of dissolved oxygen. Measurements were made using the following equipment/method(s): water temperature, Celsius mercury thermometer calibrated up to 0.1°C; hydrogen ion concentration, digital pH meter (Microprocessor pH System-1011E). The data obtained for different parameters at three study sites of a water body over the entire study period were pooled in order to calculate the average seasonal values.

Host and Parasite Collection

The present study was carried out between September 2011 and August 2012. In total, 101 individuals of *S. niger* were examined. Fish were caught by local fishermen using nets and further investigation was carried out in the laboratory, where total length, standard length (SL) and sex for each fish was determined. Fish were examined for the presence of *P. kashmirensis* according to standard methods (Ergens and Lom, 1970). *P. kashmirensis* were killed by pouring them in a flask containing saline and then shaken vigorously for 20 s. The scolex of the cestodes was fixed Carnoy's Fixative; (6 Ethanol l:1 Glacial acetic acid 1 :3 Chloroform) separately on a clean glass slide by placing a cover glass on it while rest of the body was fixed by placing another glass slide, on the previous slide containing the cestode. The parasites were transferred directly from Carnoy's fixative to 70 per cent alcohol to remove excess of fixative. The specimens were then preserved and were kept in glycerol alcohol (70% alcohol with 5% glycerol).

Data Analysis

Infection indices were quantified by calculating prevalence, mean intensity and mean abundance following definitions in Bush *et al.* (1997) and Margolis *et al.* (1982). Pearson correlation (rp) was used to find the correlation between different physico-chemical features and parasitic infection. The correlation among the infection indices was also calculated by using Pearson correlation rp. Correlation analysis of data was carried out using SPSS 11.5 package programme. Chi-square tests were used to see the significant differences in prevalence among the months, seasons and sex. Students t test was used to analyse the differences in intensity and abundance among the season. Parametric t tests were used for comparison of condition factor between infected and uninfected hosts. We also used scatter plot and trend lines to show the relationship between some of the environmental variables with the infection indices (prevalence and mean intensity) of *P. kashmirensis*.

Results

During the present endeavour, infection of *P. kashmirensis* in *S. niger* was studied and the results obtained are given under the following sub-headings.

Water Quality

The mean values of various physico-chemical features, calculated from data collected monthly over a span of 12 months at three study sites are presented on seasonal basis (Table 13.1). The water chemistry of river was studied and its oligotrophic nature was confirmed as per OECD and APHA (1982) standards.

Table 13.1: Seasonal variation of physico-chemical features of water in river Sindh

Paramete	Spring	Summer	Autumn	Winter
Water temp. (°C)	20.14±2.3	26.2±5.4	13.4±6.4	3.1±1.3
Air temp. (°C)	18.43±5.1	29.6±3.2	18.6±4.4	1.2±0.6
pH	7.9±0.65	7.1±0.04	7.05±0.52	7.75±0.3
Dissolved oxygen(mg/l)	3.9±1.03	2.16±0.09	2.9±0.85	4.32±0.12
Free CO_2 (mg/l)	20.3±1.5	25.1±1.4	16.3±1.6	18.5±0.7

Influence of Month and Season on the Infection Indices

Infection with *P. kashmirensis* was recorded in *S. niger* in all seasons (Table 13.2). Infection pattern followed a clear seasonal pattern with peak prevalence in summer. Statistically, seasons showed significant differences in prevalence ($p<0.031$). Monthly prevalence showed insignificant differences ($p<0.97$), whereas, the prevalence was highest in August (prevalence: 22.7%) and least in February (prevalence: 4.1%). Mean number of *Pomphorhynchus* infection varied significantly among the seasons (t test=3.4, $p=0.04$). The highest mean intensity was recorded during summer (MI=6.4±0.5) whereas it was lowest during colder months (MI=2±1.0) (Table 13.2).

Table 13.2: Seasonal variation of infection indices (Prevalence, and MI) of *Pomphorhychus kashmirensis* in *Schizothorax niger* from River Sindh

Season	Spring	Summer	Autumn	Winter	Total
Sample size	30	22	25	24	101
Infected	2	5	3	1	11
Uninfected	28	17	22	23	90
Prevalence	6.6	22.7	13	4.1	10.8
MI	3.5+1.7	6.4+0.5	5+3.8	2+1.0	7.3+1.3

Influence of Sex and Host Length on the Level of Infection

A total of 11 fish, 11.6 per cent males and 10.34 per cent females, were parasitized by *P. kashmirensis*, with total mean intensities of 4.4 and 5.6, respectively, (Fig. 13.1). The study revealed no significant differences between the sexes ($p<0.8$).

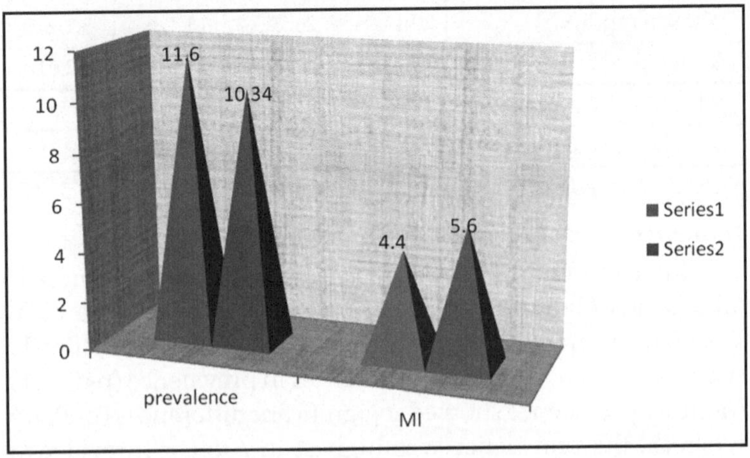

Fig. 13.1: Showing Prevalence and MI in Case of Male and Female S. niger

Infection of *P. kashmirensis* significantly increased with the increase in host length ($r=0.7$; $p=0.02$) (Table 13.3, Fig. 13.2). Thus we can say that prevalence and mean intensity showed+ve correlation with the length of the host. This depicts that with increase in the host length the number of parasites also increases.

Table 13.3: Correlation of host length and parasitic burden of *S. niger* in River Sidh

Mean Length (c_1)	No. of Parasites (c_2)
13	4
18	11
23	22
28	40

DF = 3, P-Value = 0.038, Correlation of C1 and C2 = 0.9

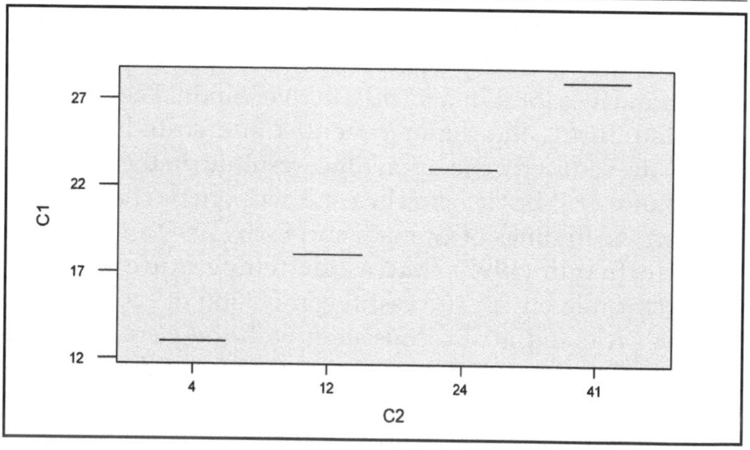

Fig. 13.2: Showing Correlation of Host Length and Parasitic Burden in *S. Niger*

Correlation between Infection Indices and Water Quality

Prevalence and mean intensity showed a significant positive correlation with the water temperature (Pearson's correlation, rp=0.7, 0.9 $p<0.01$) respectively. Furthermore, free CO_2, air temperature showed significant positive correlation with prevalence and mean intensity, whereas, free O_2, pH, showed negative correlation with prevalence and mean intensity (Table 13.4).

Table 13.4: Correlation (Pearson's correlation) between the infection indices of *Pomphorhynchus kashmirensis*

Parameters	Prevalence (r_p)	Mean intensity (r_p)
Water temperature (°c)	0.7	0.9
Air temperature (°c)	0.7	0.9
pH	-0.6	-0.7
Dissolved oxygen (mg/l)	-0.8	-0.9
Dissolved carbon dioxide (mg/l)	0.8	-0.9

(r_p) pearson correlation co-efficient.

Discussion

The above observations are being discussed in light of the already available literature as under:

Influence of Month and Season on the Infection Indices

Our results clearly depict a seasonal cycle in prevalence and abundance for *P. kashmirensis* in river Sindh. The increased infection during the summer months in our study is likely due to the reduced generation time, resulting in the increased abundance of *P. kashmirensis* in a shorter period. These results support the findings of Granath and Esch (1983) and Brouder and Hoffnagle (1997) that water temperature plays an important role on the successful completion of each stage of the life cycle and is also consistent with the view of Chubb (1980) that the impact of parasites on their hosts may increase with temperature if parasites are, as a result, able to grow more or mature more rapidly. Furthermore, the seasonal dynamics reported in this study support previous reports (Granath and Esch, 1983) that the optimum temperature for growth of parasite ranges between 25-30°C. Within limits, increase in temperature is likely to alter birth, death, and development rates in ways that could favour both parasites and their intermediate hosts. In short, the periodicities in our study could be due to extreme seasonal temperature changes which may involve freezing over of the water during winters and warmer periods during summer.

However, our results correspond very well with the findings of Bertasso and Oldewage (2005) who reported a high mean intensity during summer. The increased mean intensity in the summer may be due to metabolism as well as feeding activity of fish (Klenov, 1972). Tekin-Ozan *et al.* (2008) have suggested the same reasons for peak infection in summer season in case of *Caryophyllaeus laticeps*. However, our results are inconsistent with the results of Retief *et al.* (2007) who indicated that the mean intensity of Helminth infection increases from spring to summer, autumn and then winter, indicating that the new cohort is released in spring. This may also be due to the general effects of increased temperature which may have effects on parasite (faster embryonic development and hatching), effects on hosts (altered feeding, reduced host resistance), and effects on transmission (earlier reproduction in spring, more generations per year, potential transmission year round; Marcogliese, 2001). Abundance and availability of suitable copepod intermediate hosts plays an important role in seasonal dynamics of *P. kashmirensis* and slight change in seasonal occurrence of *P. kashmirensis* are attributed to changes in the population structure of the cyclopoid copepod community (Marcogliese *et al.* 1989). The increased prevalence of parasitic infection in summer months in our study may also be related to an increase in abundance of the intermediate hosts during these months. Our results are consistent with the observation of Beer and German (1993) who described how eutrophication increased the abundance of the intermediate hosts. Eutrophication level increases with the onset of summer in river Sindh. These conditions are favourable for macrophytes and intermediate host (copepod).

Interaction between pollution and parasitism is a complex process and one is unable to generalize the impact of pollution on disease (Lafferty, 1997). In contrast to toxic pollution, eutrophication is favourable to the occurrence of parasitism up to some degree. The water body which we studied was oligotrophic with comparatively low macrophytic growth which is more during summer season. Similar observations have been made by Marcogliese, (2001). We also suggest here that type of water body also influences the seasonal infection pattern.

Influence of Sex and Host Length on the Level of Infection

There was no significant association between sex and prevalence of parasitism. A number of workers have commented on the differences in the infection level with helminths in male and female hosts, the published papers indicating that different factors may be responsible for the unequal distribution and that the problem requires further research (Williams and Jones, 1994).

The present findings demonstrate that there exist significant positive relationship between total length and the number of worms per fish. Tekin-Ozan *et al.* (2008) concluded from their results that the prevalence of parasites increased according to length of fish host. The increase in the infection with the increase in length may be due to the ageing factor of the fish. Similarly, Brouder (1999) stated that Roundtail chubs, *Gila robusta* infected with Asian tapeworm showed a significant difference in total length compared to uninfected chubs, and a positive correlation between infection intensity and total length of fish (Brouder, 1999). Positive relationship between parasitic burden and host size in *Schizothoraz. niger* can be due to the fact that larger fish provides more surface area for the parasite attachment (Nie and Kennedy, 1991).

Condition co-efficient was found to be significantly lower in infected fish than in uninfected fish. It may be due to the fact that parasites may decrease the immune system of the hosts, which may lead to decreased growth of the fish. Decreased growth may lead to decrease in health condition of a fish (Khan and Thulin, 1991; Poulin, 1992).

Correlation between Infection Indices and Water Quality

Parasitic fauna is influenced by many natural abiotic factors like temperature, oxygen, salinity, and hydrogen ion *etc*. Many of these abiotic as well as other anthropogenic stresses influence the temporal and spatial occurrence of parasites, in particular the helminth parasites of fish (Chubb 1980). Similar view has been suggested by Dogiel and Pettruschevski, 1970 by stating that seasonal environmental changes of water (temperature, pH, conductivity) affect the occurrence of parasites of aquatic host and this may also explain the seasonal variations of *P. kashmirensis* seen in this study. Increasing water temperature was associated with the increase in prevalence of the *P. kashmirensis*. The significant positive correlation of *P. kashmirensis* prevalence with some environmental variables shows that abiotic factors play an important role in the *P. kashmirensis* occurrence. The effect of environmental variables might be attributed to interactions with biotic and abiotic factors including species abundance fluctuations in intermediate host communities composed of potential hosts with differing susceptibilities to infection (Marcogliese *et al.* 1989) and sensitivity of the different *Pomphorhychus* life cycle stages to abiotic parameters. We found that the proportions of the *Pomphorhychus* infection were positively related to some of the physico-chemical features of the water. This data is consistent with a number of studies around the world, which have found that changes to the water quality often increases the infection of the parasite (Dogiel *et al.* 1961; Dechtiar 1972; Snieszko 1974; Rumyantsev, 1988; Valtonen *et al.* 1997; Lafferty *et al.* 2005).

Concluding Remarks

Our results are important because they provide insight into the ecology of *Pomphorhychus* from important freshwater bodies of Kashmir. Furthermore, seasonal dynamics of *Pomphorhychus* infection was integrated with the seasonal changes in physico-chemical features of river Sindh. Overall study indicated that length and condition factor may influence the prevalence and intensity of *Pomphorhychus*, although further studies are needed to elucidate these and other factors affecting the occurrence of *Pomphorhychus*. Positive association between *Pomphorhychus* and some of the physico-chemical features indicate that these *Pomphorhychus* are useful indicators in pollution studies. The results in this study will be helpful to implement control methods in natural and culture systems.

REFERENCES

American Public Health Association (1998). Standard Methods for the Examination of Water and Waste Water, 20th edn. American Public Health Association, the American Water Works Association and the Water Environment Federation, Washington, p. 1220.

Bertasso A and Avevant OA (2005). Aspects of the Ecology of the Asian Tapeworm, *Bothriocephalus acheilognathi*, 1934 in the Yellowfish in Vaal Dam, South Africa. Onderstepoort. *J. Vet. Res.* 72: 207-217.

Brouder MJ and Hoffnagle T L (1997). Distribution and Prevalence of the Asian fish Tapeworm, *Bothriocephalus acheilognathi*, in the Colorado River and Tributaries, Grand Canyon, Arizona, Including Two New Host Records. *J. Helminthol. Soc. Wash.* 64: 219-226.

Brouder M J (1999). Relationship between Length of Round tail Chub and Infection Intensity of Asian Fish Tapeworm *Bothriocephalus acheilognathi*. *J. Aquat. Anim. Health*. 11: 302-304.

Beer SA and German SM (1993). Ecological Prerequisities of Worsening of the Cercariosis Situation in Cities of Russia. *Parazitologiya.* 27: 441-449.

Bush AO, Lafferty KD, Lotz JM and Shostak AW (1997). Parasitology Meets Ecology on its Own Terms: Margolis *et al.* Revisited. *J. Parasitol.* 83: 575-583.

Chubb JC (1980). Seasonal Occurrence of Helminthes in Freshwater Fishes. Part III. Larval Cestoda and Nematoda. *Adv Parasitol.* 17:141-313.

Dechtiar AO (1972). New Parasite Records for Lake Erie Fish. *Great Lakes Fish Comm Technical* Rep 17: 1-20.

Dogiel, V. A.; Petrushevski, G.K. and Polyanski, Y. I. (1961). *Parasitology of Fishes* English Translation. Edinburgh: Oliver and Boyd.

Dogiel VA and Pettruschevski G K Y (1970). Parasitology of Fishes. 3rd ed. Oliver and Boyd Ltd. English Translation by Z. Kabata.

Ergens R and Lom J (1970). Causative agents of Fish Diseases. Academia, Prague, p. 384.

Fotedar DN, Duda PL and Raina MK (1970). A New Species of the Genus *Pomphorhynchus monticelli* from *Bufo virdis* in Kashmir. *Indian J. Helminthol.* 22 (1:) 41-45.)

Fotedar DN and Dhar RL (1977). On Five Species of the Genus *Pomphorhynchus* Monticella 1905 from Fresh Water Fishes of Jammu and Kashmir, India. *Indian J. Zool.* 5: 15-29.

Granath WO and Esch GW (1983). Survivorship and Parasite-Induced Host Mortality among Mosquitofish in a Predator-free, North Carolina Cooling reservoir. *Am. Midl. Naturalist* 110: 314-323.

Kaw B L (1941). Studies of Helminth Parasites of the Fishes of Kashmir, Part 1. Description of Some new Species of the Genus *Pomphorhynchus* Monticelli, 1905. *Proc Indian Acad Sci.* 31: 369-378.

Kaw B L (1951). Helminth Parasites of Kashmir Part II. Acanthocephala. *Indian J. Helminthol.*, 3: 117-132.

Khan RA and Thulin J (1991). Influence of Pollution on Parasites of Aquatic Animals. *Adv. Parasitol.* 30: 201-238.

Klenov AP (1972). Seasonal and Age Dynamics of *Bothriocephalus acheilognathi* Infection in *Ctenopharyngodon idella*. Byulleten Vsesoyuznogo Instituta Gelmintologii. 8: 25-27.

Lafferty KD (1997). Enviromental Parasitology: what can Parasite tell us about Human Impacts on Environment? *Parasitol. Today.* 13: 251-255.

Lafferty KD and Kuris AM (2005). Parasitism and Environmental Disturbances: In *"Parasitism and Eco-systems"* pp. 113-123.

Linstov O (1908). Die Verbreitung des Bibers im Quartär. Museum fü r Naturund Heimatkunde zu Magdeburg, Abhandlungen und Berichte 1(4:) 211-387.

Mackereth FJH, Heron J and Talling JF (1978). Water Analysis: Some Revised Methods for Limnologists. Freshwater Biological Association, Scientific Publication, pp. 120.

Marcogliese DJ, Esch GW, Holmes JC, Kuris AM and Schad GA (1989). The use of Ecological Terms in Parasitology. *J. Parasitol.*, 68: 131-133.

Marcogliese DJ (2001). Implications of Climate Change for Parasitism of Animals in the Aquatic Environment. *Can. J. Zool.* 79(8:)1331-1352.

Margolis L, Esch GW, Holmes JC, Kuris AM, Schad, GA (1982). The use of Ecological Terms in Parasitology Report Bush *et al.* – Parasite Ecology and Terminology 583 of an Adhoc Committee of the American Society of Parasitologists. *J. Parasitol.*, 68: 131-133.

Meyer A (1933). Acanthocephala. In: Bronn's Klassen und Ordnungen des Tierreichs, Vol. 4 Akademische Verlagsgesellschaft MBH, Leipzig.

Monticelli FS (1905). Observatione Intorno ad Alcune Specie di Heterocotylea. Boll Soc Naturalist Napoli 18: 65-80.

Niem P, and Kennedy CR (1991). Occurrence and Seasonal Dynamics of *Pseudodactylogyrus anguillae* Yin and Sproston Monogenes in eel, *Anguilla anguilla* L., in England. *J. Fish Biol.* 39: 897-900.

OECD (1982). *Eutrophication of Waters: Monitoring, Assessment and Control.* OECD, Paris, pp. 154.

Poulin R (1992). Meta-analysis of Parasite – Induced Behavioural Changes. *Anim. Behav.* 48: 137-146.

Retief NR, Avenant O A, Preez HH (2007). Ecological Aspects of the Occurrence of Asian Tapeworm, *Bothriocephalus acheilognathi* Yamaguti, 1934 Infection in the Largemouth Yellowfish, *Labeobarbus kimberleyensis* Gilchrist and Thompson, 1913 in the Vaal Dam, South Africa. *J. Phys. Chem. Earth.* 3215-(18) 1384-1390.

Rumyantsev EA (1988). Some Aspects in the Studies of Fish Parasite Fauna in the Lakes of Different Type. In: Nauer, O.N. and Drozdov S. N.Eds Parasites of Fresh Water Fishes of North-West Europe. Materials of the International Symposium within the Programme of the Soviet-Finnish Co-operative, Petrozavodsk, U.S.S.R. pp. 130-136.

Snieszko SF (1974). The Effects of Environmental Stress on Outbreaks of Infectious Diseases of Fishes. *J. Fish. Biol.* 6: 197-208.

Tekin O S, Kir I and Barlas M (2008). Helminth Parasites of Common Carp *Cyprinus carpio* L., 1758 in Bey°ehir Lake and Population Dynamics Related to Month and Host size. *Turk. J. Fish. Aquat. Sci.* 8: 201-205.

Valtonen ET, Holmes JC and Koskivaara M (1997). Eutrophication, Pollution and Fragmentation: Effects on the Parasite Communities in Roach and Perch in Four Lakes in Central Finland. *Parassitologia.* 39: 233-236.

Williams H and Jones A (1994). Parasitic Worms of Fish. 593 pp. *London, Taylor and Francis.*

Page 170-190

Fisheries and Aquaculture
Edited by: **Prof. (Mrs.) Neelima Gupta** and **Dr. D.K. Gupta**
Edition: **2015**
ISBN: 978-93-5056-736-4
Published by: **Discovery Publishing House Pvt. Ltd., New Delhi (India)**

14

Ecology of the Asian Tapeworm *Bothriocephalus acheilognathi* Yamaguti, 1934 of Fishes in the Dal Lake of Srinagar, Kashmir

Tanveer A. Sofi, Fayaz Ahmad, Ibraq Khurshid and **Shabnam Ara**

Post-Graduate Department of Zoology, University of Kashmir, Srinagar - 190 006. Email: *stanveer96@gmail.com rajafayazali@yahoo.co.in

ABSTRACT

Seasonal surveys were conducted at the Dal Lake of Srinagar between April 2010 and January 2012. Twenty Schizothorax niger and 20 Cyprinus carpio were collected with the aid of gill nets. Surface water quality variables were included. The cestodes were identified as either Bothriocephalus acheilognathi Yamaguti, 1934 or 'other cestode species.' The majority (99.8%) of the cestodes found in both fish species were identified as B. acheilognathi (Asian tapeworm). The prevalence, mean intensity and abundance of B. acheilognathi in both fish species were calculated. Ecological parameters including species specificity, seasonality, gender specificity and relationships between fish size and the Asian tapeworm prevalence were also included. In this study, B. acheilognathi preferred Schizothorax niger over Cyprinus carpio although a low intensity was observed in Cyprinus carpio. Furthermore, the infection (in terms of prevalence, abundance and mean intensity) in Schizothorax niger was markedly higher. Seasonal patterns observed in the Asian tapeworm's infection of Cyprinus carpio are attributed to breeding and subsequent feeding patterns of this fish species with relatively high infections recorded in winter and spring. For Schizothorax niger no explanation can be given regarding the seasonal patterns observed for the mean intensity and abundance of B. acheilognathi. The maximum and minimum mean intensity and abundance values in Schizothorax niger were recorded in autumn and spring, respectively. In addition, the prevalence of B. acheilognathi was consistently high in all four seasons.

Keywords: Asian Tapeworm; *Bothriocephalus* acheilognathi; *Schizothorax niger; Cyprinus carpio;* Seasonal Prevalence.

INTRODUCTION

Surveys conducted by the fish parasitology group have shown unexpectedly high numbers of helminth parasites in fish species in the Dal Lake of Srinagar. The high number of helminth parasites can be attributed to *Bothriocephalus acheilognathi* which has been introduced with cyprinid fish into South Africa from Asia (Brandt *et al.* 1981). The Asian tapeworm, originally a parasite of the Chinese grass carp (*Ctenopharyngodon idella* Valenciennes, 1844*)* and the silver carp (*Hypothalmichthys molitrix* Valenciennes, 1844*)* in the Southern parts of China (Boomker, Huchzermeyer and Naudé 1980), has spread rapidly to other countries by means of infected fish (Pool 1987) and has adapted itself successfully to the common carp (*Cyprinus carpio* Linnaeus, 1758) (Boomker *et al.* 1980). In South Africa, bothriocephalid parasites have been found in various dams and freshwater systems in Gauteng Province. Localities in South Africa where *B. acheilognathi* has been found include the Komatipoort area (Mpumalanga Province) (Boomker *et al.* 1980), Marble Hall (Mpumalanga Province) (Brandt *et al.* 1981), Boskop Dam (KwaZulu-Natal Province) (Van *et al.* 1981), Hartbeespoort Dam (North West Province), Piet Gouws Dam (Limpopo Province) (Mashego 1982), Olifants River and Glen Alpine Dam (Limpopo

Province) (Mashego 1982), and the Vaal Dam (Gauteng Province) (Mashego 1982). The tapeworm's presence in most of the localities mentioned above can be attributed to the supply of common carp fry to commercial farmers (Boomker *et al.* 1980). However, according to Mashego (1982) its presence in the Vaal Dam cannot be accounted for. Brandt *et al.* (1981) mentioned the possibility that this tapeworm was imported into South Africa with the common carp as long ago as 1859 or with the Dinkelsbuhl Aischgrund variety of the common carp in 1952. *Cyprinus carpio* has been found in the Dal Lake but its introduction date is uncertain. *Bothriocephalus acheilognathi* was originally described as three different species from wild fish in Japan (as *B. acheilognathi* Yamaguti, 1934 and *Bothriocephalus opsariichthydis* Yamaguti, 1934) and from grass carp (*C. idella*) from South China (as *Bothriocephalus gowkongensis* Yeh, 1955) (Paperna 1996). These three species were later recognized as being identical (Korting 1975; Molnar 1977) with the name *B. acheilognathi* taking priority. Pool (1988) believes that the three species, *B. acheilognathi*, *B. kivuensis* and *B. aegyptiacus*, are identical, with *B. acheilognathi* having priority. Various authorities (as cited by Pool and Chubb 1985 and Pool 1988) noted that *Bothriocephalus opsariichthydis* Yamaguti, 1934, *Bothriocephalus fluviatilis* Yamaguti, 1952, *B. gowkongensis* Yeh, 1955, *Bothriocephalus phoxini* Molnár, 1968 and *Schyzocotyle fluviatilis* Akhmerov, 1960 are the same species as *B. acheilognathi* Yamaguti, 1934. Pool and Chubb (1985) concluded that there is only one *Bothriocephalus* species parasitizing cyprinid fish and suggested the continued use of the name *B. acheilognathi*. Cestodes in this study were identified as either *B. acheilognathi* or 'other cestode spp.' The purpose of this article is to provide a brief description of the parasite's infection, seasonality, gender specificity and species (host) specificity in the two fish species sampled. A comparison between the parasite's infection in *Cyprinus carpio* and its infection in *Schizothorax niger* is also included.

Materials and Methods

Study Location

Four surveys were conducted in the Dal Lake of Srinagar of – one per season, namely in April 2011 (early spring), June 2011 (summer), October 2011 (late autum) and January 2012 (winter).

Water Quality

Water quality data for the duration of the project were obtained from the Water Board, and were collected during routine monitoring activities made by the Water Board. Standard techniques were used by the Water Board to analyse the water samples. The following surface water variables were included: pH; temperature; electrical conductivity; dissolved oxygen; and light penetration.

Collection of Fish and Cestodes

The fish species collected during the four surveys were *Cyprinus carpio* and *Schizothorax niger*. The fish were identified based on the size of the snout as suggested by Skelton (2001). Twenty *C. carpio* and 20 *S. niger* fishes per survey were collected using gill nets consisting of four sections with varying stretched mesh sizes of 90, 110 and 130 mm, respectively. They were weighed (in grams) and measured (fork length in millimetres). The fish were killed by severing the spinal cord behind the head and were subsequently dissected by making an insertion from the anus towards the head. Once they had been dissected, the intestines were removed and placed in a normal saline solution in petri dishes for examination. Methods described by Khalil (1991) were used for processing the platyhelminth parasites found during the surveys. Parasites were collected as soon as possible after the death of the fish to prevent any deterioration. The intestines were pulled open carefully using two sharp tweezers to ensure that the cestodes were kept intact. Each cestode was carefully and slowly dislodged from the intestinal wall, ensuring that it remained intact. They were transferred to a clean sampling bottle containing normal saline solution, which was then shaken vigorously for a few minutes to dislodge debris and induce muscle fatigue in the helminths, which in turn, deters strong contraction of the scolices and relaxes them. While swirling the sampling bottle, an equal amount (equal to the amount of saline solution already present in the sampling bottle) of a hot alcohol-formaldehyde-acetic acid (AFA) solution was added to kill and fix the specimens. Specimens were then stored in 70 per cent alcohol.

Identification of Cestodes

The cestodes were stained with Grenacher's borax carmine stain (Pantin 1964) and identified.

Statistical Analyses

All specimens were counted and the total obtained was used for statistical analyses which were conducted by the University of Kashmir, Department of Statistics. Prevalence, abundance and mean intensity of *B. acheilognathi* were calculated per season for each fish species. Infection statistics were calculated by making use of the definitions set by Margolis, *et al.* (1982) and Bush, *et al.* (1997). Data was analysed to determine the seasonality (using ANOVA and then Scheffe or Dunnet T3) and species and gender specificity (using Pearson Chisquare test and t-tests) of *B. acheilognathi*. A comparison between the infections in the two fish species was done (using the t-test). In addition, the infection of *B. acheilognathi* (intensity) in each fish species was compared to the size (fork length) of the fish sampled. Regression analysis was used to determine if any correlations existed. Digital micrographs of stained specimens were taken using a Zeiss Axioplan 2 Imaging microscope.

Results

Water Quality

Surface water variables and data obtained in this study are presented in Table 14.1.

Identification of Cestodes

According to Mashego (1982), the classification of the bothriocephalid worms is based primarily on the shape of the scolex. Pool (1984) concluded from his study on *B. acheilognathi* that the identification of adults should be based on the heart-shaped scolex and prominent square apical disc. The identification of the bothriocephalid cestodes in this study was therefore based on these characteristics. Specimens found in the current study were compared to sketches provided by various authorities (Yamaguti 1934; Yeh 1955; Molnár and Murai 1973; Mashego 1982) as well as the diagnosis of *B. acheilognathi* (as *B. gowkongensis*) by Yeh (1955), as cited by Paperna (1996). Micrographs and sketches of *B. acheilognathi* collected during the four surveys are presented in Fig. 14.1. When reviewing available sketches it is the authors' opinion that the scolex of specimens from the current study compared fairly well with many of the *Bothriocephalus* species that have a heart-shaped scolex (Fig. 14.1A). As mentioned in Paperna (1996), the eggs are operculated (Fig. 14.1F) and the vitellaria laterally scattered (Fig. 14.1D). According to the diagnosis given in Paperna (1996), mature and gravid segments vary in breadth and length. However, in this study this was not the case. Most segments were broader than they were long (Fig. 14.1B and 14.1C). We however, disagree with the system of labelling the reproductive system as proposed by Yamaguti (1934), and consider that, after reviewing the available literature; it should be as indicated in Fig. 14.1E.

Table 14.1: Summary of water quality variables recorded seasonally at the Dal Lake of Srinagar

Survey	pH	Temperature	Electrical Conductivity	Dissolved Oxygen	Secchi Disc Readings
(units)	(°C)	(mS/m)	(mg/l O_2)	(cm)	
Autumn (April 2000)	7.60	–	17.00	–	–
Winter (June 2000)	7.34	19.90	16.00	12.50	30.00
Spring (October 2000)	8.00	21.40	17.00	–	28.00
Summer (January 2001)	8.26	25.00	23.00	6.30	28.00

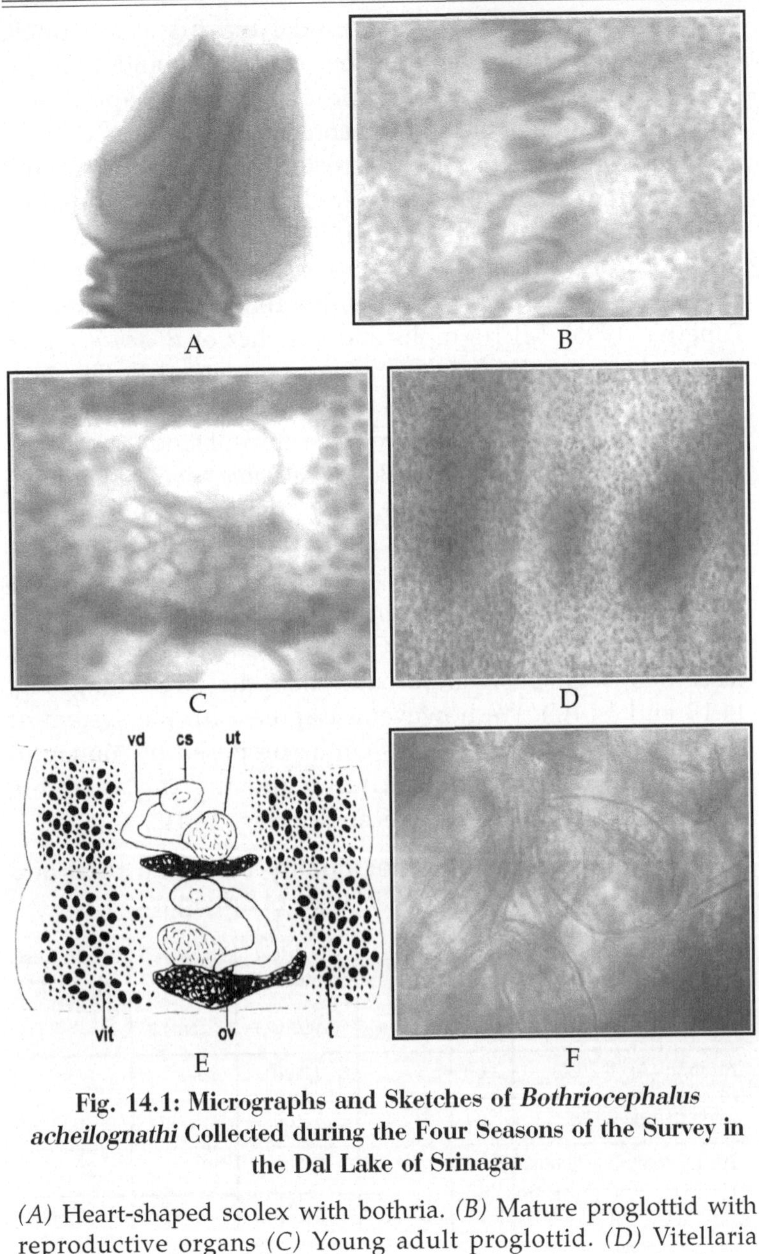

Fig. 14.1: Micrographs and Sketches of *Bothriocephalus acheilognathi* Collected during the Four Seasons of the Survey in the Dal Lake of Srinagar

(A) Heart-shaped scolex with bothria. *(B)* Mature proglottid with reproductive organs *(C)* Young adult proglottid. *(D)* Vitellaria scattered. *(E)* Sketch of a young adult proglottid *(F)* Operculated egg.

Table 14.2: Number of cestodes collected from *Cyprinus carpio* and *Schizothorax niger* at the Dal Lake of Srinagar during the four seasons

Survey	Cyprinus carpio (n=70)		Schizothorax niger (n=70)	
	B. acheilognathi	Other Cestode spp.	*B. acheilognathi*	Other Cestode spp.
Spring (April 2011)	4	0	417	4
Summer (June 2011)	298	0	651	0
Autumn (October 2011)	256	0	120	1
Winter (January 2012)	24	0	40	3
Total	582		132 8	8
Total cestodes	582		1336	

Parasite Numbers

The tapeworms encountered in this study were grouped as either *B. acheilognathi* or 'other cestode spp.'. The number of *B. acheilognathi* and other cestode spp. collected during the four seasons of the survey is tabulated in Table 14.2. Of the 140 fish sampled, only 19 out of 80 *Cyprinus carpio* harboured *B. acheilognathi* while none harboured other cestode spp.; and 68 out of 80 *Schizothorax niger* harboured *B. acheilognathi* while only six harboured other cestode spp.

Infection Statistics of B. acheilognathi

The percentage of hosts (prevalence) infected with *B. acheilognathi,* and its intensity (mean intensity) and abundance (relative density) in both *Cyprinus carpio* and *Schizothorax niger* are illustrated graphically in Fig. 14.2, 14.3 and 14.4 respectively. A statistical comparison (t-test) of the two fish species in terms of *B. acheilognathi* prevalence, abundance and mean intensity is also included to determine whether or not there are significant differences between fish species.

Prevalence

The prevalence of *B. acheilognathi* in *Schizothorax niger* was relatively constant over all seasons, ranging from 80-90 per cent, whereas the prevalence in *Cyprinus carpio* was fairly constant (10-15%) in autumn, spring and winter followed by a considerable increase in winter (55%) (Fig. 14.2). When comparing its prevalence in the two fish species, that in *Schizothorax niger* was considerably higher. Statistical analyses indicate that, there was a significant difference (t-test, P=0.001) in its prevalence in the two fish species.

Abundance (Relative Density)

During all surveys, the abundance of the Asian tapeworm was considerably higher in *S. niger* (Fig. 14.3). In this fish species, abundance values ranged from 55.0 (spring) to 170.9 (spring) while in *C. carpio* these values ranged from 0.2 (spring) to 14.9 (winter). The following seasonal trend was observed for *S. niger:* values decreased from autumn to winter and then again in spring. The latter was followed by an increase in summer. For *C. carpio* the opposite trend was observed. Values increased from autumn to winter and were followed by a decrease in spring and a further decrease in summer. Statistical analyses indicate that there was a significant difference (t-test, P=0.011) between the relative densities of *B. acheilognathi* in the two fish species sampled.

Mean Intensity

Excluding spring, the infection was considerably more intense in *S. niger* (Fig. 14.4). The highest value recorded for *S. niger* was 213.6 in spring and the lowest value was 68.8 recorded in spring. During the remaining seasons the mean intensity decreased to 102.2 and 85.8 in summer and winter respectively. Similarly, the mean intensities in *C. carpio* differed considerably from 2.00 in autumn to 78.7 in spring. During winter and summer a mean intensity of 27.1 and 4.3, respectively, was recorded. Statistical analyses indicate that, there could be a significant difference between the mean intensities of *B. acheilognathi* in the two fish species (t-test, P value was slightly above 0.05 at 0.053) but due to either the sample size being too small or the variance being too big this cannot be said for certain.

Ecological Parameters

Gender Specificity

In both fish species, there were no significant differences (t-test, *P* values>0.05) in the average number of *B. acheilognathi* found in males and females even though the average number in males and females differed. In *Cyprinus carpio* the average numbers of *B. acheilognathi* in male and in female fish were 12.85 and 2.70, respectively. In *Schizothorax niger* the average numbers were 91.43 and 107.42, respectively. In addition, the presence or absence of *B. acheilognathi* is not dependent on the gender of fish species (Pearson Chi-square test; *P* values for both fish species > 0.05). Similar numbers of male (7) and female (12) *C. carpio* and male (37) and female (31) *S. niger* were found to harbour *B. acheilognathi*. In *C. carpio,* the prevalence of *B. acheilognathi* in males and females was 0.21 and 0.26, respectively. Similarly, in *S. niger* the prevalence of *B. acheilognathi* was 0.84 in males and 0.86 in females.

Seasonality

In *Cyprinus carpio,* the highest number of *B. acheilognathi* was observed during the winter survey while in *Schizothorax niger* the highest number was observed during the spring survey (Table 14.2). From the statistical analyses (Pearson Chi-square test) performed on the data, the presence/absence of *B. acheilognathi* in *Cyprinus carpio* was dependent on the season (*P*=0.002) with the highest number of infected fish (11) being in those caught in winter and the lowest (2) being in autumn. This was not the case for *Schizothorax niger*. Similar numbers of *Schizothorax niger* (between 16 and 18) were infected with *B. acheilognathi* during all four seasons of the survey.

However, when conducting the ANOVA test to determine if there were significant differences between seasons, the results show that there were significant (*P*=0.003) seasonal differences based on the number of *B. acheilognathi* found in *S. niger*. *Post hoc* tests were then undertaken to distinguish which of the seasons differed significantly. The results of the statistical analyses (Dunnet T3 test) showed that autumn and spring differed significantly with a *P* value of 0.011. No significant seasonal differences were determined in the number of *B. acheilognathi* found in *C. carpio.*

Species Specificity

When comparing fish species, *S. niger* harboured a higher number of *B. acheilognathi* than *C. carpio* (Table 14.2). The number of *B. acheilognathi* found in *S. niger* totalled 1328, while *C. carpio* only had a total of 582 *B. acheilognathi* in the same number of hosts (70). In addition, a higher number of *S. niger* (68) were infected with *B. acheilognathi* than *C. carpio* (19). From the statistical analyses (Pearson Chi-square) performed when data is pooled according to fish species, the presence/ absence of *B. acheilognathi* was highly dependent on fish species, P values being 0.000.

Size Specificity

No correlations were observed between the sizes (fork lengths) of fishes (both *Schizothorax niger* and *Cyprinus carpio*) sampled and the number of Asian tapeworms recorded.

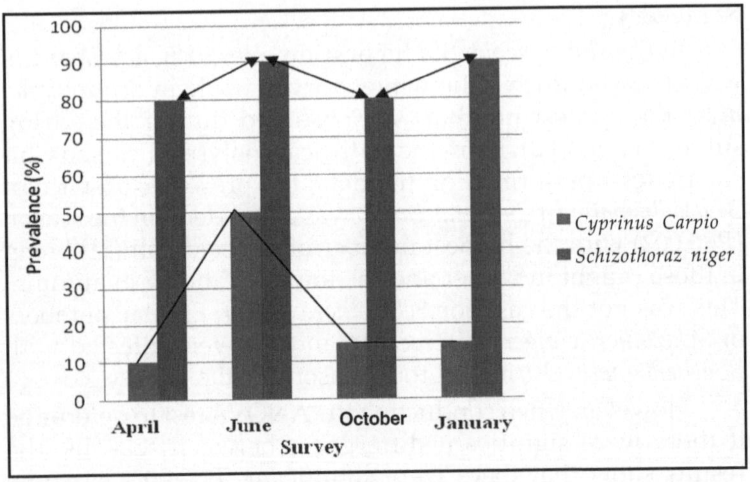

Fig. 14.2: Graph Depicting the Prevalence of *Bothriocephalus acheilognathi* in *Cyprinus carpio* and *Schizothorax niger* during the Four Seasons

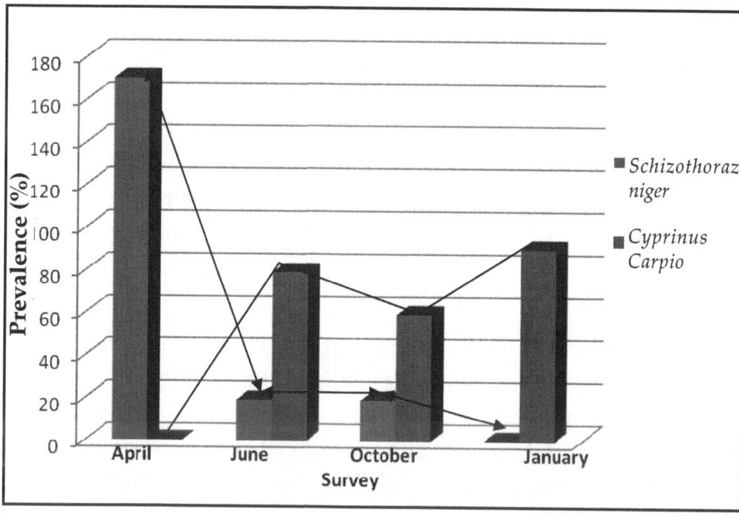

Fig.14.3: Graph Depicting the Abundance (relative density) of *Bothriocephalus acheilognathi* in *Cyprinus carpio* and *Schizothorax niger* during the Four Seasons of the Survey

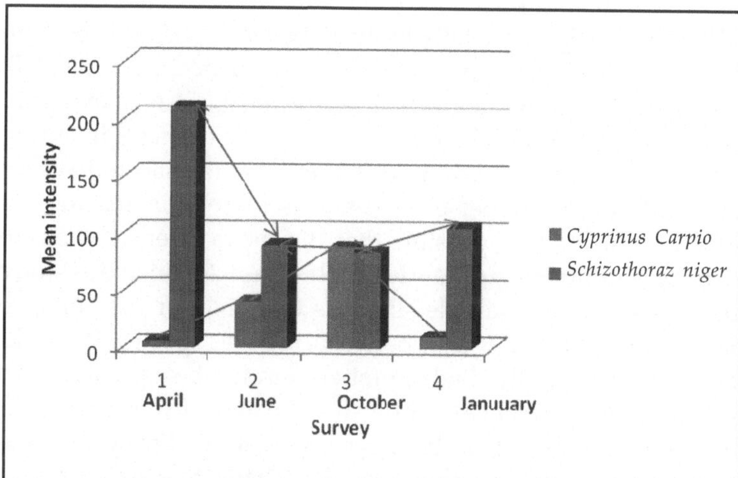

Fig 14.4: Graph Depicting the Mean Intensity of *Bothriocephalus acheilognathi* in *Cyprinus carpio* and *Schizothorax niger* during the Four Seasons

Discussion

Exceptionally high numbers of *B. acheilognathi* and low numbers (an insignificant amount) of other cestode spp. were found in the fish sampled. As highlighted by Khan and Thulin (1991), parasites are a natural part of the aquatic community and their distribution and abundance are potentially either directly or indirectly affected by a number of biotic and abiotic factors.

Infection

The infection of *B. acheilognathi* (in terms of prevalence, abundance and mean intensity) in *Schizothorax niger* was greater than that observed in *Cyprinus carpio.* Noticeably higher numbers of this tapeworm were observed in *S. niger* and a noticeably higher number of this fish species was infected. Similar prevalence and mean intensity values to those obtained in this study were recorded for *L. aeneus* and *L. kimberleyensis* in a separate preliminary study conducted by Nickanor, *et al.* (2002) in the Vaal Dam during 2001. The infection statistics indicate that both prevalence and abundance of *B. acheilognathi* differed significantly (statistically) between the fish species with *S. niger* exhibiting higher values. The mean intensity of *B. acheilognathi* was higher in *S. niger* for most seasons, except in spring and autumn when the opposite was the case. In spring and atumn a small number of *C. carpio* were infected with a relatively high number of tapeworms thereby increasing the mean intensity. It is possible that the mean intensities of the fish species differ significantly but this is uncertain in this study because either the sample size was too small or the variance was too big to distinguish between the fish species. It would be expected that the high numbers (and sub-sequently high prevalence, abundance and mean intensity) of *B. acheilognathi* found in *S. niger* in this study are linked to the life cycle of the tapeworm as the transmission of parasite to host is via an intermediate host eaten by the fish (Paperna 1996). Korting (1975) mentioned that the intermediate host of the Asian tapeworm for carp is a crustacean and that a number of crustaceans can act as intermediate hosts. When considering the food preference of largemouth yellowfish, it is found that it initially feeds on insects and crustaceans, but once it reaches a fork length of more than 300 mm it feeds on other fish (Skelton 2001). Although the majority of infected *S. niger* collected during the survey varied in fork length between 360 and 420 mm, it is possible that infected crustaceans are eaten occasionally, resulting in an infection in *S. niger.* It was unexpected, however, to find an infection as heavy as that obtained in this study. When considering the infection of *B. acheilognathi* (in terms of prevalence, mean intensity and abundance) in relation to fish size (fork length), no correlations were recorded in *S. niger*. It is important to note that *L. kimberleyensis* was the first recorded host of *B. acheilognathi* (as *B. gowkongensis*) in South Africa in 1978 (Brandt *et al.* 1981). The type of crustacean or copepod acting as an intermediate host for *B. acheilognathi* for this fish species should be determined. This opportunistic tapeworm has already adapted successfully to the common carp, *C. carpio* (Korting 1974; Boomker *et al.* 1980) in South African waters. This carp species feeds on a range of plant and animal matter (Skelton 2001) and, more specifically, carp fry, which tend to be more heavily infected with the tapeworm, feed on zooplankton (Boomker *et al.* 1980). A better understanding of the intermediate host could explain the high infection of *B. acheilognathi* in *S. niger*. Other authorities, such as: Marcogliese and Esch (1989) and Williams and Jones (1994), mention that metacestodes use planktonic or benthic copepods as intermediate hosts. If this is the case, then *L. aeneus* should be the preferred host as this fish species is broadly omnivorous with zooplankton, benthic invertebrates, vegetation, algae and detritus forming the major food of the species (Dorgeloh 1985; Skelton 2001). Although *L. aeneus* is not the preferred host (Nickanor *et al.* 2002), it still becomes infected (although low) with *B. acheilognathi*. Poulin (1998) mentioned that parasites such as the Asian tapeworm that enter their host through ingestion cannot prevent non-host species from eating the infected intermediate hosts. This method of transmission (ingestion) enables more host species to become infected.

Another reason why both fish species are infected with this tapeworm could be that the intermediate copepod host species can vary considerably. Various genera of copepods have been found to be compatible intermediate hosts (Williams and Jones 1994; Paperna 1996) and in this case it is possible that a larger crustacean, such as: a crab, acts as a paratenic host – this would explain the enigma behind the higher infection observed in largemouth yellow fish. In a study conducted by De Leon, *et al.* (2000) in Mexico it was found that helminth communities were generally more abundant in carnivorous fish species than in herbivores and detritivores. This matter needs to be researched further in order to gain a better understanding of infections by the Asian tapeworm.

Seasonal Trends

In *C. carpio*, the prevalence of *B. acheilognathi* was fairly constant except in summer when noticeably higher numbers of *C. carpio* were infected. Prevalence values in summer were approximately four to five times higher than in the remaining seasons (Fig. 14.2). This could be due to a change in feeding regime, but during the four seasonal surveys it has been found that *C. carpio* fed well (Bertasso 2004). Korting (1974) indicated that early spring, when plankton grows, is likely to be a significant season in terms of seasonal incidence and infective period. This was not the case, however, in *C. carpio* in this study. In spring, the prevalence was fairly low. The reason could be that more infected food (copepods) were available in that particular summer than is usually the case. Temperature data recorded during the winter of this study (Table 14.1) were higher than in a previous separate study conducted in the Dal Lake (Crafford 2000). In winter visibility (light penetration) in the Dal Lake was at its maximum although in the remaining three seasons similar (slightly lower) values were exhibited (Table 14.1). It can be assumed that the finding of an increased prevalence in winter is exceptional and was caused by an external unknown factor. Statistical analyses indicated that, as a result of this high prevalence in winter, the presence of *B. acheilognathi* in *C. carpio* is dependent on the season. In

S. niger, no trend was observed for prevalence of the Asian tapeworm throughout the four seasons (Fig. 14.2); a similar, very high number of fish being infected throughout the year. Abundance values in *C. carpio* exhibited a pattern similar to the prevalence values observed in the same fish species (Fig. 14.3). Values increased considerably from autumn to winter followed by a decline in spring and a further decline in summer. It is assumed that this seasonal trend is related to the breeding and subsequent feeding patterns of *C. carpio*. Feeding habits of the host account for a large percentage of the variation in the total number of parasites per host species (Williams and Jones 1994). The number of parasites in a host would depend on how much the host eats and whether the food is infected. In winter, the fish eat enough food to sustain them through the breeding season, which lasts from spring through to late summer (Skelton 2001) and explains the decrease in abundance recorded in spring and summer. As soon as the breeding season ends fish start eating again. This results in an increase in abundance from autumn to winter. In *S. niger,* the seasonal trend in abundance could not be attributed to the fish's breeding patterns. *S. niger* breed in mid to late summer (Skelton 2001) which would mean that abundance values should be higher in winter and spring, but nevertheless the opposite was observed (Fig. 14.3). A sharp decrease in abundance values was recorded from autumn to winter after which abundance values remained relatively constant decreasing slightly in spring but increasing again in summer. This seasonal trend could be related to changes in the amount of food and sub-sequently infected food available. In autumn the high abundance relative to the other three seasons was due to the considerably higher number of *B. acheilognathi* found in the *S. niger,* in the survey. A similar pattern to that recorded for the abundance of *B. acheilognathi* in *S. niger,* was recorded for the mean intensity (Fig. 14.4). This is due to the fact that most of the fish sampled during the four seasons were infected with *B. acheilognathi*. The mean intensity in *C. carpio* also exhibited a similar pattern to that of the abundance in *C. carpio,* except that the mean intensity peaked in spring rather than in winter (Fig. 14.4). Mean intensities in the *C. carpio* increased considerably from autumn to winter followed by a significant increase (three times that of winter) in spring after which the intensity decreased in summer to an intensity similar to that recorded in autumn. In spring, the mean intensity recorded in *C. carpio* was even higher than that recorded in *S. niger*. Opposite seasonal trends were recorded for the mean intensity of the two fish species. Statistical analysis indicates that the occurrence of *B. acheilognathi* in *C. carpio* is dependent on the season with the highest number of fish infected in winter. However, no statistically meaningful differences were observed in the intensity of *B. acheilognathi* found during each season. The opposite is true for the *S. nigeer* sampled in this study. Statistical analysis indicates that the occurrence of *B. acheilognathi* was not dependent on the season, even though there were significant statistical differences between the intensity of *B. acheilognathi* recorded in autumn and that recorded in spring.

Fish Gender and Species Specificity

Statistical analysis indicates that the presence of *B. acheilognathi* is highly dependent on the species of fish with *S. niger*, as mentioned above, having the highest infection of the two fish species. Poulin (1998) noted that high host specificity could be an artefact of inadequate sampling but in this study 20 fish per species per season were collected which cancels out this possibility. In addition, various studies conducted in the Dal Lake systems, in which cestode endoparasites have been incorporated, have revealed either an absence of cestodes or low infections of them in a range of fish species, namely: *Clarias gariepinus* (Marx 1996; Crafford 2000; Watson 2001), *Labeobarbus marequensis* (Watson 2001), *Oreochromis mossambicus* (Watson 2001), *Labeo capensis* and *Labeo umbratus* (Groenewald 2000). When pooling the data according to the sex of the fish, the tapeworms exhibited no preference for male or female fish. Similar numbers of male and female *S. niger* were infected. Even though there were noticeably lower numbers of infected female *C. carpio* when compared to males there was no dependency (statistically) on fish gender.

Size Specificity

In both fishes species sampled no correlations were observed between fish size and Asian tapeworm infection. The statistical *P* values were closer to 0 than 1.

Conclusion

In this study, the majority of the tapeworms were identified as *B. acheilognathi* based on the heartshaped scolex and presence of bothria. This was achieved after comparing the specimens collected with the descriptions and sketches in the literature. *B. acheilognathi* in this study was species (host) specific with a considerably higher infection (in terms of prevalence, abundance and mean intensity) recorded in *S. niger.* The reason for this has still not been determined. The Asian tapeworm in this study was not fish-gender specific. Seasonal trends were observed for prevalence, abundance and mean intensity of the tapeworm in *C. carpio* although statistical analyses indicate that no significant differences existed between seasons. Seasonal trends in *C. carpio* were attributed to breeding and subsequent feeding patterns of the fish. In *S. niger*, no seasonal trend was recorded for prevalence. The abundance and mean intensities of *B. acheilognathi,* however, varied seasonally with the highest value being recorded in autumn and the lowest value in spring. Statistical analyses indicate that there was a significant difference between the presences of *B. acheilognathi* in these two seasons. The reason for the seasonal trends observed in *S. niger* cannot be explained. Further research on *S. niger* concentrating on factors such as post-spawning migrations of the host, schooling behaviour, age of host, reproductive behaviour, host feeding behaviour, host hormone levels/state of maturity, immunological response of host, availability of infected intermediate hosts as food, site of infection, negative interaction between parasites (as outlined by Williams and Jones 1994) should be conducted to provide an explanation as to why there are seasonal variations in *B. acheilognathi*'s infections in this fish species.

REFERENCES

Bertasso A (2004). Ecological Parameters of Selected Helminth Species in *Labeobarbus aeneus* and *Labeobarbus kimberleyensis* in the Vaal Dam and an Evaluation of their Influence on Indicators of Environmental Health. M.Sc. Dissertation Rand Afrikaans University.

Boomker J, Huchzermeyer F W and Naude T W (1980). Bothriocephalosis in the Common Carp in the Eastern Transvaal. *Journal of the South African Veterinary Association* 51: 263 264.

Brandt F, Van ASJ, Schoonbee H J and Hamilton-Attwell VL (1981). The Occurrence and Treatment of *Bothriocephalus* in the Common Carp *C. Carpio* in Fish Ponds with Notes on its Presence in the Largemouth Yellow Fish *Barbus kimberleyensis* from the Vaal Dam Transvaal. *Water SA* 7: 35-42.

Bush AO, Lafferty K D, Lotz J M and Shostak A W (1997). Parasitology meets Ecology on its own Terms: Margolis *et al*. Revisited. *Journal of Parasitology* 83: 575-583.

Crafford D. (2000). Application of a Fish Health Assessment Index and Associated Parasite Index on *Clarias gariepinus* (Sharptooth Catfish) in the Vaal River System with Reference to Heavy Metals. M.Sc. Dissertation Rand Afrikaans University.

De Leon GPP, Garcia-Prieto L, Leon-Regagnon V and Choudhury A (2000). Helminth Communities of Native and Introduced Fishes in Lake Patzcuaro Michoacan Mexico. *Journal of Fish Biology* 57: 303-325.

Dorgeloh W (1985). Food Selection and Competition for Food among three Fish Species *Salmo giardneri Barbus aeneus* and *Clarias gariepinus*. *South African Journal of Science* 81: 693.

Groenewald M. (2000). Bioaccumulation of Metals and the General Health of Fish from the Vaal Dam and Vaal River Barrage. M.Sc. Dissertation Rand Afrikaans University.

Khalil L (1991). *Techniques for Identification and Investigative Helminthology*. St Albans: International Institute of Parasitology.

Khan RA and Thulin J (1991). Influence of Pollution on Parasites of Aquatic Animals. *Advances in Parasitology* 30: 201-238.

Korting W (1974). Bothriocephalosis of the Carp. *Veterinary Medical Review* 2: 165-171.

Korting W (1975). Larval Development of *Bothriocephalus* sp. (Cestoda: Pseudophyllidea) from Carp (*C. Carpio* L.) in Germany. *Journal of Fish Biology* 7: 727-733.

Marcogliese D J and Esch GW (1989). Experimental and Natural Infection of Planktonic and Benthic Copepods by the Asian Tapeworm

Bothriocephalus acheilognathi. Proceedings of the Helminthology Society of Washington 56: 151-155.

Margolis L Esch GW Holmes JC Kurtis AM and Schad G A (1982). The use of Ecological Terms in Parasitology (Report of an ad hoc Committee of the American Society of Parasitologists). *Journal of Parasitology* 68: 131-133.

Marx HM (1996). Evaluation of a Health Assessment Index with Reference to Metal Bioaccumulation in *Clarias gariepinus* and Aspects of the Biology of the Parasite *Lamproglena clariae.* M.Sc. thesis Rand Afrikaans University.

Mashego S N (1982). A Seasonal Investigation of the Helminth Parasites of *Barbus* Species in Water Bodies in Lebowa and Venda South Africa. Ph.D. thesis University of the North.

Molnar K (1977). On the Synonyms of *Bothriocephalus acheilognathi* Yamaguti 1934. *Parasitologia Hungarica* 10: 61-62.

Molnar K and Murai E (1973). Morphological Studies on *Bothriocephalus gowkongensis* Yeh 1955 and *B. phoxini* Molnár 1968 (Cestoda Pseudophyllidea). *Parasitologia Hungarica* 6: 99-108.

Nickanor N, Reynecke D P, Avenant-Oldewage A and Mashego S N (2002). A Comparative Study of Stomach and Intestine Contents in *Barbus aeneus* and *Barbus kimberleyensis* in the Vaal Dam to Clarify Variance in Tapeworm Infestation. *Journal of South African Veterinary Association* 73(3): 142-159.

Pantin CFA (1964). Notes on Microscopical Techniques for Zoologists. Cambridge: Cambridge University Press.

Paperna I (1996). Parasites Infections and Diseases of Fish in Africa – An Update. Rome: FAO (CIFA Technical Paper no. 31).

Pool D (1984). A Scanning Electron Microscope Study of the Life Cycle of *Bothriocephalus acheilognathi* Yamaguti 1934. *Journal of Fish Biology* 25: 361-364.

Pool DW and Chubb JC (1985). A Critical Scanning Electron Microscope Study of the Scolex of *Bothriocephalus acheilognathi* Yamaguti 1934 with a Review of the Taxonomic History of the Genus *Bothriocephalus* Parasitizing Cyprinid Fish. *Systematic Parasitology* 7: 199 211.

Pool DW (1987). A Note on the Synonymy of *Bothriocephalus acheilognathi* Yamaguti 1934 *B. Aegyptiacus* Rysavy and Moravec 1975 and *B. kivuensis* Baer and Fain 1958. *Parasitology Research* 73: 146-150.

Pool DW (1988). An Experimental Study of the Biology of *Bothriocephalus acheilognathi* Yamaguti 1934 (Cestoda: Pseadophyllidea). Abstract of Thesis University of Liverpool.

Poulin R (1998). Evolutionary Ecology of Parasites: From Individuals to Communities. London: Chapman and Hall.

Skelton P (2001). A Complete Guide to the Freshwater Fishes of Southern Africa 2nd ed. Halfway House: Southern Book Publishers.

Van As J G, Schoonbee H J and Brandt FDW (1981). Further Records of the Occurrence of *Bothriocephalus* (Cestoda: Pseudophyllidea) in the Transvaal. *South African Journal of Science* 77: 343.

Watson R (2001). The Evaluation of a Fish Health Assessment Index as a Biomonitoring Tool for Heavy Metal Contamination in the Olifants River Catchment Area. Ph.D. Thesis Rand Afrikaans University.

Williams H and Jones A. (1994). Parasitic Worms of Fish. London: Taylor and Francis.

Yamaguti S (1934). Studies on the Helminth Fauna of Japan. Part 4: Cestodes of fish. *Japanese Journal of Zoology* 6: 1-112.

Yeh LS (1955). On a New Tapeworm *Bothriocephalus gowkongensis* n. sp. (Cestoda: Bothriocephalidae) from Freshwater Fish in China. *Acta Zoologica Sinica* 7: 69-74.

[V]
Water Pollution and Its Impact on Fisheries

Page 193-197

Fisheries and Aquaculture
Edited by: **Prof. (Mrs.) Neelima Gupta** and **Dr. D.K. Gupta**
Edition: **2015**
ISBN: 978-93-5056-736-4
Published by: **Discovery Publishing House Pvt. Ltd., New Delhi (India)**

15

Impact of Profenofos on Gill of *Channa triatus*

Kumari Minoo and **D.N Sadhu**

Department of Zoology, Chas Mahila College, University.
Department of Zoology, Vinoba Bhave University, Hazaribag. Email:dns_hzb @yahoo.com

ABSTRACT

The aim of the present study was to evaluate the effect of sub-lethal concentration of Profenofos [an organophosphate composition of (0-(4-bromo-2-chlorophenyl) 0-ethyl s-propyl phosphorothioate] in the blood of Channa striatus. On exposure to 12.5 ppm of Profenofos, gills showed signs of histopathological lesions. Signs of impairment in tissues were more intense after exposure for 4 to 8 days. The secondary lamellae showed irregular growth of cells due to rapid multiplication. The inflammatory condition led to the occurrence of lamellar fusion in some positions, so that distinct lamellar bridge were formed. No histopathological effect was observed in the control group.

Keywords: Profenofos, Organophosporus, *Channa triatus.*

INTRODUCTION

Due to the tremendous growth in industrialization, modernization in urban scenario and use of chemicals of various kinds in the agricultural practices, there has been an increasing trend in the of level of water pollution. It appears that the pollution status has been diversified and more complexities in the water pollution have arisen with the passage of time. The water sources are losing their characteristic features with the developing pace of industrialization and a continuous process of increasing contamination is occurring day-by-day (Gaynor and Dawson, 1977; Kumar and Pant, 1981; Nath and Kumar, 1990; Jha *et al.* 1995).

The damages in the gills of fishes are most spectacular and significant in view of the fact that these causes impairment in breathing activity leading to mortality. In respect to inflammatory condition of gill epithelia, it appears that these sort of deformities occur due to penetration of pollutant in the epithelial lining and the blood capillary network of gill lamellae. Such deformities in the adult fishes have been reported earlier by Charkraborty and Konar (1974), Rao *et al.* (1979); Khangarot and Somani (1980), Srivastava and Srivastava (1984).

Material and Methods

Channa triatus were procured from Rani – Pokhar located at 20 Km., from Chas college Chas and were kept in tanks for 10 days under ambient laboratory conditions (temp. 22^{0}C ±1.2^{0}C; pH 7.5, DO 4.05 ± 0.5 ml/L)). The effect on fishes after exposure to aqueous media containing 12.5 and 16.5 ppm Profenofos for 24, 48, 72, and 96 hours, were ascertained in respect to histopathological changes in the gills. Tissues were fixed and paraffin blocks were prepared, 5-6 micron thick sections were cut and stained with haematoxylin and eosin, Heidenhain Azan stain and triple Mallory stain. The histological and histochemical preparation were thoroughly examined and those showing distinct and meaningful effects of exposure to the Profenofos media were photographed.

Result and Discussion

The gills of *Channa triatus* on exposure to 12.5 ppm of Profenofos treatment for 4-8 days showed most distinctly the signs of histopathological lesions (Fig. 15.1, 15.2). It was found that the extent of impairment of tissues increased with the duration of exposure time. However, after exposure for 4 days, the effects were limited to occurrence of uneven swelling in some parts of the epithelial lining of the primary lamellae and some signs of blood hemorrhage with the blood cells spread in the inter lamellar spaces and over the outer surface of the lamellae as well. In the specimens exposed for 8 days, these signs of impairment in tissues were more intense and therefore more pronounced. The secondary lamellae showed irregular growth of cells due rapid multiplication. The formation of inflammatory condition led to the occurrence of lamellar fusion in some areas causing formation of distinct inter lamellar bridges.

In specimens exposed for longer periods of time, an additional sign of lesion was the disintegration of blocks of cells in the epithelial lining. In extreme cases, separation of the epithelial lining from the basal cells was visible. It was noted that some specimens began to show signs of adversities soon after exposure to the insecticides media. These features clearly demonstrated sign of hyperplasia and formation of inter lamellar junction. Inter lamellar bridges were in fact due to hyperplasia.

Channa triatus after exposure of 16.5 ppm of Profenofos, in comparison to 12.5 ppm, exhibited more apparent signs of histopathological lesions as the period of intoxication prolonged. In such cases the main events comprised of the occurrence of hyperplasia due to rapid multiplication of cells, fusion of primary lamellae in some positions and formation of inter lamellar junctions. However, instances of disintegration of epithelial cells and separation of epithelial lining were visible (Fig 15.1, 15.2).

The basal cells of gill lamellae might have been induced by this factor for undergoing rapid multiplication and thereby enhancing the process of gaseous exchange. To cope with the prevalent adverse situation, the proliferation phenomenon extended the survival change, at least for a short duration.

However, after long-term exposure, specimens developed more signs of deformities in the gill lamellae leading to death (Table 15.1). This finding is in agreement with the finding of Khangarot and Somani (1980) and Akhtar (1985) who reported increased gaseous exchange rate in *Puntius sophore*.

It is evidence that Profenofos is harmful to *Channa striatus* causing damages in the gills on exposure to its sub lethal concentration. The present finding on the disorganized condition of gill epithelia of *C. triatus* are in line with other workers.

Table 15.1: Degree of toxicity of different concentrations of Profenofos to *Channa striatus* mortality rate

Concentration in PPM	1 Hrs.	5 Hrs.	12 Hrs.	24 Hrs.	48 Hrs.	72 Hrs.	96 Hrs.
12.5	Nil	Nil	Nil	Nil	Nil	3	9
13	Nil	Nil	Nil	1	2	8	12
14	Nil	Nil	Nil	3	9	14	24
15	Nil	Nil	Nil	9	15	30	43
15.5	Nil	Nil	9	12	30	45	55
16	Nil	3	10	24	47	56	60
16.5	Nil	3	12	36	50	70	77
17	Nil	4	17	38	57	75	80
18	4	8	20	50	71	85	95
19	8	21	50	70	87	91	100

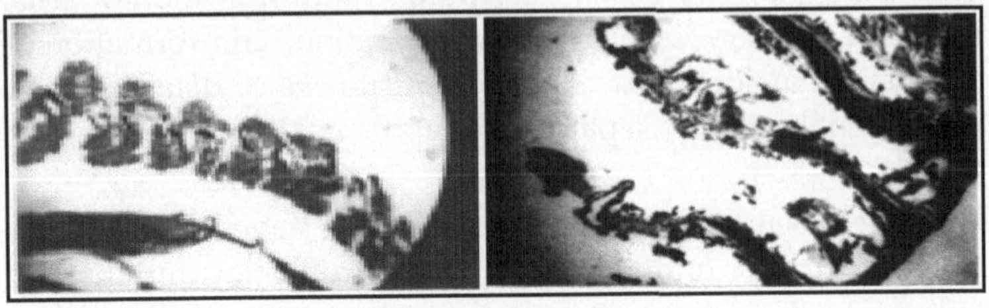

Fig. 15.1: Cross Section of Gill after Exposure of Profenofos in 12.5 PPM for 4 to 8 Days

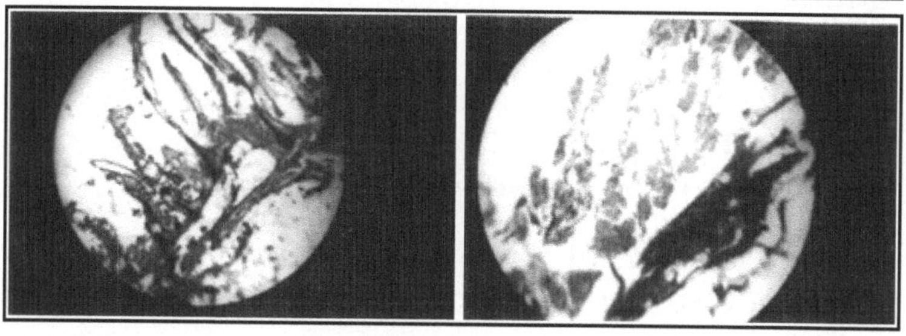

Fig. 15.2: Cross Section of Gill after Exposure of Profenofos in 16.5 PPM for 4 to 8 Days

REFFRENCES

Akhtar M N (1985). Toxicity of Pesticide Folithion 50 to Paddy Field Proc. 72nd *Indian Sci Cong Asso.* Pt 3, pp. 127.

Chakraborty G, Konar, SK (1974). Cronic Effect of Sublethal Level of Pesticides on Fish Proc NaH *Acad Sci* India 44b:241-246.

Gayner W and Dawson (1977). The Acute Toxicity of 47 Industrial Chemical of Fish and Salt Water Fishes. *J. Hazard. Mat.* 1: 305-318.

Jha BS, Jha MM and M K (1995). Impact of Nickel Toxicity on the Ovary of the Fresh Water Teleost, *Anabus testudineus (Bloch).* A Histopathological Study - 5. Environ and Poll. 2 (1): 1-4.

Khangarot and Somani RC (1980). Toxic Effects of Mercury on the Gills of a Fresh Water Teleost, *Puntius sophore.* Hamilton, Curr. Sci. 49: 832-834.

Kumar S and Pant S C (1981). Histopathologic Effects on Gills, Liver, and Kidney of *Puntinus conchonius. Indian J. Exp. Biol.* 19(2): 191-194.

Nath K and Kumar N (1990). Gonadal Histopathology following Nickel Intoxication in the *Grant* Gourami *Colisa fasciatus* (Bloch and Schn) a Fresh Water Perch *Bull. Environ. Contam Toxicol. 45(2).299-30* Nemerow, N.i (1978). Industrial water Pollution, *Addison Weslery Pub. Conpany, Inc.*

Rao SP and Rao KVR (1979). Effect of Sublethal Concentration of Methyl Parathion on Selected Oxidative Enzymes and Organic Concentrations in the Tissue of Fresh Water Fish, *Tilapia mossambica* (Peters) Curr.Sci. 48 (12): 526.528.

Srivastava AK and Srivastava A (1984). Histopathological Changes of Gills of *Channa gachua* Exposed to Sub-lethal Concentration of Malathion and Chlordane. *Proc Sem. Pest. Ag fan.*

Page 198-203

Fisheries and Aquaculture
Edited by: **Prof. (Mrs.) Neelima Gupta** and **Dr. D.K. Gupta**
Edition: **2015**
ISBN: 978-93-5056-736-4
Published by: **Discovery Publishing House Pvt. Ltd., New Delhi (India)**

16

Effect of Carbofuran on Nitric Oxide Content in Ovary of Catfish *Heteropneustes fossilis* (Bloch.)

Amar Singh* and **V. Tripathi**

Department of Animal Science, M.J.P. Rohilkhand University, Bareilly, U.P. India. E-mail: *amrsngh84@rediffmail.com

ABSTRACT

The present study was designed to evaluate the total nitric oxide (NO) content in ovary and serum after exposure to sub-lethal concentration of carbofuran to female freshwater catfish H. fossilis (Bloch.) during previtellogenic phase of the annual reproductive cycle. Carbofuran (2, 3-dihydro-2, 2-dimethyl-7-benzofuranyl-N-methylcarbamate) is a broad spectrum N-methyl carbamate insecticide widely used in agriculture for the control of insects, mites, and nematodes in soil or for fruit, vegetables, and crops. Fish were exposed to sublethal concentration of carbofuran (0 and 1 mg/L). The fish were sacrificed after 1, 3, 5 and 7 days of pesticide exposure. Ovary and serum NO level was investigated in the form of total nitrite/nitrate content, which is a stable metabolite of NO. The carbofuran at the dose 1 mg/L significantly ($P<0.05$) elevated the total NO content in ovary and serum in comparison to control fish.

At the first day, exposure of sublethal concentration of carbofuran significantly increased total nitrite/nitrate content in both ovary and serum compared to control fish which increased gradually as time of carbofuran exposure increased. The results indicate possible implications of carbofuran on NO mediated ovarian functions.

INTRODUCTION

Pesticide pollution from agricultural areas is widely regarded as one of the greatest causes of contamination of surface waters (Line *et al.* 1997; Loague *et al.* 1998; Gangbazo *et al.* 1999) and alters the chemical composition of water. Alterations in the chemical composition of the natural aquatic environment usually affect the behavioral and physiological systems of the inhabitants, particularly those of the fish. Carbofuran at sublethal concentration inhibits oocyte maturational process in *Heteropneustes fossilis* (Chatterjee *et al.* 1997). Nitric oxide (NO) is a free radical gaseous molecule that has a widespread distribution in different biological system, shows its ubiquity (Dixit and Parvizi, 2001). Tripathi and Krishna (2008) have shown the presence and localization of all three isoforms of NOS and seasonal variation in the production of NO in the ovary of female catfish *H. fossilis,* which has a close association with follicular development and oocyte maturation. The present study was designed to evaluate the total nitric oxide (NO) content in ovary and serum after exposure to sub-lethal concentration of carbofuran to female freshwater catfish *H. fossilis*.

Material and Methods

Fish

Alive and healthy female *Heteropneustes fossilis* (25-35 gm.) during previtellogenic phase of the annual reproductive cycle were procured from local ponds and brought to laboratory. The fish were acclimatized to the laboratory conditions for seven days prior to experiment and fed at morning hours minced goat liver which fish had access to *ad libitum*. No mortality was observed during acclimatization.

Carbofuran

Carbofuran was purchased from the local market supplier of Bareilly, Uttar Pradesh, India, manufactured by Nagarjuna Agrichem Ltd. Hyderabad, Andhra Pradesh, India.

Experimental Procedure

Fish were exposed to sublethal concentration of carbofuran (0 and 1 mg/L). The fish were sacrificed after 1, 3, 5 and 7 days of pesticide exposure. For NO estimation, blood was collected by caudal cut, allow to clot at 4^0C after clotting centrifuged at 1500g and serum separated out in Microcentrifuge tube. Ovaries were dissected out after decapitation and stored at - 20^0C till used.

Total Nitrite/Nitrate Estimation

The total nitrite/nitrate in sample was estimated by the method of Sastry *et al.* (2002). Tissues were processed for nitrite/nitrate (stable metabolite of NO) content, for a correlation of NO production and gonad function. The nitrite/ nitrate concentrations measured were together in the serum and tissue homogenates. Briefly, 100 ml of sample or standard (potassium nitrate) was mixed with 400 ml of 0.55M carbonate buffer. Approximately 100 mg activated copper – cadmium alloy filings were added to the samples and mixture was incubated at 30°C for 1 h with gentle shaking. Then, 100µl of 0.35M sodium hydroxide and 400µl of 0.12M zinc sulphate were added and incubated for 10 min at room temperature. The tubes were centrifuged at 4000 rpm for 10 min and the supernatant (150µl) was transferred to wells of microtiter plates in triplicate. Then, 75µl of 1 per cent (w/v) sulphanilamide and 75µl of 0.1 per cent (w/v) *N*-naphthalenediamine were gently added, incubation for 10 min and the absorbance was measured at 545 nm in a micro plate reader (ECIL MS5605A, India) (Fig. 16.1).

Statistical Analysis

All values were expressed as mean ± SE. All the data were analyzed by one-way ANOVA followed by Duncan's multiple range test. Differences were considered significant at $P<0.05$.

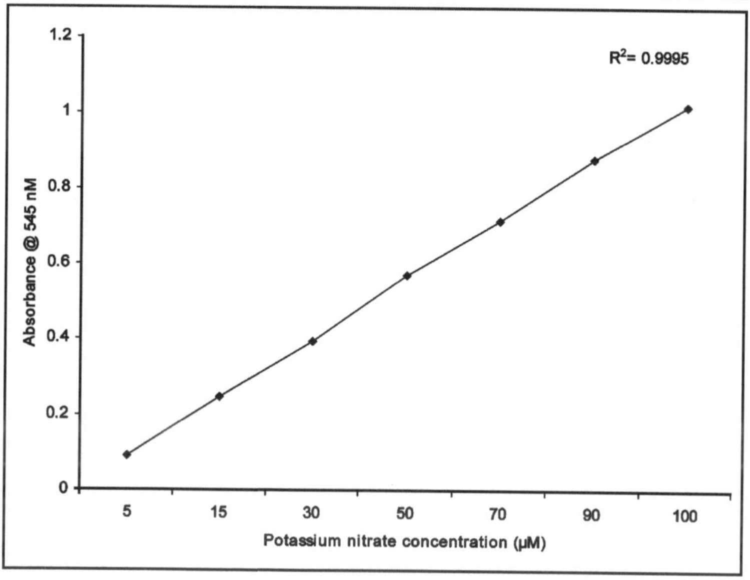

Fig. 16.1: Standard Curve for Total Nitrite/Nitrate Concentration Obtained by Method Described under Total Nitrite/Nitrate Estimation

Results

The carbofuran at the dose 1 mg/L significantly ($P<0.05$) elevated the total NO content in ovary and serum in comparison to control fish. At the first day, exposure of sublethal concentration of carbofuran significantly increased total nitrite/nitrate content in both ovary and serum compared to control fish which increased gradually as time of carbofuran exposure increased (Fig. 16.2 and 16.3). No significantly change was observed in gonadosomatic index during the experiment.

Fig. 16.2, showing total nitrite/nitrate level in ovary after exposure of sub-lethal concentration of carbofuran in *Heteropneustes fossilis* during Previtellogenic Phase. Values are expressed as ± SEM. Values are expressed with superscript (a and b). Values with different superscript significantly different $P<0.05$ and values with similar superscript are not statistically different $P>0.05$ from each other (based on Duncan's multiple range test n=5).

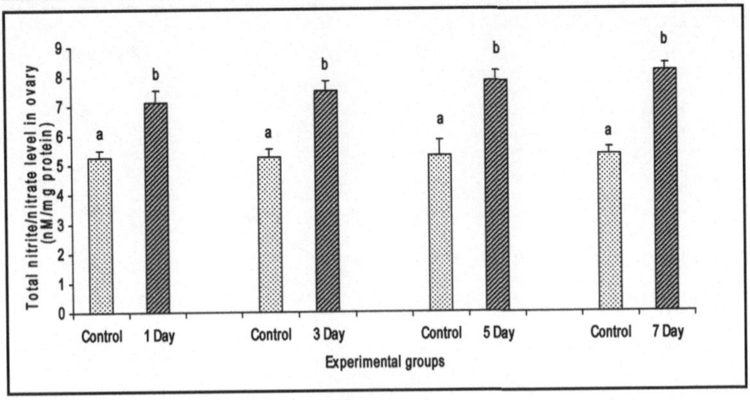

Fig. 16.2

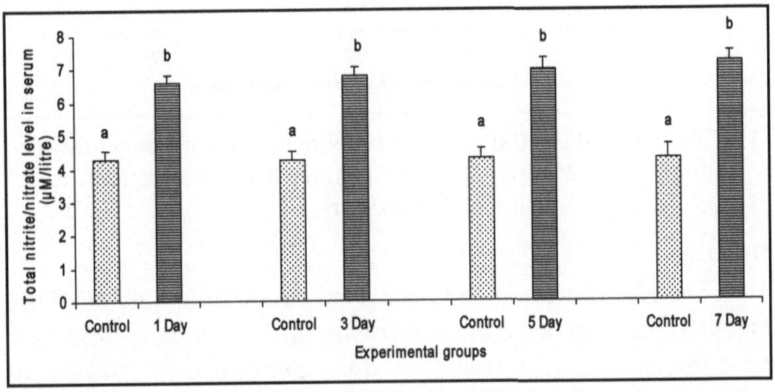

Fig. 16.3

Fig. 16.3, showing total nitrite/nitrate level in serum after exposure of sublethal concentration of carbofuran in *Heteropneustes fossilis* during previtellogenic phase. Values are expressed as ± SEM. Values are expressed with superscript (a and b). Values with different superscript significantly different $P<0.05$ and values with similar superscript are not statistically different $P>0.05$ from each other (based on Duncan's multiple range test n=5).

Discussion

This study demonstrate that after exposure of sublethal concentration of carbofuran significantly ($P<0.05$) elevated total nitrite/nitrate content in ovary and serum compared to control. However, few reports are available which shows that sublethal concentration of carbofuran ultimately affects to oocyte maturation in *H. fossilis* (Chaterjee *et al.* 1997, Ghosh *et al.* 1999). It has been also shown that nitric oxide also affects oocyte maturation in *H. fossilis* (Tripathi and Krishna, 2008). Therefore, the data suggest that elevated total nitrite/nitrate content seems to be having possible implications on ovarian functions.

REFERENCES

Chatterjee S, Dutta A B and Ghosh R (1997). Impact of Carbofuran in the Oocyte Maturatuion of Catfish, *Heteropneustes fossilis* Bloch.). *Arch. Emviron. Contam. Toxicol.* 32: 426-430.

Dixit V D and Parvizi N (2001). Nitric Oxide and the Control of Reproduction. *Ani. Reprod. Sci.* 65: 1-16.

Gangbazo G, Cluis D, and Bernard C (1999). Knowledge Acquired on Agricultural Non-point Pollution in Quebec – 1993-98: Analysis and Perspectives. *Vecteur Environ.* 32: 36-45.

Ghosh R, Chatterjee S and Dasmahapatra A. K. (1999). Action of Carbofuran Technical on Tissue Lipid of Fresh water Catfish, *Heteropneustes fossilis* Bloch.). *Asi. Fish. Sci.* 12: 235-247.

Line DE, Osmond DL, Coffey SW, McLaughlin RA, Jennings GD, Gale JA and Spooner J (1997). Non-point Sources. *Water Environ. Res.* 69: 844-860.

Loague K, Corwin DL, and Ellsworth TR (1998). The Challenge of Predicting Non-point Source Pollution. *Environ. Sci. Technol.* 32: 130-133.

Sastry KVH, Moudgal RP, Mohan J, Tyagi JS and Rao GS (2002). Spectrophotometric Determination of Serum Nitrite and Nitrate by Copper – Cadmium Alloy. *Anal. Biochem.* 306: 79-82.

Tripathi V and Krishna A (2008). Changes in Nitric Oxide NOsynthase Isoforms and NO in the Ovary of *Heteropneustes fossilis* Bloch., During the Reproductive Cycle *J. Endocrinol.* 199: 307-316.

Page 204-214

Fisheries and Aquaculture
Edited by: **Prof. (Mrs.) Neelima Gupta** and **Dr. D.K. Gupta**
Edition: **2015**
ISBN: 978-93-5056-736-4
Published by: **Discovery Publishing House Pvt. Ltd., New Delhi (India)**

17

A Study on Histopathological Alterations in Liver and Kidney of Indian Major Carp, *Labeo rohita* (Hamilton) Due to Mercury Contamination from Parichha Dam, Jhansi

Vineeta Yadav and **R.K. Porwal**

Post-Graduate Department of Zoology, S.M.P.G. College, Chandausi, Sambhal (U.P.), India. *Email: *vineetayadav6987@gmail.com

ABSTRACT

Mercury is a harmful poisonous metallic element, found in soil, air and water bodies. It causes hazardous effects in all living organisms. The present study was aimed to investigate the histopathological effects of mercury on liver and kidney of Indian major carp, Labeo rohita of Parichha dam during 2010. The presence of mercury in water samples and fish tissues were examined by semi-micro analytical method and atomic absorption spectrophotometry. The objective of this work was to examine the histopathological effects caused by a heavy metal pollutant, mercury (Hg^{++}) in Labeo rohita. The fish samples were exposed to 10 per cent sub lethal concentration at 8 ppm (96 h LC 50) of mercury for a period of 30 days. Several histopathological alterations including vacuolar degeneration, necrosis of hepatocytes, nuclear degeneration, profuse haemorrhage and haemolysis and eccentric displacement of nuclei of hepatocytes in *liver and vacuolization of epithelial cells, endothelial thickening in tubular epithelium, severe haemorrhage in Bowman's capsule, hypertrophy of epithelial cell and necrosis by karyorrhexis and karyolysis in kidney were observed.*

Keywords: Mercury, Liver, Kidney, Histopathology, LC50, *Labeo rohita.*

INTRODUCTION

Heavy metals play a major role among pollutants of environmental concern (Singer and Zimmermann 2005). They are present throughout the eco-system and are detectable in critical amounts and their contamination may have devasting effects on ecological balance of recipient environment and diversity of aquatic organisms such as fish fauna (Farombi *et al.* 2007). Metals enter into water bodies throughdead and decomposing vegetation and animal and directly by polluted water (Abo El Ella *et al.* 2005). They are serious pollutants of aquatic environment because of their environmental persistence and ability to be accumulated by aquatic organisms such as fish (Veena *et al.* 1997).

Mercury is one of the most harmful heavy metals, Mercury is persistent, it can not be broken down in the environment, only its form can change. Mercury is one of the most toxic metals and it grouped under European economic community's blacklist pollutant because of its high toxicity, persistence and bioaccumulation in the ecosystem. Mercury is present in many aquatic media, mainly in the form of inorganic mercury or methyl mercury (CH_3Hg^+). The biological presence of mercury is dependent upon chemical and physical factors like dissolved oxygen, pH and water temperature. The largest source of mercury pollution are chloride – alkaline industry, mining, use of mercury derivatives, thermal power plants and atmospheric residue which comes from fossil fuels and garbage burning (Driscoll *et al.* 1994).

The biological accumulation of mercury in aquatic individuals is the result of direct and tropic exposures. Most compounds of mercury are natural or anthropogenic which have great capacities of penetration to the skin, epithelium of gills, digestive and excretory systems (Boudou and Ribeyre 1983, 1985).

Mercury predominantly accumulates in gills of fish but also accumulates in muscles, liver and kidneys through absorption. During absorption there are four possible routes for metals to enter in a fish: the food ingested; simple diffusion of metallic ions through gill pores; trough drinking water and by skin absorption. The bioaccumulation of heavy metals in the different fish tissues have been studied by several investigators (Ashraf 2005, Catla and Canpolat 2006, Uluturhan and Kucuksezgin 2007, Fernandes *et al.* 2008). Heavy metals cause several histopathological alterations in different visceral organs of fish which have been studied by many authors (Athikesavan *et al.* 2006; Van Dyk *et al.* 2007).

This study is concerned with the histopathological alterations in liver and kidney due to mercury (Hg^{++}) contamination of Indian major carp, *Labeo rohita* of Parichha dam, Jhansi during 2010.

Material and Method

Study Area

Parichha dam built on the bank of Betwa river, is about 25 Km., away from Jhansi, Uttar Pradesh on NH 25 in India, extending about 15 km., in length. It has 4 Zones (Parichha head to Ujyanghat, Ujyanghat to Tilaithaghat, Tilaithaghat to Kolbaghat, and Kolbaghat to Notghat).

Sampling

Water Sampling

During 2010, water samples (1L) were collected from Zone-I, Zone-II, Zone-III and Zone-IV of Parichha dam, in polyethylene bottles, separately. The samples were acidified by nitric acid and transferred to the laboratory in an ice-box for further analysis.

Fish Sampling

At the same time, samples of *Labeo rohita* were collected from the same zones. The fish measured about 30.2 to 50.5

cm in total length and 540 to 720 g in weight and were acclimatized to laboratory conditions for 30 days. Fish were fed with minced goat liver and water was renewed every 24 hr., with routine cleaning of the aquaria, leaving no faecal matter, unconsumed food or dead fish. Five groups of ten fish each were exposed to 20 L of 46.25 mg /L mercury (E. Merck, India). Each of 8 ppm (10% of 96 h LC50) solution of mercury was prepared in well water having dissolved oxygen 6.52 mg/L, PH=7.2, water hardness 23.3mg/L and water temperature 28±20°C. Parallel control groups of fish were kept in 20 L of plain tap water containing no mercury. Fish all groups were fed throughout the tenure of experiments. Five fish, each from the experimental as well as control groups were sacrificed to analyze mercury accumulation, the remaining fish were sacrificed for histopathological analyses.

Estimation of Mercury and Water Sample and Fish Tissues

Mercury analysis of water was carried out using semi-micro analytical method (SMAM) and atomic absorption spectrophotometer. The liver and kidney of *Labeo rohita* were dried in oven at 80° C for 12h. Tissues were digested overnight in concentrated nitric acid and perchloric acid (3:1) at 100°C. These samples were diluted in de-ionised water and mercury concentration was determined by atomic absorption spectrophotometry.

Histopathological Analysis

Liver and kidney were fixed in Bouin's fluid and 10 per cent neutral buffered formalin, dehydrated, embedded in paraffin wax and sectioned at 5-6µm then stained with haematoxylin and eosin. The sections were examined microscopically.

Results

Control

In the control fish liver, the cords of hepatocytes were arranged in a radial net like pattern around the central vein which make liver lobules. Each lobule is connected with the other by connective tissues, Gilsson's capsules. Polyhedral hepatocytes have distinct central nucleus and homogenous cytoplasm. Between the hepatocytes, sinusoids are distributed irregularly. In connective tissues, interlobular veins and arteries, bile ducts are present. The biliary system occurs as intercellular bile canaliculi which eventually anastomose to form typical bile ducts. Haemopoetic tissues are found around the large vessels of the liver (Fig. 17.1).

Exposed

The liver of *Labeo rohita* after mercury exposure for 30 days show retardation in hepatocytes. The plasma membrane of some hepatocytes were broken down at different places (Fig. 17.2). Their nuclei were eccentric (Fig. 17.3). Nuclear degeneration of hepatocytes, hyperaemia in hepatocyte (Fig. 17.3) were evident. Between hepatocytes and blood capillaries, profuse haemorrhage and haemolysis and severe degeneration and vacuolation between hepatocytes were observed (Figs. 17.3, 17.4).

Histopathological Alteration in Kidney

- *Control:* In control fish, kidney is structurally and functionally differentiated into head and trunk kidney. Trunk kidney is rich in uriniferous tubules which is lined with columnar epithelial cell with distinct nuclei. Trunk kidney performs excretory function. Interstitial tissues are found in intertubular spaces. These tissues have parenchymatous nucleated cells (Fig. 17.5).
- *Exposed:* After thirty days exposure to mercury, the interstitial leucocyte infiltrations and endothelial wall thickening were observed at the glomerular capillaries level. Mild degenerative changes of tubular epithelium were noticed (Fig. 17.6). Tubular epithelium showed necrosis characterized by karyorrhexis and karyolysis. Vacuolization of epithelial cells, necrosis of hematopoietic tissue and hyperplasia were promount (Fig. 17.6, 17.7). Hypertrophy of epithelial cells of convoluted tubule and profuse haemorrhage were observed (Fig. 17.6).

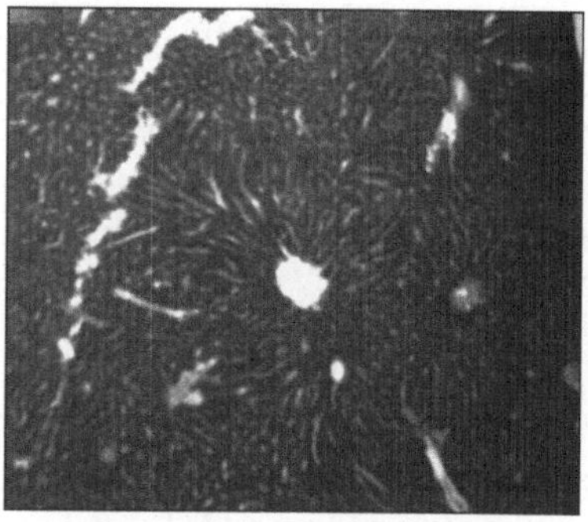

Fig.17.1: T.S. of Liver of Controlled Fish, *Labeo Rohita* Showing Normal Hepatocytes, Central Vein, Sinusoids (Haematoxylene-Eosine stain 4x)

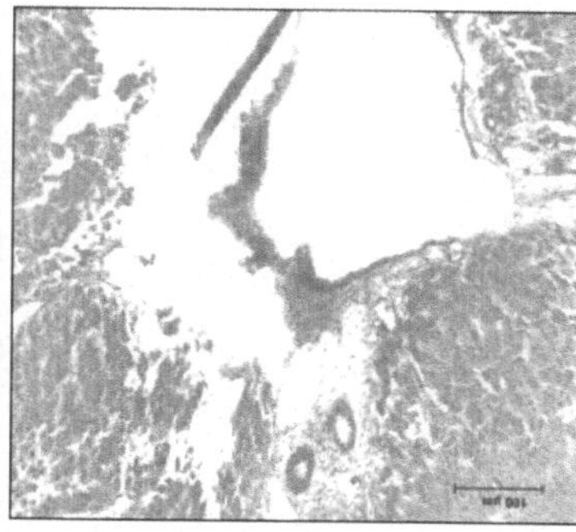

Fig. 17.2: T.S. of Liver of *Labeo Rohita* Showing Necrosis, Ruptured Plasma Memberane and Vacuolar Degeneration of Hepatocytes (10x)

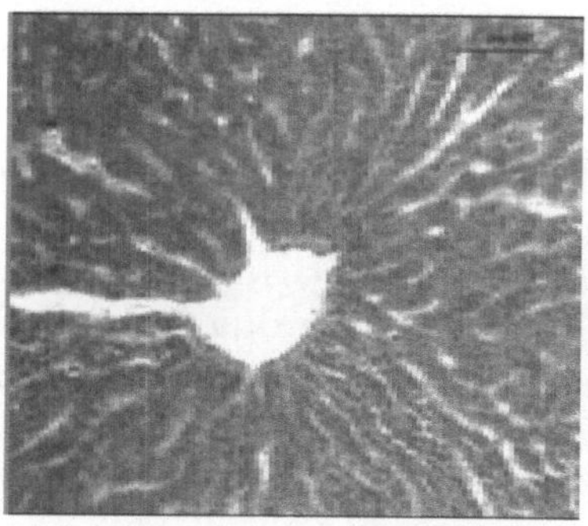

Fig. 17.3: T.S.of Liver of *Labeo Rohita* Showing Eccentric Displacement of Nuclei of Hepatocytes, Haemorrhage and Oedema in Hepatocytes (10x)

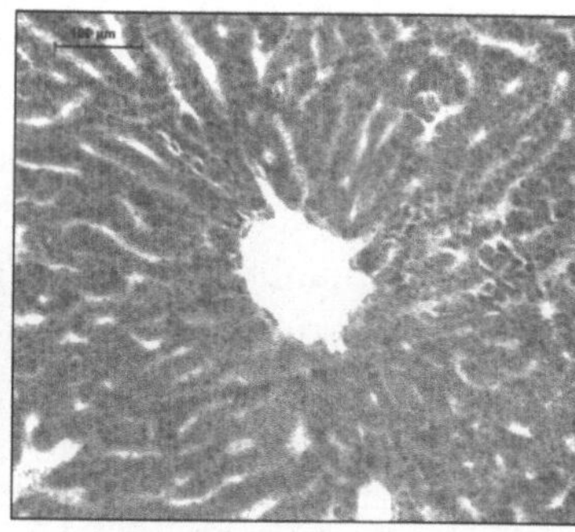

Fig. 17.4: T.S. of Liver of *Labeo Rohita* Showing Necrosis of Hepatocytes (10x)

Discussion

The histological alterations noticed in the present study are in accordance to thirty days mercury exposure. The surface area of hepatocytes decreased, may be due to increase in intrabiliary fibre-connective tissue and degeneration of hepatocytes in the liver of both sexes of *C. carpio* after $HgCl_2$ exposure at 0.1 ppm for 45 and 60 days as shown by Masud *et al.* (2003).

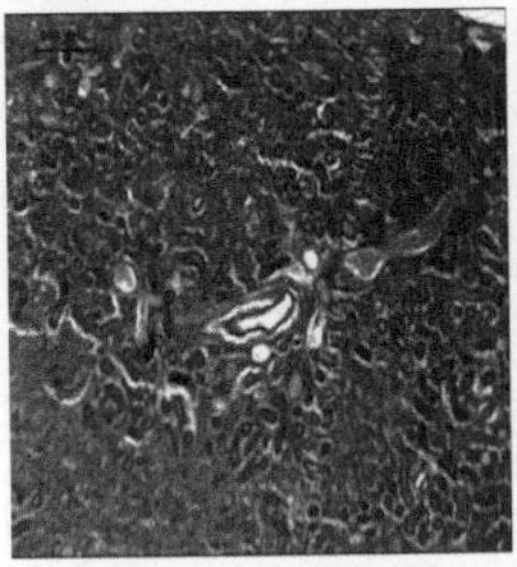

Fig. 17.5: T.S. of Trunk Kidney of Controlled Fish, *Labeo Rohita* Showing Normal Structure (Haemotoxylene-Eosine stain 10x)

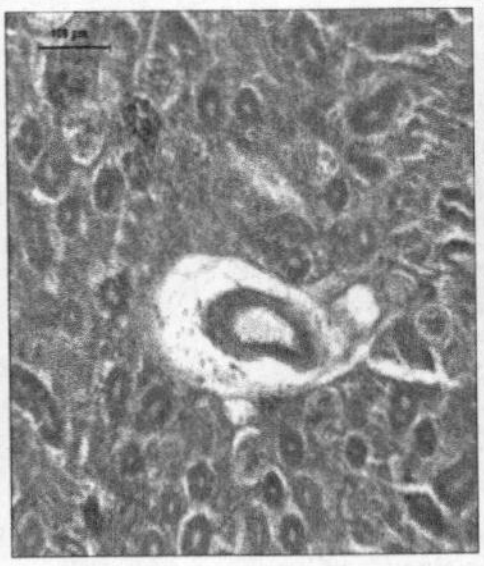

Fig. 17.6: T.S. of Trunk Kidney of *Labeo Rohita* Showing Profuse Haemorrhage and Endothelial Wall Thickening (10x).

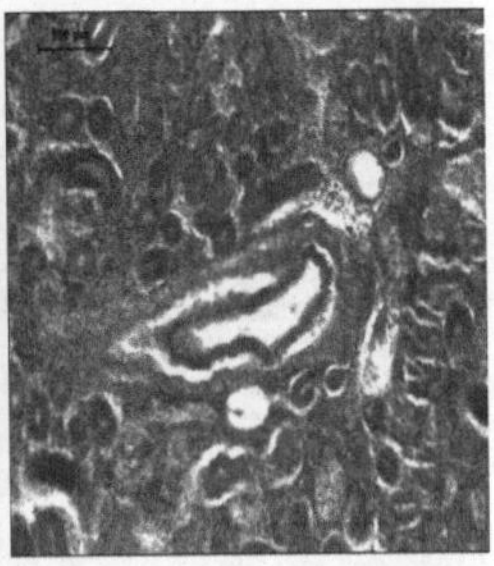

Fig.17.7: T.S. of Trunk Kidney of *Labeo Rohita* Showing Endothelial Wall Thickening of Tubules, Hyperplasia, Necrosis of Epithelial Cells

The histopathological lesions observed in the liver were rupture of sinusoid with haemorrhage at several places, broken central vein and mild swelling in the hepatocytes. Peebua *et al*. (2008) also observed similar changes in the liver of Nile tilapia *Oreochromis niloticus* due to alachlor exposure. The cellular degeneration in liver might be due to oxygen deficiency as a result of gill degeneration (Mohamed, 2001). Rana (2007) observed disintegration of hepatic cells, separation of hepatic cells from the blood vessel and proliferation in the pancreatic tissues. Broken hepatocytes and clear atrophy were also seen in the nucleus of hepatocytes in urea exposed fish, *Anabas testudineus*.

Nassr-Allah and Abdel-Hameid (2007) observed inflammation, central necrosis cellular degeneration in liver tissue of *O. aureus* juvenile exposed to phenol. The damage caused in liver might be due to the cumulative action of toxicant on blood and ultimately on other cellular structures. There seems to be a definite correlation between tissue damage and certain physiological alterations. Liver is the major metabolic centre and any damage to this organ would cause other physiological disturbance leading to subsequent mortality of fish. The hepatic damage observed in the present investigation is in accordance to the observations made by different researchers during exposure to different pollutants. Some authors have reported high degree of liver damage in treatment of various heavy metal compounds in *Channa punctatus* (Patil 1995).

Fatmaand Mohamed (2008) studied bioaccumulation of selected metals in water and different visceral organs of *Oreochromi niloticus* and *Lateniloticus* from lake Nasser-Egypt and reported several histopathological alterations, including vacuolar degeneration with focal areas of necrosis in liver. The high accumulation of lead and cadmium in the liver, which was also noted by Gbem *et al.* (2001) is related to the fact that liver plays a role in accumulation and detoxification. It appears to be a general feature of the liver of intoxicated fish that the degree of structural heterogeneity is enhanced with increasing concentration of the toxicant.

Figueiredo-Fernandes *et al.* (2007) reported that the hepatic parenchyma of fish exposed to copper showed hepatocellular necrosis and cytoplasmic vacuolation. Damage of blood capillaries in the liver along with disarray of hepatic cords, supports the view of previous workers that metals cause haemorrhage in the internal organs (Singh and Bhati 1994).

Mazher and Boja (2007) observed vacuolation, damaged blood vessels, hepatic leison with necrosis and accumulation of cytoplasmic granules in the liver of *Tilapia mossambica* due to the toxicity of copper sulphate, lead nitrate and zinc sulphate.

In fishes, kidney is the main organ of excretion therefore the toxicant has to pass through it in its degraded from which may be more toxic as the histological units of kidney are more delicate. Kidney is highly susceptible to toxic injury because of its high blood supply. Prashanth (2011) reported dilation of the lumen of the kidney tubules, degeneration and necrosis of mesenchymal cells at low dose treated fish.

Anita Susan and Tilak (2003) reported severe necrosis, hemorrhage and vacuoles around renal tubules. Degeneration of epithelium, necrosis of haemopoetic tissues, shrinkage and degenerated glomeruli and haemorrhages from thin blood capillaries in the kidney of *Channa triatus* after heavy metal poisoning were reported by Kulshreshtha *et al.* (1984).

The kidney of fish receives the largest proportion of postbranchial blood and therefore renal lesions might be expected to be good indicators of environmental pollution (Ortiz *et al.* 2003).

In conclusion, the present histopathological study proved that the heavy metal mercury causes several histopathological alterations in liver and kidney of the Indian major carp, *Labeo rohita* after thirty days exposure.

REFERENCES

Abo El Ella S M, Hosny MM and Bakry MF (2005). Utilizing fish and Aquatic Weeds Infestation as Bioindicators for Water Pollution in Lake Nubia Sudan. *Egypt J Aquat Biol Fish* 9: 63-84.

Ashraf W (2005). Accumulation of Heavy Metals in Kidney and Heart Tissues of *Epinpehelus microdon* Fish from the Arabian Gulf Environmental Monitoring and Assessment. 101:311-316.

Athikesavan S, Vincent S, Ambrose T and Velmurugan B (2006). Nickel Induced Histopathological Changes in the Different Tissues of Fresh Water Fish *Hypophthalamichthys molitrix* Valeciennes. *J. Env. Biol.* 27: 391-395.

Boudou A and Ribeyre F (1983). Aquatic Toxicology Nriagu JOEd J Wiley and Sons; New York. 73-116.

Boudou A and Ribeyre F (1985). Experimental Study of Tropic Contamination of *Salmo gairdneri* by two Mercury Compounds $HgCl_2$ and CH_3HgCl-Analysis at the Organism and Organ Levels Water Air and Soil Pollution. 26: 137-148.

Catla M and Canpolat O (2006). The Comparison of Three Cyprinid Species in Terms of Heavy Metals Accumulation in Some Tissues *Water Environmental Research*. 78: 548-551.

Driscoll CT, Yan C, Schofiel L, Munson R and Holsapple J (1994). The Mercury Cycle and Fish in Adirondak Lakes. *Env. Sci.Technol.* 28: 136-143.

Farombi EO, Adelowo and Arioso (2007). Biomarkers of Oxidative Stress and Heavy Metal Levels as Indicator of Environmental Pollution in African *Clarias gariepinus* from Nigeria Ogun River. *Intl. J. Env. Res.Pub. Hlth.* 4: 158-165.

Fatma, Mohamed AS (2008). Bioaccumulation of Selected Metals and Histopathological Alterations in Tissues of *Oreochromis niloticus* and *Lates niloticus* from Lake. Nasser. Egypt. *Global. Vet.* 2:205-218.

Fernandes C , Fontainhas-Fernandes A Cabral D and Salgado M (2008). Heavy Metals in Water Sediment and Tissues of *Liza saliens* from Esmoriz-Paramos Lagoon Portugal. *Env. Mon. Assess.* 136: 267-275.

Figueiredo-Fernandes A, Ferreira- Cardoso JV, Garcia-Santos S, Monteiro SM, Carrola J, Matos P and Fontai-nhas-Fernandes A (2007). Histopathological Changes in Liver and Gill Epithelium of Nile Tilapia *Oreochromis niloticus* Exposed to Water Borne Copper. *Pesq. Vet. Bras.* 27: 103-109.

Gbem TT, Balogun J, Lawal FA and Annune PA (2001). Trace Metal Accumulation in *Clarias gariepinus* Teugels Exposed to Sub-lethal Levels of Tannery Effluent. *Sci. Total. Environ.* 271: 1-9.

Kulshreshtha SK, Shrivastava RS and Arora N (1984). Toxicity of Two Pesticides to the Kidney of Fresh water Teleost *Channa punctatus* Bloch. *Proc. Sem. Eff. Post. Ag. Fau.* 63-70.

Masud S, Singh IJ Ram RN (2003). First Maturity and Related Changes in Female *Cyprinus carpio* after a Long-term Exposure to Mercurial Compound. *J. Ecophysiol. Occup. Health.* 3:1-14.

Mazher S and RA Boja (2007). Histopathological Lesion Induced by Copper Sulphate Lead Nitrate and Zinc Sulphate in the Liver Intestine and Kidney of *Tilapia mossambica. J. Aqua. Biol.* 22: 189-192.

Mohamed FA (2001). Impact of Environmental Pollution in the Southern Region of Lake Manzalah Egypt on Histological Structure of the Liver and Intestine of *Oreochromis niloticus* and *Tilapia zilli. J. Egypt. Acad .Soci. Environ. Dev.* 2: 25-42.

Nassr-Allah H and Abdel-Hameid (2007). Physiological and Histopathological Alteration Induced by Phenol Exposure on *Oreochromis aureus* Juveniles. *Turk. J. Fish. Aqua. Sci.* 7:131-138.

Ortiz JB, De Canales MLG and Sarasquete C (2003). Histopathological Changes Induced by Lindane Gamma-HCH in Various Organs of Fishes. *Sci. Mar.* 67: 53-61.

Patil GP (1995). Studies on Some Aspect of Endocrine Regulation Due to Heavy Metal Pollution in the Fresh Water fish *Channa punctatus* Bloch: Ph D. Thesis SGB Amaravati Uni Amaravati MS.

Peebua P, Kruatrachua M, Pokethitiyook and Singhkaew S (2008), Histopathological Alterations of Nile Tilapia *Oreochromis niloticus* in Acute and Subchronic Alachlor Exposure. *J. Environ. Biol.* 29: 325-331.

Prashanth MS (2011). Histopathological Changes Observed in the Kidney of Fresh Water Fish *Cirrhinus mrigala* Hamilton Exposed to Cypermethrin. *Rec. Res. Sci. Tech.* 3: 59-65.

Rana A (2007). Histopathological Alterations Induced by Fertilizer urea on the Liver of *Anabas testudineus* Bloch. *Proc. Zool. Soc India.* 6: 121-127.

Singer C and Zimmermann S (2005). Induction of Heat Stock Protein hsp 70 in the Zebra Mussel *Drcissena polymorpha* following Exposure to Platinum gp Metals Platinum Palladium and Rhodium: Comparison with Lead Cadmium Exposures. *Aquatic Toxicology.* 75: 65-75.

Singh S and Bhati PS (1994). Effect of Zinc Chloride on Certain Morphological Parameters of Blood in *Channa punctatus* Bloch. *Poll. Res.* 13 (4): 381-384.

Sudan AT and Tilak K S (2003). Histopathological Changes in the Vital Tissues of the Fish *Cirrhinus mrigala* Exposed to Fenvalerate Technical Grade. *Poll. Res.* 22 2: 179-184.

Uluturhan E and Kucuksezgin F (2007). Heavy Metal Contaminants in Red Pandora *Pagellus erythrinus* Tissues from the Eastern Aegean Sea. *Turkey Water Research.* 41: 1185-1192.

Index

*****